THE VAISNAVA LITERATURE OF MEDIAEVAL BENGAL

THE VAISNAVA LITERATURE OF MEDIAEVAL BENGAL

RAI BAHADUR DINESH CHANDRA SEN

GYAN

Published by

Gyan Publishing House
5, Ansari Road
Daryaganj, New Delhi-110002
Phone: 011-47034999, 9811692060
E-mail: books@gyanbooks.com

Distribution Network
gyanbooks.com
India, USA, Canada, UK, Australia

ISBN: 978-93-6780-277-9 (HB)

First Published, 1917

2nd Impression 2024

Printed at: Gyan Press, Delhi.

THE VAISNAVA LITERATURE OF MEDIAEVAL BENGAL
Author: RAI BAHADUR DINESH CHANDRA SEN

THE VAISNAVA LITERATURE OF MEDIÆVAL BENGAL

THE
VAISNAVA LITERATURE
OF
Mediæval Bengal

(Being Lectures delivered as Reader to the University of Calcutta in 1913).

By

RAI SAHIB DINESCHANDRA SEN, B.A.

Fellow and Head Examiner, Calcutta University, Associate Member,—Asiatic Society of Bengal, Author of 'History of Bengali Language and Literature,' 'Typical Selections from Bengali Literature,' 'Banga Bhasa-O-Sahitya' and other works.

WITH A PREFACE
BY
J. D. ANDERSON, Esq., I.C.S., (*Retired*).

Published by the

UNIVERSITY OF CALCUTTA

1917

DEDICATED

WITH GRATEFUL ESTEEM

BY

THE AUTHOR

To that Great Bengali

WHO OPENED

THE PORTALS OF THE CALCUTTA UNIVERSITY

TO OUR MUCH NEGLECTED LANGUAGE

AND

OF WHOM IT HAS BEEN APTLY SAID

"HIS NOBLEST ACHIEVEMENT, SUREST OF ALL,
THE PLACE FOR HIS MOTHER TONGUE IN STEP-MOTHER'S HALL."

PREFACE.

The author of these lectures (his audience must have found them equally instructive and delightful) has asked me to write a few words of preface to his volume. He has old claims upon my friendship and regard, which make it impossible for me to plead my incompetency. There is, I suppose, no Englishman living who can speak with any show of authority on the subject of these lectures, the Vaiṣṇava poetry of Bengal in the sixteenth and seventeenth centuries of our era. To me at least, the perusal of my friend's book has been an introduction to a world only hitherto known to me by hearsay and (partly) by vague memories of hymns sung to me in my distant childhood in Calcutta. I was half inclined to refuse a task for which I can plead no special fitness. On second thoughts, however, it seems to me that there are two matters of which I can speak in such fashion as may possibly be of use to readers of this book.

When I mention two different subjects of which I might write without excessive presumption, I am thinking of two classes of readers into whose hands these lectures will probably fall. These are, firstly, European readers who know little of the special Hindu beliefs of Bengal and to whom Chaitanya Deva is but a name. Secondly, there are those who, being themselves Bengalis or having spent many years in Bengal, will regard the poetry of which the author treats as a branch, a delightful and truly indigenous branch, of a literature with which they are already familiar. To the latter, let me in anticipation apologise for a quite summary and elementary account of the place of Chaitanya in the religion and literature of Bengal.

Dr. Nicol Macnicol has recently published an admirable conspectus of the Theistic elements in Hinduism from the Vedic to the Muhammadan Period. I might very well refer Western readers of this book to Dr. Macnicol's work, specially as it is in part based upon the Ray Sahib's excellent History of Bengali Language and Literature. But since these lectures may well be read by many who have not occasion or opportunity to peruse books on Hinduism, a brief account of the reform of Chaitanya may be interesting and useful to such readers.

The Theism of Bengal has for the most part found its inspiration in the mystic theme of the desire of the human soul to commune with the Divine Essence, personified in the divine hero Krishṇa, regarded as an Incarnation of Vishṇu. It was thought that the creature might crave for union with the Creator in such fashion as Rādhā, the favourite of Krishṇa's joyous youth, craved for her lord and lover. Vaiṣṇava mysticism adopted romantic songs of the loves of the deified pair as the expression of the pain and rapture of the soul separated from God and yet ever conscious of and yearning for his infinite perfection and love. So early as the twelfth century, a Bengali, the famous Jaya Deva, composed the *Gita Govinda*, the song of the divine Cowherd. To the devout Vaiṣṇava, the whole poem, unique for its soft and languorous style in Sanskrit literature, is an allegory of the soul striving to escape from the distraction and allurement of the senses to find peace and rest in mystical union with God. It is in the twelfth century that the Indian mind developed a doctrine of passionate personal devotion and *bhakti*, or faith towards an incarnate deity. It was, apparently, an evolution from the earlier system of Yoga,—the study of means for the absorption of the soul into the divine Essence, a system which was itself a popular modification of philosophical Pantheism. It was a doctorine which in so many ways resembles the passionate personal love of the Christian for his Redeemer that it has been suggested that it was an adaptation to Indian conditions of life and thought of Christian teaching.

Later, Vidyāpati Ṭhākur, in the Maithili dialect of Behar, and Chaṇḍidas, in Bengali, wrote of the same theme. Both lived in the days when Eastern India suffered cruelly from Mughal raids. Both dwelt wistfully on God's love for man and man's love for God, as typified in the immortal tale of the long separation and final reunion of Krishṇa and his mortal counterpart Rādhā. The lyrical poems which recounted Rādhā's wail of love and separation became the hymns of believers who deplored their severance from God. Their religion was one of absolute surrender of self to the divine will.

It was only natural that the practical working of such a creed, in a climate which has itself a strong sensuous appeal, should vary according to the varying temperaments of its followers. It cannot be denied that in some cases the mystical imagery of love poems of the most passionate and romantic type were interpreted too literally. There were those who strove to rid themselves of the importunacy of the senses by indulging them to the pitch of satiety, or persuaded themselves that the example set by scriptures ostensibly erotic might be followed without blame. It was a curious coincidence that just when monastic depravity, amid other causes, produced the Reformation of Martin Luther, there was born in Nadiyā in Bengal the Vaiṣṇava reformer Chaitanya.

It was at Gayā that Chaitanya first realised that, inspite of the clamour and perturbation of worldly affairs, of human love and ambition, there is in man's mind a thirst for righteousness, only to be adequately expressed by an ardent personal love for God. For him, God was Krishṇa, his affection for his creatures best expressed in the old legend of his love for Rādhā. The tale was to be interpreted in a strictly spiritual sense, as an expression, in terms easily understood by all men and all women in a land where marital and parental love are more than usually strong, of the desire of the Creator that his creatures should cleave to Him only in the hope of salvation, of the love of the creature for infinite perfection in the Creator. A devout follower of Chaitanya has said that the reformer "showed in his character, and preached to the world, the purest morality as an accompaniment of spiritual improvement." Morality, Chaitanya and his devout followers believe, is a necessary result of *bhakti*, of the passionate belief and love of the devout soul.

The religion of Chaitanya still lives and flourishes in Bengal, and Mr. Sen's lectures give a vivid and most interesting description of its expression in Bengali literature during the sixteenth and seventeenth centuries. Its influences may be seen in modern writings not directly Vaiṣṇava in import. The old passionate desire for union with God is still expressed in verses that do not indeed mention the name of Krishṇa and Rādhā, but employ the old imagery, sensuous in form but mystical in meaning. As Mr. R. W. Frazer has said, "five hundred years have passed away since Chaitanya spread a faith in the saving grace of Krishṇa throughout the land. Nevertheless, down to the present day, the same spirit that inspired Chaitanya continues still to dwell among his followers." Not only among his followers does this spirit survive, the teaching of Chaitanya has inspired all Bengali literature since his day. Its traces may be detected in the religious writings of Bankimchandra Chatterjee the novelist, and in the exquisite mystical verses of Sir Rabindranath Tagore. Hence the lectures here reproduced are an essential chapter in the history of Bengali literature, and may be read with profit by western admirers of Bengali writers of our time.

So much I have ventured to say by way of rapid introduction for the benefit of Western readers of my friend's book. May I now say a few words on a more technical subject for the consideration of experts in Bengali language and literature? At p. 81 of his Introduction to his "Typical Selections from Old Bengali Literature" Mr. Sen has made some allusions to sundry quite tentative speculations of my own as to accent and metre in the Bengali Language. Metre in all languages, as most of us know, is a subject of much disputation, and he would be a rash man indeed who should pretend to be dogmatic on the subject of the metre of a foreign language. Still, as Mr. Sen has quoted from my letters to him on the subject, letters containing mere suggestions on a difficult subject, I may perhaps be allowed to say, in as concise a form as I can compass, what my suggestions really are.

I take it for granted that, in all languages, the poet makes use of certain audible qualities, universally recognised in the speech he uses, to produce a definite and recognisable rhythm. Let me begin by admitting that a metrical rhythm can be imparted to words not written with a rhythmical intention, namely, by chanting them. A familiar instance is the prose version of the Hebrew Psalms commonly chanted in Christian churches. By adding melody, qualities of stress, pitch and duration are imparted to syllables which they do not possess when spoken in an ordinary tone. But when we speak of metre, we mean something that is audible in ordinary recitation without the accompaniment of melody.

In Europe we are familiar with three different kinds of metre. Firstly, there is the classical metre of quantity or comparative duration of syllabic sound. We get this in the metres of Greek and Latin. We find it again in Sanskrit literature. I am told that Pāṇini himself, at least 400 years before the Christian era, classified syllables as being *plūta*, *dīrgha* or *hraswa*, each of the two former being roughly twice as long as that which follows. This is so close a parallel to the musical classification of notes as to inspire a suspicion that quantitative verse must have been chanted. As quantitative verse is still written in some Indian languages, Indian scholars are in a position to make an authoritative analysis of quantitative metres. Quantitative verse, in imitation of Sanskrit metres, has been written in Bengali. But this is a mere matter of learned ingenuity, like Tennyson's imitations of classical metres.

Next, there is the verse in which the beat of rhythm is produced by the fixed word-stress of such languages as English. In these languages there is, no doubt, an audible phrasal stress, but the stress inherent in certain syllables is the fixed quality chosen by the poet to produce rhythm.

I have no wish to go into the many vexed questions as what constitutes English metre, but I suppose every one will admit that the rhythm of English is produced by a more or less regular alternation of word-stresses.

Thirdly, there is the type of verse we find in French, where the dominantly audible quality which constitutes metre is phrasal accent, whether of pitch or stress. Here, as in the last type, quantity does not go to the making of metre, though it may be deliberately used in the production of variety of effect. Nor is word-stress used in the making of rhythm. What is used is the accent which accompanies each phrasal unit, each group of words pronounced in one breath. In French, for example, the phrasal accent is normally on the last syllable of the phrase, it precedes and announces a pause which may be a cæsura or the end of the line In the latter case, it falls on and emphasises the rhyme. The rhythm in this type of metre is produced by interposing a fixed number of more or less atonic syllables between the accented pause-syllables. The result is what is called "syllabic" verse.

Now the question is, does Bengali verse belong to one or other of these types, or does it belong to a type of its own? I think it will be admitted that Bengali verse is not quantitative verse. That is, it is not necessary that any given syllable, no matter what its place in the verse, shall be audibly 'long' or 'short'. I think, too, that we shall all agree that Bengali verse is not stress verse, since word-stress is very faint in Bengali, whereas phrasal accent is very audible. My own suggestion is that Bengali phrasal accent, instead of being final as in French, is chiefly (though not always) initial, and that this quality is the basis of Bengali metre. I suggest, too, that there is also a rhyme-accent (not of course heard in prose) which gives prominence to the rhyme, and marks the end of a verse.

I also suggest that Bengali verse is, in the technical sense, "syllabic" verse, *i.e.*, that it consists of a fixed number of *akṣaras*. There may be other qualities in Bengali verse than those which I have mentioned. In a conversation I once had with Sir Rabindranath Tagore, he said, if I did not mistake him, that he was conscious of a deliberately introduced quantitative element. That is a matter for investigation. But it ought to be possible to say, definitely and at once, whether my statements as to the nature of Bengali rhythm are correct.

Let us take, for example, the current heroic verse of Bengal, the *payar* metre. This normally consists of 14 *akaṣras*, with a cæsura or pause after the 8th *akṣara*. I say, tentatively, that there will normally be an accent on the first, the fifth, the ninth, and the rhyming *akṣara*. I take an example, quite at random, from the Bengali version of the Mahābhārata.

Daśarath(a) śuni tave | Rāmer(a) prasthān(a)
"Hā Rām(a)" baliyā, tave | tyajila parāṇ(a).
Pūrvete āchila andha | munir(a) e śāp(a),
Putra-śoke maribā, pāibā manastāp(a).
Hena-mate nṛpatir(a) | haïla nidhan(a),
Ayodhyār(a) ghare ghare | uṭhila rodan(a).

The advantage of transliterating these lines into the English character is that it is possible to indicate the 'a mute.' I suggest that each pause is followed by a phrasal accent, which falls normally on the first, fifth, and ninth syllables. There is also a rhyme accent (which, of course, is not heard in prose). Observe that these accents are not fixed word-stresses, but depend on the position of a word in a phrase. Note, too, the *enjambement* at the fourth syllable in lines 2 and 3, and at the eighth syllable in line 4. This, I believe, is a negligence, not permitted in modern verse. The important point to note, however, is that the *payār* verses here cited are "syllabic" verses in exactly the same sense as French alexandrines. Nay more, Bengali possesses an exact counterpart of the alexandrine in the *dīrgha ekābali*, which consists of 6 + 6 syllables, each metrical phrase *beginning* however with a tonic phrasal accent, and not *concluding* with an emphatic syllable. The rhyme accent of Bengali, however, produces exactly the same metrical effect as the terminal accent of the alexandrine.

We have here a fixed number of *akṣaras* or syllables, the number being rendered audible by a medial cæsura and a final rhyme. Whether each rhythmical unit is marked by an initial accent is a more doubtful point. The accent would probably only be heard if a reader were deliberately scanning the verse, or reading it in an unintelligent and mechanical way. But it may, nevertheless, be the basis of verse. As an example of what I mean, I may say that ordinary English blank verse is commonly described as being "iambic" in rhythm, that is, it consists of ten syllables, of which the second, fourth, sixth, eighth and tenth are normally stressed. But take two lines at random from Milton, such as—

> Among innumerable false, unmoved,
> Unshaken, unseduced, unterrified.

Here, evidently, the underlying scansion is understood and implied rather than emphasised by a reader who enjoys poetry.

So, I imagine, is it with the rhythm of the *payār*. In chanting, or in scanning, the three phrasal accents and the rhyme accent will be audible in their conventional places. But when a good reader is reciting the verses, the accents will be indicated rather than dwelt upon. Once the norm is asserted, once the ear is taught that each verse consists of 8+6 *akṣ ras*, it will be unnecessary to go on hammering out the rhythm. But it remains the basis of the verse and is understood, if not audibly expressed.

I make these suggestions with much diffidence, and only because, so far as I know, there is no theoretical account of Bengali metre in print other than statements of the obvious fact that Bengali verses consists of a fixed number of *akṣaras*. One kind of verse differs from another in the number of *akṣaras* belonging to each: For instance, the *dīrgha tripadi* consists of 8+8+10=26 *akṣaras*, and so on. The order of these *akṣaras* is not a matter of quantity or of stress. But I think that each unit has an initial accent, and that there is a rhyme accent as well. The *mātrā* of Bengali verse is simply an *akṣara*, no matter what its length, and no matter how many consonants it contains, so that the old saying that "*Hrasva Svarer Ekmātrā, o dīrgha svarer dui mātrā hay*" does not apply to ordinary syllabic verse in Bengali.

It will be noticed that, in transliterating the verses I have quoted above, I have marked mute *a-kāras* thus—(a), The brackets mean that the vowel is not normally pronounced in prose. The muted (a) of Bengali corresponds in metrical effect (as it originally corresponded in sound) to the 'mutee' of French. I believe (I may be mistaken) that Sir Rabindranath Tagore has written verses in which compound consonants do the work of this final (a). I may be allowed to suggest that a complete analysis of Bengali metre with copious examples is much to be desired. It would be well if Bengali students were to direct their attention to the experimental enquiries of the Abbé Rousselot in determining the exact incidence of accent in French verse, and to such treatises as that of Dr. Eugene Landry on 'The Theory of Rhythm.'

How the expressive tone of Bengali speech differs from that of other Indian languages and why its verse comes to be syllabic rather than based upon quantity or the rhythm produced by word-stresses is another and more difficult matter. The vocabulary of Bengali is partly borrowed from its parent Prakrit, partly, in modern times, from Sanskrit and other languages. The tone of voice and the phrasal accent may possibly be an inheritance from the aboriginal speech of the province, whether Dravidian, or Tibeto-Burman, or both. This is a matter for investigation, or even a question which can now never be determined. But there is no reason whatever why the existing facts of Bengali pronunciation and verse should not be analysed and described. I attach no particular importance to my own quite provisional and experimental attempt to define the working of Bengali rhythm. I arrived at it merely by trying to teach elementary Bengali to young probationers for the Civil Service. If I venture to state my conclusions, it is only to fill a gap till some competent person shall substitute something more accurate and authoritative.

Let me, with many apologies, return to the real subject of these prefatory words, the admirable and deeply interesting lectures of my friend Mr. Sen. The undergraduates who listened to them are to be congratulated on hearing for the first time an acoount of the Vaiṣṇava poetry of their country. The world at large has only recently learned that Bengal has produced in our own time one or two men of genius. Every one has read the English version of the Gītānjali with delight. Its success has led western readers to ask with curiosity whether Bengali literature has not other gems hitherto unknown to Europe. Some have even heard of the novels of Bankim, the epics and dramas of Madhusudan. But a national literature is not to be read only in the works of its most illustrious authors. It is only in Japan that a Fusiyama rises in solitary grandeur out of flat plains. The Himalayan heights are surrounded by a vast chain of mountains that support the dazzling peaks above them. Among the summits of Bengali literature are many delightful valleys of spontaneous poetry,[1] vocal with the sound of running waters. Mr. Sen has explored these with diligence for many years, with an enthusiastic love for their beauties. There could be no better guide to a tract not well-known in Bengal itself.

Some day, perhaps, we shall have in English, renderings of Mr. Sen's charming little books taken from ancient poets, the tales of "Sati," "Phullara,"

[1] A critical friend takes exception to my use of the word "spontaneous." But my choice of the word was quite deliberate. The poetry of which Mr. Sen writes belongs to a period when prose composition was not practiced, when improvisation was easy, when verse was the most natural means of expression.

J. D. A.

"**Jaḍabharatā**," "Vehulla" and others. In these he has put the essence of old legends into a delightful prose style, more suited perhaps to western taste than the rhymed verses of poets whose inspiration was sometimes mystical and religious rather than literary. In the meanwhile, here is a learned and sympathetic account of Vaiṣṇava verse by one who, in spite of his western education and long intercourse with western friends, remains a pious and convinced Hindu. His comprehension of Vaiṣṇava poetry is one of the heart as well as of the head, such as a critic whose training has been Christian can hardly hope to possess. For my own part, I have read my friend's book with admiration and enjoyment, finding in it a delightful echo of conversations held many years ago with the kind and friendly Hindus among whom my youth was spent. It would be presumptuous in me to recommend a work of so much charm and erudition. It has some of the inevitable defects, doubtless, of an excursion into a new field, but I am not competent to point them out, even if I had the wish. I am quite honestly proud and pleased that my old friend should draw me from my retirement to say a few words of appreciation. He places on me a pleasant if unnecessary duty. "Zap-bai," as the honest Kachāri folk of Assam say, when they finish their simple stories. I have written enough, and gladly make way for the author of the following pages. If his readers do not enjoy his pleasant talk of his favourite poets, how shall they hope to understand what manner of place India is, how filled with ancient piety, resonant with old songs, and craving, in its own way, for light and leading?

Cambridge, 1915. J. D. ANDERSON.

INTRODUCTION.

The whole literature of the Vaiṣṇavas of Bengal is permeated by one dominant idea—the idea of love for God and of those visions of Him which the mystic 'the pilgrim of an inward Odyssey'[1] is privileged to see from a higher plane. It emphasises the surrender of all work and an absolute dependence on His mercy alone, and relates to that stage where the warrior soul after having struggled life-long to reach a high uncompromising ideal, receives for its reward the exiled life in the Isles of world's desertion or, to use the imagery of a far higher allusion, crucification and the Crown of Thorns. The devotee at this stage cries for mercy, and the sobbings of his soul move the Most High who comes with his assurance to the sufferer:

"সর্ব্বধর্ম্মান্ পরিত্যজ্য মামেকং শরণং ব্রজ।

অহং ত্বাং সর্ব্বপাপেভ্যঃ মোক্ষয়িষ্যামি মা শুচঃ ॥"[2]

(Leave all action[3] and cling alone unto me as thy only refuge. Do not despair, I will save thee from all sin). While describing the ways for the attainment of mystic visions, the Karṇānanda urges that "all actions and all reasonings should be abandoned." "Then alone," it says, "shall we be privileged to taste the joy of nigher

[1] Pachew uses the expression. See Revue Philosophique. July, 1902.

[2] The Gita Ch. XVIII.

[3] Çankara explains সর্ব্ব ধর্ম্মান্ as all forms of Karma (action.)

sentiments; from action and reason this will never be obtained."[1].

It is when the last vestige of faith in our own power of working out our salvation is lost, that we see the Great One peep through the windows of our house. The more we recede from ourselves, the clearer grows the vision of the Great presence. The vision is pursued till it becomes a confirmed reality, confronting us in every object of sense. The infinite expanse overhead is the throne of the Lord. But as the vast sky is reflected in a dew drop., He, the Great One, is seen also in the little baby. The Vaiṣṇava calls it His Vāla Gopāla and worships it, and the Christian calls it his Child Christ.

Suso, the German mystic, who flourished in the 14th century, kissed the Baby Christ of his vision and "uttered a cry of amazment that He who bears up the heaven is so great and yet so small, so beautiful in Heaven and so child-like in earth."[2] The Vaiṣṇava literature images the same idea in the conception of the child Kṛṣṇa.

This literature is not to be approached by the materialistic-minded people who would grapple religious problems by dint of their intellectual forces. It transcends the bounds of the so-called rational ideas, 'the frontiers of human consciousness' as it is called, and reveals a world of wonders,—of mystic lights. A parallel can always be found in the European literature on mysticism. Lacordaire

[1] আর এক কথা কহি শুনহ রাজন ।
জ্ঞান কর্ম্ম ছাড়ি কর ভাব আস্বাদন ॥
জ্ঞান কর্ম্মাদি হৈতে ইহা কভু প্রাপ্তি নহে ।
নিশ্চয় করিয়া ইহা কহিলাম তোহে ॥"

The Karṇānanda, Niryāsa V.

[2] Christian Mysticism by W. R. Inge (1913), p. 176.

said beholding the vision of God, "All at once, as if by chance, the hair stands up, the breath is caught, the skin contracts. It is the Sublime which has manifested itself."[1] Visions of the Most High have appeared in the most significant manner to our Bengali apostles of Vaiṣṇavism, whose literature we have undertaken to explore in the following pages. Throughout this literature an emotional felicity like that experienced by Lacordaire is in evidence. Madam Guyon's experiences (1640-1717 A.D.) of the pang of separation from God and of 'the dark night of the soul,' as it is called,[2] are so exactly alike those described in the Māthura songs of Bengal, that we may suppose that the Vaiṣṇava religion and Christianity must have once met somewhere and interchanged ideas with one another. Madam Guyon is not alone in experiencing this sentiment. Earlier mystics such as Suso, Rulmot, Tauler and a host of others all knew the sufferings of the loss of God-vision.[3] The spirit of their writings finds almost an exact parallel in the Vaiṣṇava songs on *virah ı*,—separation. Many European writers have suggested that Christianity owed its great impetus towards mysticism to Indian example. Origen, the Alexandrian Christian writer (186-253A.), in justifying an esoteric mystic religion for the educated and a mythical religion for the vulgar appeals to the example of the Indians. And Philostratus in his life of Apollonius of Tyena makes his hero say that while all wished to be in the presence of God, the Indians alone succeeded in doing so. The writings of Plotinus, the

[1] Lacordaire Conferences xxxviii.

[2] Mysticism by Evelyn Under Hill, p. 465. (Third edition.)

[3] Do. pp. 470-485.

Egyptian Neo-platonic writer, as well as those of his successors are evidently influenced by Indian thought according to all authorities.[1] Dr. Inge, Bampton Lecturer of the Oxford University, now Dean of St. Paul's and author of a famous work on *Christian Mysticism*, says in regard to the views of some of the European mystics "At the bottom, that God can only be described by negatives, is neither Christian nor Greek, but belongs to the old Religion of India."[2] The writer says in another place of the same work "Mysticism like most other types of religion had its cradle in the East."[3] Other scholars have advanced arguments to prove that Vaiṣṇavism is indebted to Christianity for its ideas. Mr. Growse in his History of Muttra, sums up all these points and discusses this question in detail.[4] And indeed the similarity is so striking that no one can be blamed if he puts stress on it and employs his wits to find out a historical link. One of my learned friends, however, gave a very simple solution to this problem. He said that in a class the teacher dictates a sum to be worked out by the students. Some are right and some are wrong; while the wrong workings are always dissimilar, those who are right are often found to have adopted the same process. If mystic visions are sure factors of realization at a certain stage of spiritual development, people from different parts of the world may arrive at the same conclusion without consulting one another. The local causes will differentiate the outward form of belief, whereas the underlying truth will

[1] Christian Mysticism by Inge, p. 101.

[2] Do. p. 111.

[3] Do. p. 125.

[4] Mathura by Growse, pp. 66-70. (1883).

remain the same. Thus do we see that Philo, the Alexandrian Jew of the 2nd century B. C., sings but the prelude of the songs by Wordsworth or Blake almost in our own times. The song is of the death-like torpor of the physical bady and the birth of the new soul in man,—of "That serene and blessed mood in which ....

.........the breath of this corporeal frame,

And even the motion of our human blood

Almost suspended, we are laid asleep in body and become a living soul."[1]

Tertullian called his soul at such a stage the bride of Christ and the flesh its dowry,[2] and Chandi Dās said that with sesamum and *tulsi* leaf the hody was offered as dowry to the service of Kṛṣṇa.[3] The sacred leaf and sesamum were held indispensable at one time for making a gift absolute accordidg to Hindu ideas. The difference is only in the form and superficial. But when Suso is in love with Divine Wisdom and says to himself. "Truely thou should'st make trial of thy fortune, whether this high mistress of whom thou hast heard so much will become thy love, for in truth, thy wild young heart will not remain without love,"[4] is not it the very language of the Purva Rāga of the Vaiṣṇava poets with which we are all so familiar? St. Juan's utterance "I will draw near to thee in silence and will uncover thy feet, that it may please thee to unite me to thyself. Make myself thy bride, I will rejoice in nothing till I am in thy arms."[5] is only a milder form

[1] Odes composed above Tintern Abbey by Wordsworth.

[2] de Resurr 63.

[3] "তিল তুলসী দিয়া, এ দেহ সমর্পিনু" Chandi Das.

[4] Christian mysticism by Inge, p. 174.

[5] Do. p. 228.

of that passionate cry of the soul for union with God which finds expression in Kṛṣṇakamala's divine frenzy in the lines beginning with "Do thou place thy lotus feet on my bosom."[1] Ribet speaks of "Divine touches" and Scramelli says that they are real but purely spiritual sensations by which the soul feels the intimate presence of God and tastes Him with great delight.[2] Here again we are reminded of the powerful lines of Jnānadās. "My heart was filled with love at his touch, my ear was filled with the music of his voice ; the sweet scent of *kumkum*, sandal, and *kasturi* emanated from his person, and as I touched it, my head reeled in joy. Awakened to physical consciousness I lost the divine touch."[3] The divine name is a love-token to the Christian and the Vaiṣṇava alike. Suso cut deep in his breast the name of Jesus as a love-token, so that the marks of the letters remained all his life about the length of a finger-joint.[4] The devotees of all sects in India, especially, the Vaiṣṇavas have worn the name on their breasts and Vaidyāpati gives a pathetic and devotional interest to this act in his celebrated lines "Ye maids," says Rādhā, "that are with me, and see my death imminent, write Kṛṣṇa's name all over my body".[5]

[1] আমার হৃদয়-কমলে রাখিয়া শ্রীপদ &—Divine Frenzy—See Typical Selections from old Bengali Literature p. 1606.

[2] Christian mysticism, p. 371.

[5] "আমার মরমে পৈঠল লেহ, হৃদয়ে লাগল দেহ
আমার শ্রবণে ভরল সেই বাণী।"………অঙ্গ পরিমল,
সুগন্ধি চন্দন, কুঙ্কুম কস্তুরি পারা। পরশ করিতে,
রস উপজল, আমি জাগিয়া হইনু হারা?"

See Typical Selections from old Bengali Literature Part II p. 1056.

[4] Christian Mysticism by Inge p. 195.

[5] "তোমরা যতেক সখী থেকো মোর সঙ্গে।
মরণ কালে কৃষ্ণ নাম লিখ মবু অঙ্গে।"

Vidyāpati.

The East and West in quest of the Primeval Light, of which a single ray has been caught by the glorious sun, have travelled by the same path, and when they have found the light, what wonder that their descriptions should be so similar? All shrines meet at the gate of heaven; Mecca, Jerusalem and Benares shake hands with one another in the way leading to the landing Ghat of that faith which flows from the soul and makes the waters of the Ganges and the Jordan holy.

If my lectures in connection with Vaiṣṇavism shall help, in however small a degree, in making a further step towards the East and West understanding each other in the light of the materials, contained in the following pages, most of which will be brought before you, I believe for the first time, I shall consider my labours as amply rewarded. My industry has been great; if I fail because of any lack of power, I shall deserve the forbearing indulgence of my learned audience, but not their harsh comment.

I have not taken the word medieval in its ordinary sense. In European History the medieval age begins with the period intervening between the decline of the Roman power and the Revival of letters. But the Vaiṣṇava literature in *Bengal*, the subject of my lectuees, commences from the 11th or 12th century. If by this period we may be permitted to mean its early period, the middle period will necessarily be the one that follows it. I have therefore taken the period immediately subsequent to Chaitanya as forming the scope of my lectures, and in doing so I have stepped beyond the limit of the medieval age, as defined by Hallam and other writers in regard to European History, by a century or more.

The historical portion of the Vaṣṇava Literature dealt with in these lecture, (pp. 83-182) contains much new matter and I shall be interested to know how this portion particularly is received by my readers. I have to state here that my lectures are confined to an account of the Bengali Vaiṣṇavas

In conclusion I have to offer sincere thanks to my friend Mr. J. D. Anderson for revising the book and writing a preface to it. My friend Mr. M. T. Kennedy of Calcutta kindly read some proofs and I am grateful to him for this kind act.

7, Bisvakosha Lane, Calcutta.
The 12th August, 1916.

DINESHCHANDRA SEN.

CONTENTS.

Chapter I.

PAGE.

I. The early period of Vaiṣṇava Literature pp. 1—9.

Mithilā a centre of learning after the fall of Gour ... ... 1—2
Umāpati's Rādhā-Kṛṣṇa songs ... 2—7
Mithila-court encourages Rādhā-Kṛṣṇa songs 7
Real home of Rādhā-Kṛṣṇa songs is Bengal ... ... 7—9

II. Vṛndāvana restored, its importance as a centre of Vaiṣṇava learning pp. 9—18.

Vṛndāvana monopolises all authority in regard to the literature of the Chaitanya-cult 10
Vaiṣṇava ideas become stereotyped ... 10—15
A brief survey of Vṛndāvana ancient and modern ... ... 16—18

III. The great Bengali masters who revived the glories of Vṛndāvana—their works pp. 19—65.

Mādhavendra Purī 19
The legend of Gopāla ... ... 19—21
Madhava travels to Purī 21

	Page.
The great respect in which he is held by all Vaiṣṇava apostles	21—22
Lokanātha and Bhugarva	22—23
The master's order inviolable ...	23—24
The route	24—25
A fruitless search	25—26
Sanātana and Rūpa	26—27
The pedigree	27—28
Incidents before adopting Sannyās ...	28—29
The plots of the two dramas ...	29—32
Other works	32—33
A stanza from Dānakelī Kaumaudī ...	33—35
Padmāvalī, Sankṣepa Bhāgavatāmṛta etc.	35—36
The Haribhakti Vilāsa by Sanātana ...	36—38
Sanātana's humility ...	38
About the dates	39—40
Jīva Goswāmī	40—42
His works	42—44
An interesting incident	44
Rūpa Nārāyaṇa—a way-ward child ...	44—45
His tour abroad and great learning ...	45—46
The haughty scholar	46
Meets Sanātana and Rūpa	46
His vanity and defeat	46—47
Jīva Goswāmi in disgrace	47—48
The legend of the Philosopher's stone ...	49—50
Sanātana and the image of Madana Mohana	51
The temples of Vṛndāvana	51
How the temple of Madana Mohan was built	52

	PAGE.
The temple of Govindaji and other temples	54
The appreciation of the labours of Sanātana, Rūpa and Jīva	54—57
Gopāla Bhatta	57
Kṛṣṇa Dās Kavirāj	58
The Chaitanya Charitāmṛta... ...	58—62
The author's life	62—65

IV. The works written in Bengal immediately before the middle period of Vaiṣnava Literature pp. 65—82.

Purī—the most important Vaiṣṇava centre, when Chaitanya was alive ...	65—66
The *tirodhāna* of Chaitanya and the stupor of Vaiṣṇava community ...	66—68
Their renewed activities	69—70
Vaiṣṇava works written in Bengal ...	70
Murāri Gupta's Chaitanya Charita ...	70
Kaḍchā by Swarūpa Dāmodara ...	71
Kavi Karṇapura and his works ...	71—74
Vṛndāvana Dās, his life and works ...	74—76
Chaitanya Bhāgavata	76—79
Chaitanya Mangala by Jayānanda ...	80
Lochana Dās and his Chaitanya Mangala —other works	82

Chapter II.

I. Early careers of the three great Vaisnava worthies Çrinivasā, Narattama and Syāmānanda pp. 83—105

		Pages.
The vision of Chaitanya ...	...	84
The date of Çṛnivāsa's birth	...	85
Çṛnivāsa's early life ...	...	87
The Court-yard of Cṛivāsa ...	...	87
Çrinivasā's tour ...	...	89—91
Jīva takes charge of him ...	...	92
Narottama, a second Buddha	...	93—94
His early career ...	...	95—96
The renunciation ...	...	96—97
The Princely sweeper ...	...	98
His initiation and spiritual progress	...	99—100
Syāmānanda's early career ...	...	100—104
The legend about him ...	...	104—105

II. Events in their lives after 1600 AD pp. 105—182

(a) The robbery that changed the life of a great robber pp. 106—123

The journey ...	...	107—108
A brief survey of the history of Vana-Viṣṇupur ...	...	108—109
A great treasure ...	...	110
The pursuit ...	...	110
The cart carried away with its contents ...		111

	PAGE
The news causes the death of Kṛṣṇa Dās Kavirāj	111
The friends part in deep sorrow ...	113
Vīra Hāmvīra's disappointment ...	113
Çrīnivās at Dewāli	114
Kṛṣṇa Vallabha, the young scholar ...	115
In the court of the king	116
The court pundit takes umbrage ...	117
The wonderful discourses on the texts of the Bhāgavata	117—118
A second discourse and its marvellous effect	119—120
The remorseful king and the recovery of the M.S.S.	120
His initiation	120
The discrepancies in the different acconnts	121
Viṣṇupur turns into a Vaiṣṇava centre ...	122—123

(b) *Norottama at Kheturi pp. 124—150.*

Gangā Nārāyaṇa Chakravarty ...	125—127
The great festivity at Kheturi ...	128
The padas sung	129—134
The cost of the function	134—135

(c) *The great robber-chief Chānd Roy pp. 135—146.*

A terror to the people	136
The ghost of a murdered Brahmin ...	137
The repentent soul	137
Narattama visits Rājmahal, his reception there	138—140
The initiation	140
The Nowāb's distrust	140

PAGE

A visit to Kheturi 141
Chānd made a captive and thrown into prison ... ... 141—142
His great faith 142
Declines to worship Kālī 143
The capital sentence 143
The elephant forced to retreat .. 144
The Nowab's favours ... ... 145—1

(c) *Rāmchandra Kavirāj pp. 146—150*

The meeting between Rāmachandra and Çrinivāsa ... ... 147—148
Rāma Chandra's friendship with Narottama ... ... 149—150

(*d*) *An eneounter with the scholars of the opposite school pp. 150—155*

(*e*) *Further details about the lives oj the three apostles pp. 155—163.*

Narottama declared a Brahmin ... 155—156
Çrinivās' later career and history of his family ... ... 157—158
The legend of the nose-ornament ... 159
Çyamānanda's success in Orissa .. 160—163
The various centres of Vaiṣṇavism ... 163

(*f*) *Vīrachandra's work, legend about him pp. 163—169.*

The Neḍā-Neḍis 164
The reception by the Nowab ... 166
The miracle 167

PAGE

The present of a blackstone and of the *Khunti* 167
The Vīrachandra Charita ... ... 168—169

III The historical works that describe the above narratives pp. 169—183

(*a*) *Nityānanda Dās and his Premavilāsa pp. 169—174*

The date of the Premavilāsa ... 169
An account of Nityānanda Dās ... 171—174
Life of Rūpa Nārāyaṇa 174

(*b*) *Jadunandana Dās—his Karnānanda and other works pp. 175—177.*

(*c*) *Narahari Chakravarti and his works pp. 177—180.*

A short sketch ... ... 178—179
God's cook and musician 189
Other works ... ... 181—182

Chapter III.

The Songs and their Authors pp. 183—218

(a) The Spiritual philosophy underlying the songs pp. 183—197.

	PAGE
The idea of asceticism according to the Vaiṣṇavas	184
The Purvarāga	185—187
The Goṣṭha songs	188—192
Rādha Kriṣṇa songs	192
The Gour Chandrikā	193
The Māthur ...	193, 195—197

(b) Tne Pada Kartās—Govinda Dās, pp. 197—198.

His conversion	199
The appreciation of his songs ...	200
Persecution and abondonment of home ...	201
The occupation of his last years ...	202
Some of his songs	203—208

(c) The peculiar excellence of Vaiṣṇava songs pp. 209—211.

(d) Jnāna Das p. 211.

(e) Balarāma Dās pp. 215—216.

(f) Song by a Mohamoden poet pp. 216—218.

Chapter IV.

Theological Literature

(a) *The Vaiṣṇava theology pp. 219—233.*

	PAGE
A classification of emotions	220—222
The Chaitanya cult	223
Love—the watch-word	223
The moral aspects and the rules ...	224—226
The Japa	226
Antogonism towards the orthodox religion	228—231
Passions are of great service ...	231
A list of works	232—233

(b) *The degeneracy of the Buddhists and the recruiting of Vaiṣṇava converts from their ranks pp. 233—238.*

The Buddha's reluctance to admit women into monasteries ...	234
The Strict rules	234—235
The Sahajiyā cult	235—238

(c) *Jnanādi Sādhana—A curious medley of Buddhistic and Vaiṣṇava creeds pp. 238—242.*

(d) *Christianity and Vaiṣṇavism pp. 242—248.*

THE
VAISNAVA LITERATURE
OF
Mediæval Bengal

CHAPTER I

I. The early period of Vaiṣṇava Literature.

II. Vṛndāvana restored, its importance as a centre of Vaiṣṇava learning.

III. The great Bengali masters who revived its old glories—their works.

IV. The works written in Bengal immediately before the middle period of Vaiṣṇava Literature.

I. *The early period of Vaiṣṇava Literature.*

Mithilā—a centre of learning after the fall of Gaur.

The early period of Vaiṣṇava literature in Bengal, so far as is traceable from the resources now available, commences with the lays of Jayadeva and those of another poet who lived in a still earlier age, and of whom I shall have to speak presently. Jayadeva was a contemporary of Laksmana Sen, the last Hindu King of Gaur, who reigned from 1168 to 1199 A. D. When the Sen dynasty was driven from Gaur by the invading Moslem armies in 1199 A. D., the Maithil court, which had hitherto acknowledged the suzerainty of the

Emperor of Gaur, became the resort of the Brahmin scholars and poets who no longer claimed any *locus standi* in their old capital city. The tradition of Bengali learning passed to Mithilā, which became with Benares, one of the chief centres of the scholars of the Eastern India for a few centuries. Thus do we account for the fact that the divine lyrics of Rādhā-Kṛṣṇa-love in the unparalleled melody of Jayadeva's Sanskrit were echoed a century and a half later in Vidyāpati's mellifluous Maithil verse. The conferring of the title of 'Abhinava Jayadeva',[1] a new Jayadeva, on Vidyāpati by Çiva Simha, the King of Mithilā, proves that the spirit of the great lyric-master of Bengal inspired the poet-laureate of the Maithil court.

Umāpati's Rādhā-Kṛṣṇa songs.

We find several versions of some poems of Umāpati extant both in Mithilā and Bengal. There is a tradition current in Mithilā that Umāpati was a native of that region, and a contemporary of Vidyāpati. We need not credit such traditions any more than those which were related in Bengal about Vidyāpati himself, half a century ago, announcing that the poet was born somewhere near Raniganj.[2] When a historical problem offered a puzzling point, the old man of the village of an earlier generation would not wait for evidence, but quickly solved it by consulting his fancy. Prof. Aufrecht has fixed the date of this Umāpati of Maithil tradition in the first half

[1] Vide the Copper-plate grant made to Vidyāpati by Çiva Simha by which the village Visfi was conferred on the poet.

[2] See Preface to the edition of Vidyāpati and Chaṇḍidās by Jagat Bandhu Bhadra.

of the 11th century[1] ; though Sir George Grierson accepts, without adducing any evidence, or entering into controversy, the tradition of Mithilā and takes the poet to be a contemporary of Vidyāpati.[2] The origin of the Maithil tradition is to be traced chiefly to a few couplets in which the names of both the poets appear together in the colophon.[3] We have many instances of such colophons bearing the names of two poets who belonged to widely different ages. The names of Vidyāpati and Govinda Dās occur together in a considerable number of poems, and we know that the latter poet wanted only to associate his name with that of his predecessor aspiring to the fame of saying something fine in the same strain.

We have all heard of the poet Umāpati, the author of 'Chandra-chuḍa-charita'. Jayadeva refers to the flowery style of this poet's songs. Some specimens of Umāpati Dhara's Sanskrit composition are also preserved in an inscription on a stone slab which once adorned the gate of the palace of Vijaya Sen, Lakṣmana Sen's grandfather.[4] It is possible that the vernacular songs in question were composed by this distinguished poet of Vijaya Sen's court. The language of the poems is not a test by which the native place of the poet may be infallibly ascertained . We know how Vidyāpati's verses have been Bengalicised by the people of this country. The version of Umāpati's songs, current in Mithilā, would in like manner be rendered closer to Maithili, whereas those to be found in the

[1] Z D M G, Vol xl, p. 143.

[2] Vernacular Literature of Hindusthan (1889) p. 11.

[3] Preface to Vidyāpati, edited by Nogendranāth Gupta (1908) p. 59.

[4] This Stone-slab is preserved in the Indian Museum, Calcutta.

Bengali anthologies, such as the Pada-Samudra, would retain their early Bengali forms.

Umāpati Dhara was an earlier poet than Jayadeva, and if Prof. Aufrecht's conclusions as to the date of Umāpati are to be accepted, it will not be difficult to prove the identity of the two. If this is done it will follow that Rādhā-Kṛṣṇa songs were not only first written in Sanskrit in Bengal so far back as the 12th Century, A.D., but that they were written in her vernacular tongue in a still earlier age. The sensuous legend became clothed in a mystic garb in Bengal and communicated a divine message, responded to by the whole of Âryāvarta in later times.

Umāpati Dhara was a native of Bengal and we refer our readers to Chandraprabhā—a work written by Bhārat Mallik in 1572 for further particulars about him.

In the colophon Umāpati invokes blessings on his patron whom he calls "সকল নৃপতি পতি"— 'the king of all kings'—"সকল ত্রিপতি পতি"—'the Lord of the lords of the three worlds.' Allowing a considerable margin for this hyperbole, which was a characteristic of the poet according to Jayadeva, we must admit that this description alludes to a monarch who could not be short of a paramount prince. Here also the suggestion occurs that the poet refers to Vijaya Sen and not to Çiva Siṁha.

The fact that such an eminent Sanskrit scholar and poet as Vidyāpati was eager to associate his name with Umāpati's in his songs, proves the latter to have been at least an equally distinguished man. This is certainly true of Umāpati Dhara, who was the poet laureate of the court of a paramount Hindu king in an earlier age, as Vidyāpati himself was that of Çiva Siṁha at a subsequent period.

Umāpati's songs, three of which are given in the foot-note ([1]), possess a genuine and intrinsic poetic merit. The line "সকল সরীর, কুসুম তুঅ সিরজিল,
কিঅ তুঅ হ্রিদয় পথানে।"

[1](a) "মানিনি মানহ জৌঁ মোর দোসে।
সাস্তি করিঅ, বরু ন করিঅ রোসে॥
ভৌঁই কমান, বিলোকন বানে।
বেধহ বিধুমুখি কয় সমাধানে॥
পীনপয়োধর গিরিবর সাধী।
বাহু ফাঁস, ধনি! ধরু মোহি বাঁধী॥
কী পরিণতি ভয় পরসনি হোহী।
ভুখন চরণ কমল দেহ মোহী॥
সুমতি উমাপতি ভন পরমানে।
জগমাতা হিন্দুপতি জানে॥"

(b) গগনে মগন ভেল চন্দা।
মুদি গেল কুমুদিনী, তইও তোহন ধনি,
মুদল মুখ অরবিন্দা॥
কমল বদন, কুবলয় দুহু লোচন,
অধরে মধুরি নিরমানে।
সকল সরীর, কুসুম তুঅ সিরজিল,
কিঅ তুঅ হ্রিদয় পথানে॥
অসকতি কর, কঙ্কন নঁহি পরিহসি
হ্রিদয় হার ভেল ভারে।
গিরিসম গরুঅ, মান নহি মুঞ্চসি,
অপরুব তুঅ ব্যবহারে॥
অবগুণ্ঠন পরিহরি হরখি হেরু ধনি
মানক অবধি বিহানে।
সুমতি উমাপতি, সকল ত্রিপতি পতি,
হিন্দুপতি রস জানে॥

specially, in the second poem, where Rādhā's whole body is described as built by the Creator of essential flowers except only the heart which is of stone, is wonderfully ingenious.

Whether the Umāpati of these songs is the same poet whom we find mentioned in 'the Songs Celestial' of Jaydeva or not, it is certain that the capitals of some of the Maithil kings of old had poets who, following the tradition of the court of Lakṣmana Sen, sang of Rādhā-Kṛṣṇa-love after Jayadeva. The Maithil court had already adopted Lakṣmana Sen's era known as the '*lasang*,' and it was unmistakably

(*c*) সখি হে মন জন্থ করিঅ মলানে।
অপন করম ফল, হম উপভোগব
তোহেঁ কিঅ তজহ পরাণে॥
হরি সঁ প্রেম আস করি লাওলি
পাওলি পবিভব ঠামে।
জলধর ছাহরি, তরুতলে সুতল হুঁ
আতপ ভেল পরিণামে॥
কবহুঁ নেহ, নঁহি পুন্থ পরগাসব
কেবল ফল অপমানে।
কোমল হো ন পথানে॥
পুরুষ পিরিতি রিতি, নহিঁ হোঁ সরল,
রতি হু ন হুন কর দোষে।
কত ন জতন ধরি, জোঁ প্রতিপালয়,
সাপ না মানয়ে পোসে॥
সুমতি উমাপতি হরি হোয়ত পরসন
মান হোএত অবসানে।
সকল নৃপতি পতি হিন্দুপতি জীউ
পট মহিখী বিরমানে॥

Vide 'Kavi Vidyāpati' by Trailakyanātha Bhattachārya PP. 124-125.

stamped with the influence of Bengal for a long time, though after the downfall of the Hindu power in this country Mithilā was destined to hold the premier position in learning for some centuries, till once more it was conquered by Bengal—not indeed by the invading arms of her soldiers, but by the glorious band of scholars of whom Vāsudeva Sārvabhauma and Raghunātha Çiromaṇi were the most conspicuous in the 16th century.

Maithila Court encourages Rādhā-Kṛṣṇa-songs.

We find several poets of Mithilā who sang of Rādhā and Kṛṣṇa in the 15th century. Among these we may name Nandipati, Jayānanda, Chaturbhuja, Kaviçekhara, Bhanjan and Chakrapāṇi, who were either contemporaries of Chaitanya or flourished shortly after him. The court of Mithilā continued to keep tradition of appointing poets laureate to sing songs on Rādhā and Kṛṣṇa in the vernacular dialect up to quite recent times. We have come across such poems written by a successive generation of poets such as Sarasarāma, the favourite poet of Rājā Sundara Simha who reigned from 1642-1662 A.D., Modanārāyaṇa and Keçava, the poets of the court of Rājā Pratāpa Simha (1760-1776) and Bhānunātha, the poet laureate of Rājā Maheçvara Simha (1850-1860 A.D.).

But the real home of Rādhā-Kṛṣṇa songs is Bengal.

But it appears that though the Maithil kings tried to keep up the poetical tradition of the court of the Sen-kings of Bengal by appointing these 'Abhinava Jayadevas' to singing songs of Rādhā-Kṛṣṇa-love, the people there did not truely appreciate this class of poetry as keenly as the Bengalis did. In Bengal Rādhā-Kṛṣṇa-songs were an indigenous growth and had been loved in her cities and her villages alike, long before

Chaitanya flourished. New tunes and modes of music were invented in particular epochs and improved upon by succeeding generations in order to sing these songs with effect. In Mithílā this class of poetry, as I have just stated, had no great attraction for the people. Even the celestial songs of Vidyāpati had but few listeners in his own native land. Babu Nagendra nātha Gupta, the learned editor of Vidyāpati's poems writes : "In Mithila the people scarcely sing Vidyāpati's songs on Rādhā-Kṛṣna," ([1]) whereas in Bengal they are on the lips of every street-beggar."

The ingenuity of Bengali scholars is apparent in them; they have partially paraphrased these songs, introducing into them a considerable number of Bengali words. The lyrical master-pieces have thus been made understandable of the people in the mixed and quaint form current in this country. The extensive popularity of the Rādhā-Kṛiṣṇa-songs of Vidyāpati in Bengal is no doubt due to the appreciation in which they were held by Chaitanya; but it is also largely due to the natural aptitude and capacity of the Bengalis for grasping the mystic interpretations of emotional poetry more readily than any other people of India. The perfect imagery of Vidyāpati, of which it will be difficult to find the equal in the lyrical literature of Bengal, is due to the influence of the scholarly atmosphere of the Maithil court poetry; whereas the songs of the Vaiṣṇava poets of Bengal voice the mystic yearnings of the soul for its beloved, not always in the high strained metaphorical language of the Maithil lyrics, but giving a far truer

([1]) See P. 7 of the Preface to Vidyāpati's songs edited by Babu Nagendranāth Gupta (1912).

interpretation of the emotional ideals of the popular mind, than is to be found elsewhere in India.

We thus see that the early literature of the Vaiṣṇavas of Bengal begins with Umāpati, if our contention in regard to his identity with Umāpati Dhara is admitted. It grows in its rythmical wealth of language with Jayadeva who is known to European scholars by his Gītagovinda translated into English verse by Griffiths and Sir Edwin Arnold. This literature reaches its full development in the songs of Vidyāpati, Chandidās and Narahari Sarkār, and subsequently in the biographies of Chaitanya and in the works giving an exposition of the Vaiṣṇava theology which became gradually stereotyped, after Chaitanya's direct influence was gone. The views propounded in these later works of the Bengali Vaiṣṇavas showed a marked departure from the tenets of Maddhāchārya—the admitted founder of their sect—and earned for their exponents and followers the distinctive name of 'Gauḍiya Vaiṣṇavas.'

———o———

II. Vṛndāvana restored, its importance as a centre of Vaiṣṇava learning.

The three great masters, the apostles of the new faith, were of course Chaitanya, Nityānanda and Advaita. Next in rank were the six Gosvāmīs who were distinguished alike for their profound scholarship and the piety of their lives. These were Rūpa, Sanātanā, Raghunātha Dās,

Raghunātha Bhatta, Gopāla Bhatta and Jīva Gosvāmī.

Vṛindāvana monopolises all authority in regard to the literature of the Chaitanya-cult.

They all lived in Vṛndāvana during a considerable portion of their lives. This city had thus already become a centre of Vaiṣṇava learning. No book that did not bear the stamp and seal of these six Gosvāmīs of Vṛndāvana was recognised as a standard authority in the 16th century. No saintly person of that period among the Bengali Vaiṣṇavas who had not sat at the feet of at least some one of these masters and received instruction from him, inspired perfect confidence in the Vaiṣṇava community. There was none among the Vaiṣṇavas of this period in Bengal who did not consider it the highest goal of his life—'the butt-end and the sea-mark of his utmost sail'—to be privileged to live at least for a while in the blessed country where the early years of Kṛṣṇa's life were spent. The Bengali works written by the Vaiṣṇavas in the latter part of the 16th century are full of passionate panegyrics of the holy city of Vṛndāvana. Numerous works such as the Vrajaparikramā by Narahari Chakravarti give an exact topography of the sacred shrine, detailing the legendary tales of Kṛṣṇa's life with which each favoured spot there is associated.

Vaiṣṇava ideas become stereotyped.

The six masters—the Gosvāmīs—gave exposition of the highest religious philosophy of the Vaiṣṇavas in their works written in Sanskrit. But while they possess the unique value of great scholarship and the stamp of the unspotted lives that their writers led, these great works, it must be admitted, were more or less of a sectarian character. The cult of emotion was explained in its minute details and was stereotyped and conventional. Certain fixed ideas supported by great learning were allowed to take strong hold of the Vaiṣṇava community, who would not admit anything in regard to Vaiṣṇavism beyond these. They would not listen to or credit any information about Chaitanya which did not directly or indirectly emanate from the six masters. Chaitanya Charitāmṛta and Chaitanya Bhāgavata are admittedly the two great standard biographies of the Master ; the latter work specially is marked by stupendous learning and ardent faith derived from the direct influence of the six Gosvāmīs. But both these works contain matter which none but the orthodox Vaiṣṇava could be expected to believe. Details derived from extraneous sources, even if recorded in contemporary writings, were not credited by the orthodox Vaiṣṇavas if they did not conform to the account given in these two biographies. Yet these two works often give but meagre accounts of particular episodes of the life of the Master, having been written long after he had passed away from this world ; whereas there are contemporary works which give true and vivid information about such points, but are held in disregard, because some of the facts inserted in them do not tally with those to be found in the 'standard works.' I may refer for instance to the famous Karchā which gives an account of a portion of Chaitanya's life, written by Govinda Dās who was an eye-witness of what he described. In it we find that Chaitanya displayed ecstasies of devotion at the sight of the temples of Kālī and Gaṇeça. Wherever people paid their tribute of worship to God, under whatever form or name they might do so, the Master found something to inspire his emotion, and passed into a state of trance at the remembrance. The orthodox Vaiṣṇava community took a hostile attitude towards Kālī-worship and could not, for obvious reasons, credit such catholic statements. This is also the case with the accounts left by another biographer and contemporary of Chaitanya—Jayānanda. This author has described the manner in which Chaitanya passed away from this world. It is stated that in August, 1533, Chaitanya received a hurt in his left foot from a brickbat from a fall when absorbed in an ecstatic trance during the Car-festivity of Jagannātha. On the 3rd day pain increased and he got fever, and on the 6th he quitted this mortal frame. The biographers of Chaitanya do not state when and how he breathed his last. They did not love to touch a subject which caused them pain. The tradition of the country is that his body having nothing material in it passed into that of Jagannātha, or according to other accounts, into that of Gopīnātha at Puri. The *pāndās* the priests of the shrine, relate this story and earn something from the pious pilgrims by doing so. The account given by Jayānanda dispels this halo of supernatural glory, and shows Chaitanya as liable to the common fate of men. Hence Jayānanda's Chaitanya Maṇgal is discredited by the orthodox Vaiṣṇavas, though the work describes many points in Chaitanya's life which carry an undeniable authenticity and illuminate some of the obscure corners of the social and political history of the times.

Thus do we see that the works written under the direct or indirect control of the six Gosvāmīs, or in a few cases such as the Chaitanya Chandrodaya by Kavikarṇapura and the Chaitanya Maṅgala by Lochana Dās, written by the order of some of the reputed personal friends of

Chaitanya as Murāri Gupta and Narahari Sarkār, carried the highest authority among the Vaiṣṇavas. Stray literary or historical attempts which were not submitted to these scholars for scrutiny failed for obvious reasons to obtain recognition from them, though some of them possessed unquestionable authenticity. Facts had to be observed and interpreted in the light of the propaganda of the later Vaiṣṇava worthies, otherwise they were not credited. Thus do we see that the Chaitanya Bhāgavata, which was written by Vṛindāvana Dās while living at the village of Denur in the district of Burdwan in the year 1573, had to be sent to Vṛndāvana for the approval of the six *gosvāmīs* and their learned companions such as Lokanātha and Bhūgarva. The work received their full approval and Chaitanya Mangal, the original name of the book, was changed by these masters into Chaitanya Bhāgavata[1]; for the ingenuity of the author had made this biography of Chaitanya correspond in its wire-drawn comparisons to the accounts of Kṛṣṇa's life as told in the Bhāgavata. This helped to raise Chaitanya to the status of an incarnation of Kṛṣṇa. The Sanskrit and Bengali works written by the six *gosvāmīs* were sent to Bengal, where a large number of copies of each was prepared and circulated among believers. All later books on Vaiṣṇavism, in order to claim any recognition, had to quote from these authoritative works in support of the views and even facts that were promulgated. We find that five hundred copies of the Premavilāsa, a work to which I shall have

[1] ভাগবতের অনুরূপ চৈতন্যমঙ্গল।
দেখিয়া বৃন্দাবনবাসী ভকত সকল॥
চৈতন্য ভাগবত নাম দিলা তার।

The Prema Vilāsa.

to refer later on, were prepared immediately after it was written and circulated among the Vaiṣṇavas.[1]

We have thus seen the importance of the works written in Vṛndāvana in the 16th century and their bearing on the succeeding literature of the Vaiṣṇavas. Our present scope will include those works which elaborate and supplement the Chaitanya literature produced during his life-time, and embody the account of all important later developments in the Vaiṣṇava history. This takes us to the affairs after 1534, the year in which Chaitanya quitted this world. The literature of this period ends with the Bhaktiratnākara written in 1723 A.D.

The modern period, if any account of it should be written, dates from after this time. But we are not at present concerned with its history.

Though I shall describe at some length the period 1534-1725 A.D., I must first of all mention the important works of the immediately preceding period, without a reference to which facts regarding the history of the epoch with which we shall more directly concern ourselves in course of these lectures will not be fully illustrated or explained. A review of the success achieved by the great Vaiṣṇava worthies at Vṛindāvana and an enumeration of their works will form the indispensible back-ground against which a history of the Vaiṣṇavas of the later period will have to be shown.

As the luminous figures of the three great apostles, Chaitanya, Nityānanda and Advaita, pass away from the

[1] See index to the 16th Chapter of the printed Premavilāsa, edited by Jasodālal Banik.
"এক এক অধ্যায় রচি যবে সমাপ্ত করিত।
পাঁচশত ভক্ত তাহা লিখিয়া লইত ॥"

horizon of Vaiṣṇava history, the spectacle of another brilliant trio, blended in the harmony of sweet faith and spiritual ideal, rises to our view, and the success they attained appears even more striking since the great lives which preceded them had already prepared the field and created a congenial atmosphere for their work. The recognition the Vaiṣṇava community has given to Çrīnivāsa, Narottama and Çyamānanda will appear from the fact that the first is revered by them as an incarnation of Chaitanya himself, the second of Nityānanda, and the third of Advaita.[1] A vast literature sprang up describing the works of the trio, and the Rādhā-Kṛṣṇa-songs once more found an inspiring impetus from their lives as they had done in a previous era from those of the three apostles headed by Chaitanya. Nityānanda Dās, Narahari Chakravarti, Govinda Dās, Rāmachandra Dās, Valarāma Dās, Jnāna Dās and a host of other gifted writers belong to this period of Vaiṣṇava history. But before we come to them we propose to reconnoitre the back ground first, specially the history of Vṛndāvana glorified and restored by the Bengali Vaiṣṇavas—a history which as I have already stated—has such a large bearing on the development of the Vaiṣṇava movement of the succeeding period.

———o———

Vṛndāvana has, from the most ancient times, enjoyed high repute as a celebrated Hindu shrine. It is some-

[1] শ্রীমহাপ্রভুর শক্তি শ্রীনিবাস হয় ।
নিত্যানন্দ শক্তি নরোত্তমেরে কহয় ॥
অদ্বৈত প্রভুর শক্তি হয় শ্যামানন্দ ।
যার কৃপায় উৎকলীয়া পাইল আনন্দ ॥”

Prema Vilāsa, 20th Vilāsa.

A brief survey of the history of Vṛndavana, ancient and modern.

six miles to the north of Mathurā and is washed on three sides by the river Jamunā "which first makes an abrupt turn to the north and then as sudden a return upon its accustomed southern course".[1] For many centuries, however, it was a wild and uninhabited jungle visited by pious pilgrims at long intervals of time and looked very much like the present Bhāndirvana, on the opposite bank of the Jamunā,—a place of equal sanctity in ancient Sanskrit literature. The word 'Vṛndā' means the 'Tulasi' plant (Ocymmum sanctum) and the shrine seems to have been originally named after the sacred aromatic herb, though in later times the legend of a Gopi named Vṛindā was invented to give a poetic colour and a sacredness to the place. "The neighbouring country teems with cattle; the straggling herds of oxen and buffaloes, often outnumbering the human population" now graze where the god of the cow-herds had once sweetly played on the banks of the sacred Jamunā.

Mathurā, and indeed the whole of the adjacent country known as the Braja-mandala, was full of the finest temples and buildings that India could boast of in the period immediately before the Mahomedan invasion. From 1017 A.D. there descended on this flourishing city a series of invading raids of Muslim iconoclasts in rapid succession reducing its great temples and architectural monuments to dust. The *Tarikhi jamina* a record of the life of Sultan Mahmud, says:

"If any emperor would ever dream of building palaces and temples like those of Mathūrā, he would

1 History of Mathurā by Growse (1882) p. 184.

have to spend thousands of golden drachmes. But it is doubtful if the best sculptors and artists of the world would be able to build a city like this working uninterruptedly for two hundred years".

The temples of Mathurā, by the evidence of the same historian, contained five images of solid gold, each 15 feet high, the eyes of the images were made of diamonds, each worth not less than 5,000 golden drachmes, the emeralds in which they were set surpassed in transparency and brightness the most brilliant crystals and the pure water of hill streams. On the 2nd December, 1018 the city with its unmatched splendour was destroyed by Sultan Mahmud. During 1488-1515, when it had only partially recovered from this calamity, it was again a scene of devastation owing to the raids of Sekandar Lodi. In 1636 Mursed Ali was appointed governor of Mathurā and of the Mahāvana by Shajahan. He had orders laid upon him to destroy every vestige of all sacred places of Hindu worship. In 1661, Auranzeb's General Abdun Navi again attacked the ill-fated city, and used the materials of its temples to build mosques on the banks of the Jamunā. The magnificent temple of Keçava Deva had been repaired by Vīrasiṁha of Urcha at a cost of 33 lakhs of Rupees. This was demolished by Auranzeb.

Thus the whole of the tract called the Brajamandala extending over 1453 sq. miles and specially the Vṛndāvana—the scene of Kṛṣṇa's childhood—lay desolate and filled with jungles, where the Hindu pilgrims dreamt of the past glory of their race and shed tears over the departed splendour and the sanctity which still attached itself to the name of the place. Tod, the author of the history of Rājasthān, writes ;—

"Though the groves of Vṛndā, in which Kṛṣṇa disported with the Gopis, no longer resound to the echoes of his flute; though the waters of the Jamunā are daily polluted with the blood of the sacred kine, still it is the holy land of the pilgrim, the sacred Jordan of his fancy, on whose banks he may sit and weep, as did the banished Israelite of old, for the glories of Mathura—his Jerusalem."

Though the dreams of the monarchs anxious to found temples of unsurpassed beauty and splendour—dreams realized by the herculine efforts of sculptors and artists for ages,—vanished for ever, it was reserved for Vṛndāvana to redeem, in however small degree, its ancient glory in the 16th century. All on a sudden her structures rose "as by the touch of a magician's wand" and the city became once more a seat of temples of rare architectural beauty. How this happened is a tale worth telling to Bengali students, for most of you have no doubt heard that this was done by the influence of Chaitanya and some of his colleagues, although they were but ascetics and beggars and had nothing themselves to contribute to the material development of the place. Says Mr. Growse, the historian of Mathurā, " The community of the Bengali Vaiṣṇavas had a more marked influence over Vṛindāvana than of the others (sects of Vaiṣṇavas) since it was Chaitanya, the founder of the sect, whose immediate disciples were its first temple builders." [1]

Growse's History of Mathurā, p. 197.

III The Great Bengali masters who revived the glories of Vṛndāvana—their works.

Mādhavendra Purī.

In my previous lectures in connection with Ramtanu Lahiri Fellowship I dwelt upon some facts regarding Mādhavendra Purī and Lokanatha Gosvāmi. As they were the pioneers of the Vaiṣṇava movements which reached their full development in the 16th century, I shall, with your permission, give a summary of some facts about them already told by me, and shall expand others which have a bearing on the history of Vṛndāvana.

The great Bengali ascetic who, charmed with its association with Kṛṣṇa, first dwelt for a long period of his life on the banks of the dark watered Jamunā—in the groves known as the Vṛndāvana, was Madhavendra Purī—a disciple of Laksmī tīrtha of the Maddhi sect of the Vāiṣṇavas. His pious life and fervid faith cast a spell on the sacred shrine attracting a number of Bengali pilgrims, who became his disciples and admirers. We have already narrated the beautiful legend told about the manner in which he recovered the image of Gopāla (the young Kṛṣna) in the holy city. It was not his custom to seek alms of any one. He lived upon what chance brought him without begging, and day and night contemplated Kṛṣṇa's dark blue image, which, repeated in the blue-tinted dark ranks of summer clouds became to his fascinated gaze a source of ever new delights and a symbol of the Infinite. As often as he saw the storm-clouds arise, and watched a flash of lightning passing through its bosom, the vision of his Kṛṣṇa clothed in

The legend of Gopāla.

purple became distinct to his mind's eye and he swooned in ecstasy of joy.[1] These visions followed him every where and intoxicated him with joy to such a degree that in the words of the great Bengali poet of the 18th century, Rāmaprasāda, it could be truly said of the Vaiṣṇava saint that 'It was his emotions that made him mad, but the drunkards thought that he was drunk with wine.'[2]

On reaching Vṛndāvana Mādhava sat under a tree in the evening and cared not that he had eaten nothing the whole day. It was the vision that fed his spiritual life and what mattered it, if his body was starving? Here a cowherd stood before him offering him a jar full of milk. The lad's dusky complexion resembling that of Kṛṣṇa pleased the saint more than the offered draught. He accepted the gift; whereupon the cowherd disappeared. During the whole night Mādhava thought of his God and communed with him, so that the material world altogether vanished from the plane of his exalted emotion. In the latter part of the night when sleep for a short while came upon his eye-lids, he saw the same young cowherd standing before him with an imploring look. "There in the dense forest on the Anna-kuta hill," said he, "I am buried under earth by the fostering care of a Brāhmin who wanted to save me from the iconoclast's hands. I am ill at ease, Mādhava, I am the lord of these groves. Save me if you can, long have I waited for you, for you

১ "মাধবেন্দ্র পুরীর কথা অকথ্য কথন।
মেঘ দরশন মাত্র হয় অচেতন ॥"

Chaitanya Bhāgavata.

২ "আমার মন মাতালে মাতাল কৈল, মদ্ মাতালে মাতাল বলে।"

Rāmaprasāda.

are one of the few who have loved me with a whole heart." The story of how Mādhava recovered the image of Gopāla with the help of Brajavāsīs has been fully related by me in my previous lectures. Mādhava brought two priests from Bengal who became the first Bengali custodians of a Vaiṣṇava temple at Vṛndāvana.

Mādhava travels to Puri.

Mādhava travelled to Puri all alone passing through many trials and troubles by the way and heedless as ever of physical pain, at a time when the main road from the upcountry was blocked by warfare amongst local rulers —in order to bring scented sandal woods and *aguru* for decorating the image of Gopāla. It was Mādhavendra who imparted *bhakti* to Advaitāchārya, and it was at the feet of this celebrated master that Nityānanda sat at Vṛndāvana to receive instruction in the Vaiṣṇava Çāstras. Mādhavendra was once in the valley of Çriparvata in the Deccan, and there also Nityānanda saw the ascetic in one of his trances and clasped his feet, and held them to his

The great respect in which he is held by all Vaiṣṇava- apostles.

bosom, saying 'Oh lucky day! the reward of visiting all these shrines God has vouchsafed me to-day. I have seen the feet of my venerable master. The sight of thy wonderful faith has hallowed my life.[1]" We have stated elsewhere that among the Bengali disciples of Mādhavendra were Keçava Bhāratī and Içwara Purī, the Gurus of Chaitanya, Pundarīka Vidyānidhi whom Chaitanya revered

১ "নিত্যানন্দ বলে যত তীর্থ করিলাঙ।
সম্যক তাহার ফল আজি পাইলাঙ॥
নয়নে দেখিলুঁ মাধবেন্দ্রের চরণ।
এ প্রেম দেখিয়া ধন্য হইল জীবন॥"

Chaitanya Bhāgavata, Chapter VI.

as father, and Mādhava Miçra, the father of Gadādhara, the celebrated follower of Chaitanya.

Chaitanya himself, though he had not the good fortune of meeting Mādhavendra, as the latter died when Chaitanya was a mere child, often paid a respectful tribute of admiration to the memory of the illustrious leader of the Maddhi sect. He always spoke in terms of great appreciation of his venerable predecessor who first lighted the torch of *bhākti* in Bengal. At Purī he once recited the famous çloka beginning with "হে দীন দয়ার্দ্র নাথ" composed by Mādhavendra, with a voice trembling with emotion of joy and saying that as the diamond Kaustuva was the most valued amongst all precious stones, the couplet he recited was unmatched in all human poetry.[1]

Narottama, the princely ascetic of the 16th century, began his work Sādhanātatwa with the following hymn in praise of Mādhavendra:

"All honour to Mādhavendra Purī—from whom flowed the first stream of *bhakti* (in Bengal)."[2].

———o———

Lokanaātha & Bhugarva.

Nearly half a century passed away after Mādhavendra Purī placed the image of Gopāla on the Govardhana hill in Vṛndāvana when two way-farers again crossed the borders

1 "রত্নগণ মধ্যে যৈছে কৌস্তুভ বাখানি।
কাব্য মধ্যে তৈছে এই শ্লোক গণি॥"

Chaitanya Charitāmṛta, Madhyakhanda.

2 "সাবধানে বন্দিব আজ শ্রীমাধবপুরী।
বিষ্ণু ভক্তি পথের প্রথম অবতরি॥"

Sādhya Sādhana Tattva.

For a full account of Mādhavendra Purī the reader is referred to Charitanya Charitāmṛta.

of Bengal in order to visit the holy city of the Vaiṣṇavas—nay to live there permanently by the order of Chaitanya. These two Bengalis were Lokanātha Goswāmī and Bhugarva.

Lokanāth was a son of Padmanātha Chakravarti of Talgoria in Jessore. His mother's name was Sītā. The family enjoyed a great respectability as *kulin* Brahmins. He was a diligent student of Sanskrit Philosophy in his early years, and, it is said, showed indications of turning a hermit when only 20. His parents were alarmed and proposed a match for him. But he fled from Talgoria

The Master's orders inviolable.

one night in 1510 A.D[1]. Içana Nāgara in his 'Advaita Prākaça' says that Lokanāth was a fellow student of Chaitanya in the *tol* of Gangā Dās Pundit and had travelled with him in Eastern Bengal. Be that as it may, he came to Navadwip in 1510 once more, and saw the Master who received him with kindness; but ordered that he should at once go to Vṛndāvana to identify the places sacred by the association with Kriṣṇa. Lokanāth fell at the Master's feet and asked why of all others he should be selected for the task and be deprived of the pleasure of being in his god-like presence. In reply Chaitanya said "Lokanāth, you and I are not meant for

1 This date is obtained from the circumstance that Lokanatha paid his visit to Chaitānya immediately before his *Samyāsa* which took place in 1510 A.D. The particulars of Lokanātha's life are to be found in Narottama Vilāsa by Narahari Chakravarty written early in the eighteenth century and in the Premvilāsa which is an earlier historical work (written about 1630 A.D). Babu Sisirkumar Ghosh who depended on the materials obtained from the above two and other books such as the Anurāga-Valli has given an excellent sketch of Lokanātha in his Narottama Charita.

this world's pleasures. Our paths will be other than those followed by common folk A higher duty calls you there. It is the propagation of faith outside Bengal by reclaiming the ancient shrine of Vṛndāvana."[1]

The route.

With a heavy heart Lokanāth left Navadwipa with Bhugarva Achārya—a disciple of Gadādhara Pandit—to fulfill the mission the Master had proposed for him. The pair of friends lightened the fatigue of the journey by dwelling again and again upon their one favoured topic—the wonderful story of Chaitanya's devotion to God. They often wept to think of him. "The five days I spent in his company at Nadiā last time" said Lokanatha "have been the greatest period of my life. They have opened to me a new heaven and a real one".

They came to Rajamuhāl and heard reports of the great robber-gangs who infested the land. The people of the locality said that it would not be possible for them to travel to Vṛndāvana in the disturbed state of the country. They had to change their route and go by Tājpur. They reached Purneah, staying there for a short while, and went thence to Ajodhyā. They next halted at Lucknow and it took them three days to reach Agrā from there. They drank the holy waters of the Jumunā, and felt blessed thereby. On reaching Vṛndāvana they lived for some time in a state of unspeakable joy, visiting the places where Kṛṣṇa had sported with his fellow cowherds and with the *gopis*. The people of Vṛndāvana were attracted by their holy lives and by their great faith. The first joys of visiting a shrine so dear to the Vaiṣṇavas by its association

1 See Narottama Charita by Sisirkumar Ghosh.

with Kṛṣṇa, however, passed away and they felt a pang at the thought of never being permitted to return to Bengal as was the Master's command. The Premavilāsa indicates the pathos of the situation in the touching words of Lokanātha. "I shall no longer see, Oh Lord, (Chaitanya) thy blessed feet. The fulfilment of your command is the great object for which alone I endure my life. The heavenly delights of your company are vouchsafed to your other followers but they are not for me!" [1] Anurāgavallī describes him as a man always given to contemplation and of a self-scrutinising habit. He did not speak much; when he did, his words were sweet to hear and powerfully impressed those who heard them.[2]

A fruitless search.

Chaitanya went to the Deccan in 1511. Lokanātha started from Vṛndāvana in search of him, in the hope of meeting him somewhere outside Bengal. He however missed him at several stations arriving there after Chaitanya had left them. While still travelling in Southern India he heard that Chaitanya had reached Vṛndāvana. But when Lokanātha returned on receiving this information, Chaitanya had already left the holy city. The wished-for interview never took place; but Lokanātha did not swerve an inch from the Master's instructions. He practised austerities befitting a true hermit and led the

[1] "আর না দেখিব গোরা তোমার চরণ।
রহিলাম আজ্ঞামাত্র করিয়া ধারণ॥
ভক্তগণ সঙ্গে প্রভু যে করিলা লীলা।
বঞ্চিত করিয়া মোরে হেথা পাঠাইলা॥"

Prema Vilāsa.

[2] "পরম বিরক্ত কথা নাহি কারো সনে।
যে কহয়ে সে অতি মধুর বচনে॥"

life of quiet spiritual joy which attracted the young generation of Vaiṣṇava scholars, some of whom like Narottama sat at his feet to receive instruction and distinguished themselves in the following age. He was no seeker of, nay, he despised all earthly glory and did not allow Kṛṣṇa Dās Kavirāja to make mention of him in his great Memoir of Chaitanya.[1]

—o—

Sanātana and Rūpa.

Some facts about these worthies are given in detail in my lectures as Ramtanu Lahiri Research Fellow. The two brothers exercised great influence on the people of Vṛndāvāna and its vicinity in the 16th century.[2]

Born to princely fortunes they had surrendered their wealth. They were high officers of the Mahomedan Emperor of Gaur, but this exalted situation they gladly renounced to join the Master, and became hermits like him. They came to Vṛndāvana at the behest of Chaitanya and lived a long life of continued work and piety there. Their reputation as scholars, as poets, and above all as holy men who had made great sacrifices for the cause of religion, was so high that the Emperor Akbar himself came to pay a visit to them at Vṛndāvana and became their

Akbar pays them a visit.

[1] See Prema Vilāsa.

[2] "The recognised leaders of Vṛndāvana community were by name Rūpa and Santāna" Growse's History of Mathura, p. 198.

ardent admirer.[1] When the Muhamedan Emperor showed such appreciation of their distinguished career, what marvel that his General Mān Singh built the wonderful temple of Govindaji to enshrine the images of Kṛṣṇa, which the ascetics worshipped, at a cost of a crore of Rupees. The pedigree and an account of the lives of Sanātana and Rūpa are given below. [I shall only barely touch upon those points detailed by me elsewhere in connection with their interview with Chaitanya. I ask you, to read them again for the purpose of appreciating their great sacrifices and the high ideal that inspired them throughout their long lives which covered all but a full century.]

Jagat Guru, a Maratha Brahmin, became the King of Karnat in the Deccan in 1381 A.D. and reigned till 1414 A.D. Jagat Guru's son was Aniruddha who by his two wives had two sons, named Rūpeçwara and Harihara. Aniruddha, the king, died in 1416 A.D. Before his death, however, he had contracted a friendship with the Mahomedan King of Gaur who had paid a visit to his kingdom while travelling in Southern India. On the death of Aniruddha, there ensued a struggle between the half-brothers—Rūpeçwara and Harihara; Rūpeçwara was driven out of the kingdom and sought refuge in the court of the king of Gaur, who was his father's friend. He got the post

The Pedigree.

[1] "Their fame spread so rapidly that in 1573 A.D. the Emperor Akbar was induced to pay them a visit, and was taken blind-fold into the sacred enclosures of the Nidhuvana, where such a marvellous vision was revealed to him, that he was fain to acknowledge the place as indeed a holy ground. Hence the cordial support which he gave to the attendant Rajas, when they expressed their wish to erect a series of buildings more worthy of the local divinity." Growse's History of Mathura, p. 241.

of Minister to the Emperor and remained so till his death in 1433 A.D. Padmanāva his son succeeded him in the post and built a country-house at Naihati. He had five sons,—Purusottama, Jagannātha, Narāyaṇa, Murāri and Mukunda. Mukunda, the youngest son, had a son named Kumāra Deva, who settled at Fateyabad in Backerganj. Kumardeva married an accomplished girl named Revatī—a daughter of · Harinārāyaṇa Viçārada of Mādhāipur near Gaur. Mādhāipur is two miles to the east of village Shāhpur on the Mahānanda river in the district of Māldaha. Kumāra Deva lived for a time in his father-in-law's house at Mādhāipur.

By Revatī, Kumāra had three sons,-Sanātana, Rūpa and Vallabha, (*alias* Anupama.) Sanātana and Rūpa were the names given to the brothers by Chaitanya. The names by which they were known in childhood were Amara and Santoṣa, respectively. Vallaba (*alias* Anupama) who was a great scholar and zealous worshipper of Rāma died in 1517 A.D. Amara and Santoṣa adopted the Mahomedan faith and were known as Dabir Khās and Sākar Mallik,

Incidents before adopting Sanayās.

respectively till their conversion to Vaiṣṇavism in 1516 A.D. from which date they have been known as Sanātana and Rūpa, the names, as I have already said, which Chaitanya gave them. Sanātana and Rūpa settled in a village named Rāmakeli close to Gour. Hither the brothers brought a colony of Karnat Brahmins with whom they frequently discussed religious and other topics. Sanātana and Rūpa were deeply versed in Sanskrit, Persian and Arabic. Their teacher of Sanskrit was the renowned Sarvānanda Vāchaspati of Naihati and they also mastered Arabic and

Persian with the help of Syed Fakir-ud-Din, a reputed scholar and Zemindar of Satgaon.[1]

Sanātana become the minister of Husen Sāhā and Rūpa also held a high position in that ruler's court. They first met Chaitanya at Rāmakeli in 1516. Husen Sāhā had deputed one of his officers named Keçava Chatri to make enquiries about Chaitanya in the meantime; and the subject of his wonderful devotion to God was discussed in the Moslem court. The Master had evoked enthusiastic admiration in the locality and the Emperor is said to have become one of his admirers himself.[2]

After the interview, Rūpa and his brother Anupama renounced home and turned hermits. They travelled to Allahabad where they met the Master once more. They accompanied him to Benares and begged leave to go to Puri with him. But Chaitanya requested them to visit Vṛndāvana first and then come to Bengal and meet him again at Puri. Rūpa went to Vṛndāvana with his brother. On their way back the latter died. It was while travelling to Puri that Rūpa conceived the idea of writing some dramas in Sanskrit. The plot of one was roughly drawn up.[3]

The plots of the two dramas.

In this play he thought of commemorating the events of Kṛṣṇa's life in Vṛndāvana and Mathurā. Some preliminary verses were written on the way and he contemplated a further development of the plot and characters. He came to a

[1] These accounts of their pedigree are found in the notes in Sanskrit left by Jīva Goswāmi, the reputed nephew of Sanātana and Rūpa; some of the details are to be found in a Bengali work named "Kavi Vidyāpaty" by Trailakyanāth Bhattācharya.

[2] Chaitanya Charitāmṛta, Madhya Khanda.

[3] Chaitanya Charitāmṛta Madhya Khanda

place named Satyavamāpura by boat. There he dreamt that Satyavamā, the queen of Kṛṣṇa, appeared to him and ordered him not to embody the incidents of Vṛndāvana and Mathurā in the same drama, but to deal with them separately. On reaching Puri he mentioned the plot of his drama, as he had conceived it, to the Master who said that the Kṛṣṇa of Vṛindāvan and the Kṛṣṇa of Mathurā were not at all alike. While the former was love's very self and an embodiment of sweetness (*mādhurya*), the latter manifested power (*aiçvarya*) as a monarch, establishing his unapproachable superiority and might by his intellectual greatness and force of arms. The atmosphere of Vṛndāvana was one of absolute resignation, love for love's sake, unconscious sacrifices of the highest order, and these should not be confused with material glories.

The Vidagdha Mādhava and the Lalita Mādhava.

Rūpa had already advanced considerably with the plot of his drama; so he had to take considerable pains in recasting the original plan and in disintegrating it in two of its main features. The Chaitanya Charitāmṛta relates the circumstances in which some of the verses were written at Puri, and how greatly Chaitanya and Rāma Ray, the Minister of Pratāpa Rudra, admired them. But the two dramas were not completed till long after this time. The Vidagdha-Mādhava was finished in 1532 and Lalita Mādhava in 1546 A.D. I give below a résumé of these two wonderful dramas together with the same author's Dānakelīkaumadī which are among the masterpieces of literary composition in Sanskrit in the 16th century. No writer in Sanskrit from the 15th century downwards has shown poetical powers of such high order as Rūpa.

The Vidagdha Mādhava consists of seven acts. The 1st is called the Benuninādavilāsa—the effect of the music of the divine flute; the 2nd—Manmathalekba—letters inspired by the God of Love; the 3rd, Radhāsangama—the meeting of Rādhā with Kṛṣṇa; 4th—The Venuharaṇa —or the stealing of the flute; 5th Radhāprāsādhana—the toilet of Rādhā; 6th Çaratvihāra—the courtship of Autumn; 7th—Gauritīrtha Vihāra—the joys of the shrine called Gauritīrtha.

Lalita Mādhava consists of ten acts. The 1st is named Sayan Utsava or the evening plays; 2nd—Çaṁkhachuḍavadha or killing of the demon Çankhachuḍa; the 3rd Unmatta Rādhikā—Rādhikā gone mad with love; 4th Rādhābhisāra or the stealing out of Rādhā to meet her lover, 5th Chandrāvalilīlābha—the meeting with Chandrāvali; 6th Lalitāprāpti—the meeting with Lalitā; 7th Nava Vṛndāvanasangama—the first meeting at Vṛndāvana; 8th Vṛndāvanavihāra—the dallying at Vṛndāvana; 9th Chitradarçaṇa or the Sight of the Picture; 10th Purṇamanaratha—Fulfilment of Desire.

Their spiritual meaning

It should be stated here that the love discussed in the above plays is spiritual, inspite of the fact that it is occasionally presented in a sensuous garb. Spiritual love was no phantom or willow-the-wisp with Rūpa or with other followers of Chaitanya. Sanātana and Rūpa were hermits of unspotted life and asceticism. They were mystics initiated in their blessed experience of communion with God by Chaitanya himself. Chaitanya Charitāmṛta devotes two chapters to Chaitanya's instructions imparted to Rūpa on rhetoric and on the exalted emotions of the spiritual plane. In fact some of the *Çlokas* in the dramas, such as

> "তুণ্ডে তাণ্ডবিনী রতিং বিতনুতে তুণ্ডাবলী লব্ধয়ে ।
> কর্ণ ক্রোড় কড়ম্বিনী ঘটয়তে কর্ণার্ব্বুদেভ্যঃ স্পৃহাম্ ॥
> চেতঃ প্রাঙ্গন সঙ্গিনী বিজয়তে সর্ব্বেন্দ্রিয়াণাং কৃতিং ।
> নো জানে জনিতা কিয়দ্ভিরমৃতৈঃ কৃষ্ণেতিবর্ণদ্বয়ী ॥"

Vidagdha Mādhava, Canto 1, Verse XVII.

were composed on the spot, as Rūpa witnessed Chaitanya's ecstasies of spiritual joy. It is therefore but natural that the works of Rūpa, inspite of their occasional apparent sensuousness, are revered as sacred books by the Vaiṣṇavas. They only prove that religion and faith are no bitter doses for deseased souls, and that asceticism is not to be always associated with skeleton forms tortured by self denial and austerities. Sentiments of devotion to God are fountains of never-ceasing joy—the ambrosia of heaven vouchsafed to men and are sweet, delicious and congenial food for the soul. Many annotators have tried to interpret the works of Rūpa and Sanātana in their proper spiritual light, and none of them is so conspicuous as Jīva Goswāmi, their nephew and disciple, and son of Anupama who died in 1517.

Other works.

Of the other works of Rūpa, all of which are in Sanskrit, the following are the most noted. The Ujjalanīlamaṇi describes the emotions of love and classifies them in 360 groups. The niceties of the feelings of a woman's heart are traced in all possible variety and treated in a scientific way with illustrations from Sanskrit classics. A brief résumé of the contents of this book is to be found in the Bengali works Chaitanya Charitāmṛta and Bhaktiratnākara.

Bhaktiratnāmṛtasindhu is a work treating the subject *bhakti* in an exhaustive manner. It is a complete survey of the emotional features of the Vaiṣṇava religion and illustrates its principles from the lives of the saints. It was written in the year 1541 A.D.

Nātakchandrikā, a work on Drama and Rhetoric.

Dānakelīkaumadī, a drama which has already been mentioned. Its subject is the amours of Rādhā and Kṛṣṇa. The artificial forms of Sanskrit style prevail in the works of Rūpa. But though imagery and figures are constantly drawn from the inexhaustible source of Sanskrit literature which had already reached a finished stage of rhetorical ornamentation, Rūpa's eyes, like those of all true poets, discover beauty for themselves, and do not blindly follow the classical traditions.

The first stanza of Dānakelīkaumudī for instance may be taken as a typical one. It runs thus:

"অন্তঃ স্মেরতয়োজ্জ্বলা জলকণব্যাকীর্ণ পক্ষাঙ্কুরা ।
কিঞ্চিৎ পাটলিতাঞ্চলা রসিকোৎসিক্তাপুরঃ কুঞ্চতি ॥
রুদ্ধায়া পথি মাধবেন মধুর ব্যাভূগ্নতারোত্তরা ।
রাধায়াঃ কিলকিঞ্চিৎ স্তবকিনী দৃষ্টিঃ শ্রিয়ং বঃ ক্রিয়াৎ ॥"

A stanza from the Dānakelīkaumudī.

In order to understand this verse one must first know what is meant by the word "কিলকিঞ্চিৎ". In Sanskrit poetics the word is used to mean a combination of seven different emotions. The *çloka* traces these emotions in the glance of Rādhā, who all unexpectedly in the path to the market, is obstructed by Kṛṣṇa. She is happy beyond measure at meeting her lover, but angry at his want of prudence, her eyes redden with just wrath; she is a wife and if discovered in in her lover's company, woe will attend her, this fear brings a tear drop to her eyes;

while she enjoys the humour of her situation inspite of her danger, her eyes also indicate that she is proud of the attentions of her lover and is inwardly pleased. Rādhā, thus caught in the arms of Kṛṣṇa, manifests a complexity of emotion which is apparent in her glance; it is sweet, it is reproving, it is tearful, it is half-abashed, it is indicative of an inward joy and sense of appreciative humour, it is proud and at the same time slightly tinged with the flash of anger. Jīva Goswāmī in his commentary, the inspiration of which, no doubt, came from his uncle—the poet himself, details these emotions and at the same time emphasises the word স্তবকিনী and dwells upon the beauty of the stanza from another point of view, *viz.*, that of the glance as compared to a blooming flower. There is a stage in the growth of a flower, when the bud bursts into blossom, still wet with dew, it seems to smile covertly, it opens its blossoms with what may well seem to be coyness, it resists the force of the air and yet yields to it gradually, and the flush on the petals may be interpreted to signify the momentary anger of the lover's heart. The growth of the bud to flower at this stage images the beauty of Rādhā's glance in all its niceties in her puzzling situation. These are ingenously brought out by the commentator as he tries to explain the hidden beauties of the suggestive stanza. The word "স্তবকিনী" has a direct reference to a bud that is bursting, and the poet, without saying anything that the commentator has brought out, suggests the whole group of vision by this single word, though throughout the verse all other words chosen are apt to carry the simile of the bud without its being made too prominent or striking.

Verses like these inspite of their apparent ingenuity have a simple beauty of their own. They are not to be ascribed to the craze for strained similes and metaphors which characterises the writings of the mediæval poets. Chaitanya displayed a hundred niceties of exalted emotion in his love of God and, these were fountains of never-ceasing beauty to the admiring eyes of those who witnessed them. It is no wonder that the shades of tender feeling introduced by these poets sprang from minute observation of the Master's ecstasies of love. The whole thing was conceived from the sight of a mystic world—hitherto unknown to the people, and though put in the outward forms and phraseology of the material world, it always symbolised the spiritual and the abstract, brought within the range of human comprehension by Chaitanya's own life.

The Padmāvalī is an anthology of Rādhā Kṛṣṇa songs containing 392 stanzas. It was annoted by Vīrchandra, son of Nityānanda, and the commentary was called Rasikarangadā—the giver of delight to one who is an adept in love. An edition of this work was published by Pundit Rāmnārayaṇa of Berhampur in 1881 and a second edition was called for in 1910.

The Sankhepa Bhāgabatāmṛta—as its name implies, briefly relates some of the stories of the Bhāgavata.

Haṁsadūta and Uddhavasandeça—in these two poems Rādhā laments her separation from Kṛṣṇa. Both of them describe messages of love on the model of Kāli Dās's famous Meghaduta.

Stavamālā—religious hymns addressed to Chaitanya and Rādhā Kṛṣṇa.

Kṛṣṇer janmatithi.

Gaṇadveçadīpikā—(in two parts). This work describes the great apostles of the Vaiṣṇava faith as incarnations of the *gopis* of the Rādhā-Kṛṣṇa legend.

Ānandamahodidhi.

Prajuktakṣachandrikā.

Mathurāmahatmya—a topography of Mathurā and a description of her glories.

Govinda Virudāvalī.

While Rūpa's works are characterised by a genial poetic flow and soaring flights of imagination, those of Sanātana, his elder brother, display a profundity of study and a mastery of the details of the Vaiṣṇava scriptures, for which he now stands as the great law-giver and authority in matters concerning the customs of Vaiṣṇava society.

The Hari-bhakti Vilasa by Sanatana.

Chaitanya had suggested the lines on which the great work, Haribhakti Vilasā, of Sanātana was written. This work gives a complete code of the ritual of Vaiṣṇavism. Chaitanya Charitāmṛta (Maddhyakhanda, Chap. 24) gives a synopsis of the suggestions made by Chaitanya which were elaborated by Sanātana. The work gives details how images are to be made and how temples are to be founded, with an enumeration of various ceremonies which a Vaiṣṇava should perform at the various stages of his life. It also gives details of chaste life according to the Vaiṣṇava conception of morality and is full of interesting particulars as to the ceremonial portion of Vaiṣṇavism, which for the purpose of comparative theology will be useful by offering a historical clue to the transformation of ancient Hindu and Buddhistic thought into comparatively modern forms.

The authorship of this monumental work shewing, as it does, extraordinary learning and a patient collation of facts on the part of Sanātana, is now ascribed to Gopāla Bhatta. Chaitanya desired Sanātana not to introduce any matter into the work which could not be supported by some ancient authority, and so the author had to take immense pains to discover old texts while enunciating rules of conduct as briefly suggested by Chaitanya. Gopāla Bhatta simply expanded the work of Sanātana with some further illustrations; and the work as it now stands is as great in size as in its usefulness to the Vaiṣṇava community of Bengal. They are guided by the texts of the Haribhakti Vilāsa in all matters of daily life.

It was by Sanātana's wish that the book was published in the name of Gopāla Bhatta. For before renouncing the world as a hermit, he had lived despised in Hindu society having once been a Mahomedan convert. Though by his great sacrifices, by his unique scholarship and by the unspotted character of his life he had now earned an exalted rank among the advanced Vaiṣṇavas and was reckoned as Goswami or Guru by them, the whisper of the lay Hindu and even the Vaiṣṇava community branded him with infamy; and no penance and sacrifice could induce the Hindu community of those days to look with respect and goodwill upon one who had even temporarily foregone the faith of his fathers. His sin was not expiated even by his becoming an ascetic—a Sādhu—of the first rank. The tradition of the grim and orthodox intolerance which Rūpa and Sanātana met from the populace still lingers in the circumstance that at Ramakeli—their native village—no Hindu, even up to the present day, touches the water of the tank which was excavated by the orders of the brothers and still bears their names.[1]

Sanātana's humility

No one was more alive to the popular sentiment than Sanātana himself, whose humility was without limit. He considered himself despised of others and was content with the sweetness which sprang from within him. He never viewed the sentiments of the people with anger or even a proud indifference. Humiliated by public opinion, he considered himself the most humble of all living men. This humility, which was spontaneous, adorned his moral life and gave him a genuine respect for others. Thus did Sanātana publish his *magnum opus* in Gopāla Bhatta's name, wishing that its codes might be accepted by the Hindu community the more readily as coming from one who in their eyes was a genuine Brahmin. He, however, allowed the commentary called the Dikprakaçikā, which he himself wrote on the work, to stand in his own name. But it is an open secret now to the people who have any culture in Vaiṣṇava history, that it was Sanātana and not Gopāla Bhatta who composed the original work. This is indicated in Chaitanya Charitamṛta (Chap. 24, Madhyakhanda) ; Jīva Goswami, Sanātana's nephew, at the close of his commentary on the 10th Skanda of Bhāgavata mentions Haribhaktivilāsa and the commentary on it as being both the work of his uncle. In 1554 A.D. Sanātana finished the celebrated commentary on the Bhāgavata named Vaiṣṇava-toṣiṇī. The Loghutoṣiṇī—an abridgement of the same—was compiled by Jīva when Sanātana was still alive. Sanātana also wrote the Bhagavatāmṛta in two parts, and supplemented them with commentaries of his own. This is

[1] See Kavi Vidyāpati by Trailokyanatha Bhattāchārya.

mentioned in the works of Kṛṣṇa Dās Adhikāri, a pupil of Jīva.

Rūpa was born in 1490, and Sanātana in 1492. In some of the modern Vaiṣṇava works the dates of the death of Sanātana and Rūpa are given as 1559 and 1565 A.D. respectively. But we have a large mass of evidence to prove that both the brothers died in 1591 having lived the full span of a century.

About the dates.

In the first place let me refer to the date on which the celebrated temple of Govindaji was built by Mān Singh at Vṛndāvana. The inscription says that the temple was completed in 1590 by the direction of the Gurus of Mān Singh, Sanātana and Rūpa. We know that ingenious arguments may be advanced to the effect that the temple might have taken long years for its completion and though it was begun at the instance of Sanātana and Rūpa, the brothers might not have lived to see it completed. This view is not, however, correct. For we know that Çrinivāsa paid a visit to Vṛndāvana in the year 1592 when he found the temple of Govindaji complete. He was told on his arrival that it was only four months since Sanātana had died and that Rūpa had died only four days before. He, therefore, failed to meet the venerable saints while they yet lived. The year 1559 as the date on which Sanātana is said to have died is incredible also from another point of view. He was alive in 1583, this we know for certain, as Jīva wrote his Loghutoṣiṇī in that year taking advice from him. Çrinivasa stayed in Vṛndāvana for not less than 6 or 7 years. He left it after 1597. This is borne out by the authentic records preserved in the court of the Rājās of Viṣṇupur.[1] All this evidence undisputedly

[1] See the word "Viṣṇupur" in the Viçwakoṣa.

proves that Sanātana and Rūpa died about the year 1591 and at an interval of a little more than four months.

JĪVA GOSWAMI

Jīva, the distinguished nephew of Sanātana and Rūpa and son of Anupama, is described in the Premavilāsa as being already very old when his uncles died. He could not have been less than 80 years of age at the time. He was, therefore, born early in the 16th century. He was a young lad when his father died and his uncles turned hermits. They had distributed their vast property among the poor and Brahmin scholars before renouncing home, reserving one fifth of the whole for the maintenance of their family, and even this was great wealth for Jīva—the sole heir to this share of the property. Sanātana and Rūpa had removed their wives and other members of the family to Fatehabad before they followed Chaitanya. This was evidently with the object of making their family and property safe from the hands of the infuriated Emperor of Gaur who had sent Sanātana to jail from which the latter made his escape by the help of Mir Habul, the jailer.

How Jīva takes Sannyāsa.

The widowed mother was full of admiration for the sacrifices made to religion by Sanātana and Rūpa and by her own husband too, who had died prematurely. Chaitanya's name was a household word and each of his acts was described to Jīva, when a mere boy, in detail by the admiring mother with a fervour of faith which could not but make a lasting impression on her young son.

Chaitanya disappeared from the world in 1533, and Jīva was a mere lad about this time.[1] One day he asked his mother how a man became a hermit. She with tearful eyes described the pathetic details of renunciation. The ochre-coloured cloth was to be put on, the daily meal was to be simple and earned by begging. A hermit must sleep under a tree, drive away all desires and anxieties from his heart, and sing the praises of the Lord alone. "And, mother," asked her attentive son, "did my dear father and uncles pass through all these hardships? They were immensely rich and accustomed to the comforts of high life; how could they endure privation?" The mother wept and said that they gladly suffered all hardship for the sake of religion and for the love they bore to Chaitanya; the sight of Chaitanya was so charming that men forgot all about the earth at the sight of him and cared not for the pains of physical life. Another day the lad put on an ochre-coloured cloth and took a staff in his hand and came to his mother and smiling said, "Mother, do I now look like a hermit?" "Yes, boy, how glorious you look—like a saviour of the world," answered the unsuspecting mother. But the boy laughed only and said, "So mother what a big saint am I now! people should bow to me from henceforth." The mother said, "But the hermit must shave his head." The next day, Jīva, a youth of about 20, had his head shaven and still dressed in ochre-coloured cloth came to his mother and said, "Mother, the goal of my father and uncles is mine too. Earth has lost all

[1] This anecdote is taken from the account of Jīva Goswami given in the 23rd chapter of the Premavilāsa.

attractions for me. May the bliss attained by my uncles be mine from to-day. Adieu to world and adieu to you, dear mother." So saying he left home and his mother. She, taken by surprise and struck as by a thunder-bolt, swooned away in grief.

Remarkably handsome was Jīva and accustomed to the ease of prosperous people. The hardships of a solitary journey on bare foot in those days, when there were no good roads, must have been great. He came to Nadia and saw Nityānanda in the house of Çrivāsa. The celebrated courtyard which still bore the dust of Chaitanya's feet was now a shrine, and with tearful eyes did the young hermit touch its ground reverentially.

He next went to Benares where for some years he studied the Upanishads with a great scholar named Madhusūdana Vāchaspati and mastered the subject. He became gradually renowned as a prodigy of learning, and coming to his uncles at Vṛndāvana received a full course of instructions in the Bhakti Çāstras.

His works.

He wrote 25 works in Sanskrit, all of which are distinguished by great erudition and evident power of grasping current religious problems and solving them to his satisfaction. Some of these works are mentioned below.

1. Harināmāmṛta Vyākarana—in which grammatical terminology is, as far as possible, associated with the name of Kṛṣṇa.

2. Commentary on the Bhāgavata called the Kramasandarva.

3. Ṣatsandarva—a very remarkable work containing a dissertation on Vaiṣṇava philosophy and the higher metaphysics.

4. Sarva Saṁvādinī—an elaborate philosophical commentary of his own Ṣatsandarva.

5. Gopāla-Champū—a work in prose and verse chiefly treating of the love of Rādhā-Kṛṣṇa.

6. Durgama Sangamanī—or a guide to obscure paths, being a commentary on the Bhaktiratnāmṛtasindhu by Rūpa.

7. A commentary on the Bramhasaṁhitā which was brought to Orissa by Chaitanya himself from a place named Mallhara on the Payoṣṇi river in the Deccan. It was found in the temple of Ādi Keçava there.

8. A commentary on Kṛṣṇa Karṇāmṛta by Vilwa Mangala Thakur. This work also was brought by Chaitanya from the Deccan.

9. Sūtramālikā—A grammatical work treating of the derivation of words.

10. Kṛṣṇārchanadīpikā which treats of the details of the ritual of Kṛṣṇa-worship.

A description of the contents of these works and of the remaining 15, most of which are commentaries on standard Vaiṣṇava works, will be found in the first Taranga of the Bhaktiratnākara.

Some of these works were brought to Bengal about the year 1599 by Çrinivasa Āchāryva. We are in possession of a large mass of correspondence between Jīva Goswami and some of his friends and admirers in Bengal. From these we learn that a number of his works, such as the Uttara-Champū, the Harinamāmṛta Vyākaraṇa and the Mādhava-Māhātmya were completed and fully revised before 1599, but his Laghutoṣiṇī, Durgamasangamanī and Gopāla-Champū were not completed till some time after that year. The latter works were sent to Bengal by one Çyāmādās Āchāryya, a noted player of the *mṛdanga* and a son of Vyāsachārya, the court-pundit of Rājā Vīra Hamvīra of Vana Viṣṇupura. These letters also show that if any difficulties as to the interpretation of the sacred texts arose in Bengal, they were referred to Jīva Goswami, and his verdict on the points raised was accepted as final. Çrinivāsa was much afflicted by the news of the death of his Guru Gopāla Bhatta. Jīva Goswami, when he heard the news, wrote him thus :—

The universally respected scholar.

"Indulgence in grief does not remove it but enhances it. Çrinivāsa, know that griefs are unholy, showing the heart unreconciled to the will of Kṛṣṇa. Both body and mind are always liable to pain, a conquest over them is true heroism."[1]

We also find from this correspondence in what high esteem Jīva held the vernacular songs of Govinda Dās, the renowned Vaiṣṇava poet about whom I shall have to speak later on.

An interesting incident.

An interesting incident showing the manner of life led by Sanātana, Rūpa and Jīva, and the high ideal which inspired the Vaiṣṇavas of Vṛndāvana, is related in the Premavilāsa by Nityānanda Dās. I shall briefly mention it here:[2]

Rūpa Nārāyana, as a wayward child.

In a village named Bhitādiyā near 'Egāra Sindūra'—once the capital of the Hindu kingdom Kāmarūpa (Assam), lived a Brahmin scholar named Lakṣminārāyaṇa, the husband of Kamalā Devī, an accomplished woman and a beauty. He was a Vārendra Brahmin and a Kulin. Rūpa Nārāyaṇa

[1] The Prema-Vilāsa. The Arddha-Vilasa. Letter III.

[2] See the 19th Vilāsa.

was their only son who, though of handsome features, was a wayward lad and mixed in bad company. He neglected his lessons though his father tried his utmost to reform him. Finally in despair the father ordered his wife to give the wicked son pieces of burnt wood for his meal instead of rice. The good lady remonstrated with her husband against so cruel a punishment, but as a faithful wife she dared not violate her husband's commands and when serving his meal to young Rūpanārāyaṇa, she placed a bit of burnt wood on the plate by the side of the rice. Rūpanārāyana asked his mother as to what that piece of wood meant and she was obliged to confess her kindly stratagem. The young boy refused to eat the rice and said "Adieu to you dear mother, I shall mind my lessons from to-day, but you shall not see me for a long time." He fled from home and went to a village named Panchavatī, where he studied Sanskrit grammar. He next lived for some years at Nadia closely studying Logic and other branches of metaphysics. He was at Orissa about the year 1528, where he paid a visit to Chaitanya.

His tour abroad.

The young aspirant to learning did not, however, wait at Puri long, but went to Benares to complete his education. He got the title of Āchārya and visited Poona, which was in the 16th century a great seat of Sanskrit learning. He studied the Vedas and Upanishads with Maratha Brahmins and got the title of Saraswatī.

and great learning.

As a child he was wayward and strong-willed; as a scholar he became proud and self-assertive. He went about the country challenging learned scholars to discussion in which he always proved invincible. No scholar in southern and upper India could hold his own in controversial discussion with Rūpanārāyaṇa Saraswatī, whose scholarship was as great as his talents, so that even veteran scholars older than him by many years held him in dread. He assumed the title of Dikvijayi "or a conquerer of the four quarters."

The haughty scholar

By the time Sanātana and Rūpa were known all over Northern India as its greatest scholars. Rūpanārāyaṇa came to Vṛndāvana and in his usual arrogant tone challenged them to a free discussion on any subject they liked. The hermits said they were not inclined to enter into any controversy with any one. "Are you not great scholars as people say ?" asked Rūpanārāyaṇa jestingly. In reply they showed extreme meekness and said that their worth was exaggerated and that they were not fit persons to cope with such a young lion of scholarship as their assailant was. "Then you should give me a 'Jayapatra'—a letter acknowledging your complete defeat at my hands," said Rūpanārāyaṇa, and the brothers gladly gave him such a letter, writing what Rūpanārāyaṇa himself dictated. It was not a document that they wrote and signed under compulsion but was the outcome of the overflowing and natural meekness of their spiritual souls.

Meets Sanātana and Rūpa.

Full of vanity that the Goswāmis did not venture to hold a disputation with him, Rūpanārāyaṇa heard that there was yet a nephew of the two scholars, who might be his match and a worthy adversary. He visited Jīva, who heard from his assailant himself that his uncles had given him a

His vanity and defeat.

letter of victory which the proud scholar construed as a result of fear. Jīva—himself a young man, was very angry at Rūpnārāyaṇa's boasting, and at the humilation of his uncles. He held a disputation with him on the banks of the Jamuna. For five days they were on equal teims but on the sixth day Rūpanārāyaṇa seemed to lose ground, and on the 7th his defeat was complete. The Advaitavāda or the theory of non-duality advocated by Rūpanārāyaṇa was completely demolished and that of duality which promulgated the belief in a personal god—the key-stone to Vaiṣṇava theology, was established. Bhakti was proved to be superior to Jñāna.

Rūpanārāyaṇa was now full of remorse on recollecting his arrogant attitude towards Sanātana and Rūpa. He came with tears in his eyes before them and said that he was a great sinner having belittled his masters out of sheer folly and ignorance.

Rūpanārāyaṇa left Vṛndāvana in the year 1534, a completely reformed man and in later years accepted the post of councellor of Rājā Narasiṁha Ray of Pakapalli (Pāikpara). About whom we shall have to write hereafter.

After the scholar had gone away Rūpa called his nephew Jīva to him and said :—

"You fool, you have put on the robes of an ascetic prematurely, you have not been able yet to conquer your pride and anger. In the blessed shrine of Vṛndāvana no one should dwell who asserts his ownself and takes pride in humiliating others. Get out from my sight. You are unfit to live in this holy place."

Jīva Goswāmi in disgrace.

Jīva bowed to his uncle and left his presence at this order, and made a small hut on the outskrits of the shrine, where he ceased to speak with any body, and observed his vow of silence for a year, after which by the intercession of Sanātana, Rūpa's anger abated and his nephew was readmitted to Vṛndāvana. Rūpa is said to have got pardon from Sanātana for Jīva by a curious pun on the latter's name. One of the cardinal doctrines of Vaiṣṇavism is "Jive Dayā" or "Kindness to all living beings." Jīva "means a living being." Now Sanātāna wishing to intercede for Jīva called on his brother one day and asked him what were the great doctrines of their faith. Rūpa mentioned among others "Jive dayā" and Sanātana immediately interrupted him by asking him why was he then so cruel to Jīva. Here by "Jīva" Rūpa of course meant his nephew and not "a living being"—the literal meaning of the word.

Sanātana, Rūpa and Jīva were apostles of Vaiṣṇavism, who thus lived for long years in the holy city of the Vaiṣṇavas, converting it into a distinguished seat of learning and of religious speculation in those historic days. In 1573 the Emperor Akbar paid a visit to these distinguished hermits, known as the Goswamis: and he is said to have been greatly impressed by a marvellous vision which he saw at the holy place. "Hence the cordial support which he gave to the attendant Rājās when they expressed their wish to erect a series of buildings more worthy of the local divinity." Of this, however, we have spoken already.

The saintly lives of these men and their great influence exerted upon all who came in contact with them created legends which are now inseparable from the popular belief. One of them is recorded in the Bhaktamālā by Nāvāji, translated into Bengali by Kṛṣṇa Dās in the 17th century.

It says that once upon a time Sanātana happened to possess "a *sparça maṇi*" or the fabled philosopher's stone which he buried in the earth thinking that if a poor man should come to him for help, he would give it to him. Now there was a Brahmin named Jīvana, a native of the village Mankar in the southern part of the district of Burdwan who constantly prayed to God to give him riches. So greatly did the idea of getting riches by the grace of God possess him, that one day he dreamt that the God Mahādeva appeared to him and said that if he went to Sanātana who lived in Vṛndāvana he would give him a philosopher's stone. Jīvana came to Vṛndāvana and found Sanātana seated on the banks of the Jumna absorbed in prayer. He humbly solicited his help in obtaining riches. Sanātana meekly said that he was a beggar himself and could give nothing to others. He had not remembered then that a philosopher's stone lay buried near him. But the Brahmin said—"Mahādeva himself has appeared to me and said that you could give me a valuable stone. If the words of the great god fail me, I will commit suicide." Sanātana, thus reminded, pointed to a spot with his finger and said "There; dig it up; there it is." And so the poor man dug up the earth and found the stone there. He asked Sanātana to help him in getting it out from the earth, but the hermit said—"Filthy riches of the world I will not touch any more." Jīvana extracted the stone himself and found that whatever he touched with it became gold in a moment. Full of joy he proceeded on his way homeward, but on the road another thought occupied him. "What has the hermit got, that he rejected this most valuable stone which even a monarch might be proud of possessing?" As he thought

The legend of the philosopher's stone.

thus, the hermit appeared to the poor Brāhmin's fancy as a perfect man. The bliss apparent on his face, Jivana thought, "is not of earth, it must have come from heaven itself." He longed for a sight of the hermit to whom that precious stone was of little worth. He returned from Balasore to which city he had already journeyed and coming back to Sanātana, asked him "Father, will you tell me what riches you have got that are so much better than this that you have given me?" Sanātana said nothing but only smiled. The Brahmin was the more struck by the apparent contentment of the holy man whose happiness depended not on anything the world could give him. He said "Father, you would not touch filthy lucre, you said, I will not do so from to-day. Give me a little of what you have got. I have known no peace for all these years and I am sure the possession of this stone will increase my trouble instead of removing it." So saying he flung away the precious stone into the waters of the Jumna and became a disciple of Sanātana. The supplementary portion of the Bhaktamāla relates that Jīvana had a son named Bhāgavata whose descendants lived in the village of Kātāmārgāon at the time when Kṛṣṇa Dās translated the book. Katāmārgāon, the author says, was known afterwards as Mārgāon in the Burdwan district. The legend goes on to describe how the Emperor Akbar heard of the precious stone and sent a large number of elephants bound in iron chains to search for it in the waters of the Jumna. It is said that some of the chains became gold coming in contact with the fabled stone. But the stone itself could not be found.[1]

[1] See Bhakta Mālā, by Kṛṣṇadās, Chapter II.

The Premavilāsa describes some of the noble traits of Sanātana's character. I refer to that passage particularly which describes his arrival at Vṛndāvana. A large crowd assembled round him, the hermit asking them questions about their prefessions, their joys and sorrows, and particulars about their domestic lives, and often did he melt into tears hearing the story of a poor man's distresses, and give him such sympathy as assuaged the grief of the afflicted heart.

Sanātana and the image of Madana Mohana.

We have found in the Chaitanya Charitāmṛta that Avaitāchārya on his visit to Vṛndāvana had first discovered the image of Madana Mohana said to have been made by the orders of Kuvjā herself—one of the queens of Kṛṣna.[1] The Mahomedans paid their usual visit to the temple and Advaita concealing the image succeeded in saving it from robbery. He, however, made it over to one Mathura Chaubey who worshipped it with great devotion. Sanātana got it from Mathura Chaubey, and the Bhaktamāla says that the hermit had nothing to offer to the deity but a few pieces of coarse bread without salt. He made a straw-hut which was its first temple in a villa near Surya Ghāt; and when offering the deity the bread without salt the hermit often suppressed a tear and said "This is all that I can offer you, Lord, if you must needs dwell with a man like me!" He was, however, resolved that he would not ask help of any wealthy man, not even for the deity whom he adored.[2]

The temples of Vṛndāvana.

One day a merchant named Rāma Dās but known more familiarly as Kapuri, a Kṣettri by caste came from Multan

[2] See Bhakta Māla, by Kṛṣṇadās, Chapter II.

[2] See Bhakta Māla, by Kṛṣṇadās, Do.

down the Jumna with a boat-load of merchandise bound for Agra; but the boat stuck on a sand bank near the Kālidaha Ghāt. After trying in vain for three days to get it off, he saw Sanātana seated on the banks of the Jumna lost in profound meditation. The very sight of the holy man inspired the merchant with reverence and he implored him most humbly if he could help him any way out of the difficulty. Sanātana advised him to implore the help of God and remained silent. But the merchant said "If by the grace of God on whom you have asked me to depend I am saved from this difficulty, I shall employ all my profits of this year in building a temple for Madana Mohana—the deity whom you worship in that straw hut of yours." Sanātana said nothing to this and the merchant on reaching the banks of the Jumna really found that the boat had begun to float. The large amount of money that Rāma Dās (alias Kāpuri) earned that year, was employed by him in building the great temple of Madana Mohana. This history is to be found in such Hindi works as the Bhaktamāla by Nāvāji and Bhakatisindhu by Lachman Dās. But the earlier authority for the tale is the Bengali Chaitanya Charitamṛta by Kṛṣnadās Kavirāj written in 1583 A.D. For other particulars as to this temple the reader is referred to pp. 250-251 of the History of Mathurā by Growse. "The original image of Madana Mohana is now at Karauli, where Rāja Gopāla Siṁha who reigned from 1725-1759, built a new temple for its reception, after he had obtained it from his brother, the Raja of Jaipur. The Gossain whom he placed in charge was a Bengali from Murshidabad by name Rāmkisora."

How the temple of Madana Mohana was built.

But by far the greatest temple of Vaiṣṇavas at Vṛndavana is that of Govindaji built by Man Singh in 1590. The inscription in this temple says that it was built by Man Sirg " under the directions of the two Gurus Rūpa and Sanātana. " In the north west chapel there is another inscription which says " In the 34th year of the era inaugurated by the reign of the Emperor Akbar, Çri Man Singha Deva son of Maharaja Bhagwan Dās, of the family of Maharaj Pritthwī Rāj, founded, at the holy station of Vṛndavana, this temple of Govindadev. The head of the works Kalyān Dās, the Assistant Superintendent Mānik Chānd Chopar, the architect Govinda Dās of Delhi, the mason Gorokh Dās. " As to this temple Mr. Growse observes " It is the most impressive religious edifice that the Hindu art has ever produced, at least in Upper India. It is not a little strange that of all the architects who have described this famous building, not one has noticed its most characteristic feature—the harmonious combination of dome and spire—which is still noted as the great crux of modern art, though nearly 300 years ago, the difficulty was solved by the Hindus with characteristic grace and ingenuity."[1] Mr. Growse describes the particulars of this temple at great length, but we need not take further extracts from him here, a treatise on Art being the place where the details of such description may more aptly be quoted.

The temple of Govindaji.

I want merely to show what marvellous material results were achieved by the saintly Rūpa and Sanātana without seeking them. In fact it was the holiness

[1] Growse's History of Mathura p. 252.

of their lives that made Vṛndāvana holier than ever in popular estimation. And not only pious pilgrims thronged there from all parts of India with an admiration that was never witnessed before for the ancient shrine but even princes and potentates vied with one another in contributing to the grandeur of its temples and religious edifices, so that at the present time there is a noble array of more than a thousand temples in Vṛndavana, whereas before Rūpa and Sanātana came thither there was not one though the place had a sanctity of very ancient origin.

Other Temples.

The temple of Jugala Kisora was founded by one Nonkaraṇ in the year 1627. The image known as Jugala Kisora belonged to Jīva Goswami.

Regarding other temples with which the names of the Vaiṣṇava hermits of Bengal are associated, a full and graphic account will be found in Mr. Growse's interesting pages. And we need not enumerate them here.

Mr. Growse says "The recognised leaders of the Vaiṣṇava community were by name Rūpa and Sanātana —the authors of several doctrinal commentaries and also it is said of Mathura Mahātya. With them was associated a nephew named Jīva who founded the temple of Rādhā Damodara." Mr. Growse says further that Brahma Vaivarta Purāṇa was composed by Rūpa. We do not know from what source Mr. Growse obtained this curious information.

The Bhaktamāla by Nāvāji—the standard biographical work of the Vaiṣṇavas pays this tribute of honour to the memories of the Bengal hermits.

The appreciation of the labours of Sanātana, Rūpa and Jīva.

শ্রীরূপসনাতন ভক্তিজল শ্রীজীব গুসাঁই সর গম্ভীর।
বেলা ভজন সুপক্ক কষায়ণ কবহু ন লাগী ॥
বৃন্দাবন দৃঢ়বাস যুগল চরণ অনুরাগী।
পোয়ো লেখনি পাঁনি অঘট অক্ষরচিত দোলোঁ।
সদগ্রন্থন কোঁ সাব সর্ব্বে হস্তামল কোনৌ।
সন্দেহ গ্রন্থচ্ছেদন সমর্থ রস বাসি উপাসিক পরম ধীর।
শ্রীরূপসনাতন ভক্তিজল শ্রীজীব গুসাঁই সর গম্ভীর ॥

"Çri Rūpa and Sanātan and Çri Jīva Goswami were as a deep lake filled with the water of devotion. With them prayer was ever ripe and in season, and never bitter to the taste. Firmly fixed at Vṛndavana, full of devotion to the feet of the Dual God, with their hands writing books and with their souls fixed on the formless idea, they held in their grasp all the essence of divine love, able to resolve the mysteries of the scriptures, worshippers of the all blissful, ever staunch in faith. Cri Ṛūpa and Sanātana and Çri Jīva Gossain were as a deep lake filled with the water of devotion." [1]

In the next stanza of the Bhaktamāla we find the mention of the following names among others as worthy of high honour.

Gopal Bhatta, "the great sage" "Lokanātha, Kṛṣṇa Dās and Bhugarbha" the "rigid ascetic."

They were all followers of Chaitanya. Among others we have already written at some length about Lokanātha and Bhugarva.

Many Hindi books written in the 17th century and even in comparatively modern times give accounts of the great Vaiṣṇavas of Bengal who contributed to the building of the glories of the present Vṛndāvana. The Bhaktisindhu and

[1] History of Mathura by Growse p. 198.

the Rūpāstaka supplement the accounts of the Bhaktamāla which was freely translated by Kṛṣna Dās into Bengali in the middle of the 17th century. "Often did Chaitanya's companions at Puri" says the Chaitanya Charitamṛta [1] "ask the pilgrims who returned from Vṛndāvana 'say how are the two brothers (Sanātana and Rūpa)—what is the mode of their lives?" The pilgrims would admiringly say "They seldom sleep under a roof but mostly under a tree. Each night they sleep under a new tree. They beg not more than a handful of meal for their subsistence. Dry bread and uncooked grains they eat, and never taste any delicious food. The beggar's bowls are their only property and torn rags their only raiments. They speak of Kṛṣna only and take delight in no other thought. Four Dandas (one hour and fifty

[1] "কেহ যদি দেশ যায় দেখি বৃন্দাবন।
তারে প্রশ্ন করেন প্রভুর পারিষদগণ ॥
কহ তাহাঁ কৈছে রহেন সনাতন।
কৈছে রহে কৈছে বৈরাগ্য কৈছে ভোজন।
তবে প্রশংসিয়া কহে সেহ ভক্তগণ ॥
অনিকেতন দুঁহে রহে যত বৃক্ষগণ।
একৈক বৃক্ষের তলে একৈক রাত্রি শয়ন ॥
গৃহে স্থল ভিক্ষা কাঁহা মাধুকরি।
শুষ্করুটী চেনা চাবায় ভোগ পরিহরি ॥
করোঙ্গা মাত্র হাতে ছিঁড়া বহির্ব্বাস।
কৃষ্ণ কথা নাম কীর্ত্তন উল্লাস ॥
অষ্ট-প্রহর কৃষ্ণ ভজন চারিদণ্ড শয়নে।
নাম সংকীর্ত্তন প্রেমে নহে কোন দিনে
কভু ভক্তি বশ শাস্ত্র করয়ে লিখনে ॥
চৈতন্য কথা শুনি করে চৈতন্য চিন্তনে।"

minutes) they sleep, the rest of the day and night they spend either in singing the glories of Kṛiṣna or writing poems and theological works in Sanskrit enunciating the creed of Bhakti. They are delighted if any one speaks of Chaitanya and always think of him in order to be inspired in their holy work.' "

Another biographer says that the three fold spiritual virtues *viz.* ascticism, devotion and humility were personified in Hari Dās, Rūpa and Sanātana respectively.

Of the other Vaiṣṇava hermits who rose to distinction at Vṛndāvana by their pious lives and literary renown we have already in a previous lecture in connection with the Rāmtanu Fellowship given a somewhat elaborate account of Raghunātha Dās, popularly known as the 'Dās Goswāmi'. He was one of the greatest of the six Goswāmis.

Of the others Gopāla Bhatta son of Venkata Bhatta, deserves a mention here. Venkata Bhatta was a Marhatta Brāhmin who belonged to the village of Bhattamāri in the Deccan. He had three sons, *viz.* Trimalla, Prabodhānanda and Gopāla Bhatta. Gopāla Bhatta was trained by Prabodhānanda and became a great scholar. Their father Venkata Bhatta was himself a distinguished man of learning. Dharmarāj Adhīrendra in his celebrated commentary on the Upanishadas refers to Venkata Bhatta as his Guru.

Gopāla Bhatta.

We have already stated that the Hari Bhakti Vilāsa written by Sanātana was elaborated by Gopāla Bhatta with illustrations and published in his name by the desire of the author. Bhaktamāla recounts a legend that the Sālgrāma stone called Rādhā Ramaṇa warshipped by Gopāla Bhatta, turned into an image of Kṛṣṇa by the exercise of his miraculous power.

Gopāla Bhatta was a follower of Chaitanya and a great scholar, held as authority in regard to all matters touching the doctrinal rules for the guidance of a Vaiṣṇava's life.

We have thus seen that Chaitanyaism planted its deep root in Vṛndāvana owing to the devoted labours of Lokanātha, Bhugarva, Sanātana, Rūpa, Jīva, Raghunātha Bhatta and Gopāla Bhatta.

After these came from Bengal another fervent soul to this sacred city, who also like Sanātana, Rūpa and Jīva, is distinguished for his pure life and devotion as well as for his great literary talents. The venerable Kṛiṣṇa Dās Kavirāj has written the most erudite and instructive book in Bengali about Chaitanya and his followers. It is not only a storehouse of vast information regarding the growth and development of Vaiṣṇavism in Bengal, but gives a most scholarly exposition of the Vaiṣṇava philosophy. Its language is Bengali mixed with Hindi, terse though not always elegant, suggestive, though not always, it must be admitted, clear. The book embodies the lessons which a gifted writer and hermit took more than half a century in mastering. It is not to be cursorily read; very few men in Bengal have the power to grasp the theological portion of the work, the fruit of the author's vast learning in all departments of the Hindu philosophy; for it not only requires that the student shall be a good Sanskrit scholar in order to do so, but he must have, besides, a thorough knowledge of the old vernacular of

Kṛṣṇa Dās Kavirāja

The Chaitanya Charitamṛta.

Bengal as also of the Prakrit language that was current in the country in a previous age. Yet it is wonderful that the lowest class of men among Vaiṣṇavas whom we would condemn as illiterate often display a perfect knowledge of this monumental work, and many a problem which had appeared to us as gordian knots has been solved to our satisfaction by some Kīrtaniyā or other, men who generally hail from the lowest stratum of society.

Chaitanya ,after he had left Nadia, became an object of worship in that place. There sprang up a hundred legends attributing divine powers to him ; and these stories pious Kṛiṣṇa Dās with all his acumen of intellectual reasoning, could not help believing. He has given some of them in his book as he heard them from others. But he had a fund of first-hand information also from the most authentic sources. He had the opportunity of hearing from Sanātana and Raghunātha, Gopāla Bhatta, Bhugarva and Lokanātha what they had personally seen of the Master, and thus he got an opportunity of enriching his classical work with some of the most interesting dialogues of Chaitanya. There we find the portrait of the Master vividly drawn. There is, as I have stated, a certain degree of alloy in his gold, but where could a mine be found in which gold was ever found without the mixture of a grosser matter ? This fact detracts but little from the great intrinsic value of this monument of human patience and scholarship. I give below a synopsis of the work. It is divided into three parts, *viz* : The Adilīlā or childhood, The Madhyālīlā or the middle period, the Antalīlā or the last period.

The Adilīlā contains 17 chapters headed as follow :

1. The preliminary hymns. 2. A philosophical interpretation of Chaitanya's life. 3. Its external bearings. 4. Chaitanya's mission to himself. 5. On Nityānanda. 6. On Advaita. 7. A description of the five spiritual principles. 8. The need of another biography of Chaitanya besides the Chaitanya Bhāgavata. 9. The Bhakti-cult. 10. Chaitanya as its founder, with a list of his noted followers. 11. On the disciples of Nityānanda. 12. On those of Advaita. 13. The birth of Chaitanya. 14. His childhood 15, 16 and 17. His first youth.

The Maddyhalīlā contains 25 chapters as follow:

1. The Author's account of the lines on which Chaitanya's life is described in his work. 2. The love-ecstasies of Chaitanya and their interpretation. 3. Chaitanya's adoption of Sannyās and his brief stay at the house of Advaita at Sāntipur. 4. A description of Madhavendra Purī. 5. An account of Sākṣi Gopāla or Kṛiṣṇa as witness. 6. Vāsudeva Sārvabhauma's acceptance of Chaitanya as his Guru 7. A visit to the shrines. 8. An interview with Ramananda Ray. 9. A tour in the Deccan. 10. A noted assembly of Vaiṣṇavas and religious processions near the temple of Jagannath 12. The washing and cleansing of the Puri Temple. 13. The Car-festivity and Chaitanya's trances. 14. Descriptions of some Vaiṣṇava festivities and processions; and religious questions discussed by Swarupa. 15. The qualities of a true Vaiṣṇava described by Chaitanya. 16. The proposed tour to Vṛndāvana *via* Bengal and a return to Puri from the village Kānāi's Nātçāla. 17. A visit to Muthra and Vṛndāvan through woodland-paths, 18. Stay at Vṛndāvana and his work there 19. From Muttra to Allahabad and spiritual instructions to Rūpa. 20. An interview with Sanātana,

Discourses on the Kṛsna cult 22. The various spiritual goals. 23. The superiority of the religion of Love and Faith. 24. The stage of beatitude according to Vaiṣṇava theology. 25. Conversion of the people of Benares to the Vaiṣṇava creed and a return to Puri from Benares.

The Anta Khanda or the last period contains 20 Chapters as detailed below:

1. Chaitanya's interview with Rūpa. 2. The anecdote of the unfortunate junior Hari Dās. 3. Particulars about the devotion and spiritual life led by Hari Dās (the senior). 4. The religious instructions given by Chaitanya to Sanātana. 5. An account of Pradyumna Miçra. 6. The interview of Raghunātha Dās with Chaitanya. 7. The discussions Chaitanya had with Ballava Bhatta. 8. The details of Chaitanya's interview with Rāma Chandra Purī and the former's practising greater abstinence in regard to meal than before. 9. An account of Gopinātha Pattanāyaka's escape from capital punishment through Chaitanya's grace. 10. Some anecdotes relating to Chaitanya's acceptance of certain dainties prepared by his admirers. 11. The passing away of Hari Dās from this earth. 12. An account of Jagadānanda's breaking a jar full of perfumed oil in a fit of anger against Chaitanya. 13. Jagadānanda's tour to Vṛndāvana. 14. The divine frenzy of Chaitanya at the sight of the Chataka Hills. 15. An account of Chaitanya's trances at the sight of the groves of Vṛndāvana. 16. The love-ecstasies of Chaitanya and his appreciation of Kāli Dāsa's doing away with all caste-prejudices. 17. The narrative of Chaitanya's frenzies and of exulted emotions. 18. An account of his jumping into the sea in a fit of frenzy.

19. His growing frenzies, emaciation of physical body and losing of all control over himself at the sight of the God-vision. 20. An index to the contents of the book.

The above is a brief index to the subjects treated in the Chaitanya Charitāmṛta. No praise, however great, is adequate for the full and exhaustive treatment of Vaiṣṇava philosophy which forms one of the most important features of the work. Kṛṣṇadās quotes his authority from various Sanskrit works in support of every little point that he establishes, while the historical portion is full of minute details which throw light on the state of the country and aspirations of the people in the 16th century. It is a work of rare merit for which there is no parallel in the whole of Bengali literature.

Kṛṣṇa Dās Kavirāja was born in the year 1496 A.D. at Jhāmatpur in the District of Burdwan and was a Vaidya by caste. His father Bhagīratha died when Kṛṣṇa Das was yet a boy, and the widowed mother Sunandā did not survive her husband by many months. Kṛṣṇa Dās had a brother named Çyamā Dās whose sceptical views caused him much pain. He consequently left home in his early youth for good, and lived a long life as a hermit and a celibate at Vṛndāvana, devoting himself to religious pursuits and to the writing of Sanskrit treatises on various subjects. When he was in his 79th year, the Vaiṣṇavas of Vṛndāvan asked him to compile a work on Chaitanya's life. They urged upon him the necessity of doing so, as, according to them, he was the only fit person to undertake the task. They said that the Chaitanya Bhāgavata by Vṛndāvana Dās, though excellent in many respects, did not contain particulars about the latter period of the Master's life. Kṛṣṇa Dās took the

The author's life.

permission of Vṛndāvana Dās,—the earlier biographer of Chaitanya, to write a book which he meant to be merely a supplement to the latter's work. After the patient labour of seven years Kṛṣṇa Dās completed the Chaitanya Charitāmṛta in 1582 A.D.[1] Other particulars about the author and his work will be found in my *History of the Bengali Language and Literature.*

Kṛṣṇa Dās wrote many Sanskrit works. One of them, Govinda-līlāmṛta is much admired. It is full of poetical descriptions of the amours of Rādhā and Kṛṣṇa at Vṛndāvana and was translated into elegant Bengali verses by Jadunandana Dās in the year 1610 A.D.

Kṛṣṇa Dās also wrote a learned commentary on the Kṛṣṇa-Karṇamṛta by Villamangala. This was named Sarangarangadā; the late Rāmnarāyaṇa Vidyāratna who published an edition of the original and its commentary in 1889 calls the latter Rasikarangadā. This work was also translated into Bengali verse by Jadunandana Dās.

Among other works of Kṛṣṇa Dās we may name Chousatti Danda Nirṇaya, Premaratnāvalī, Vaiṣṇavāstaka, Rāgamāla and Rāgamaya Kaṇ. Some of the small Bengali pamphlets discussing the Sahajiyā cult are attributed to Kṛṣṇa Dās Kavirāja. But his authorship of these is disputed by all respectable Vaiṣṇava scholars who seem to be generally hostile to that cult.

It is stated in the Prema Vilāsa that old Kṛṣṇa Dās, when he heard that the only copy of his great work Chaitanya-

[1] "শাকেঽগ্নি বিন্দুবাণেন্দৌ
জ্যৈষ্ঠে বৃন্দাবনান্তরে
সূর্য্যোহ হ্যসিত পঞ্চম্যাং
গ্রন্থোঽয়ং পূর্ণতাং গতঃ। Saka 1503.

Charitāmṛta was lost, the particulars of which will be described later on, fell senseless on the ground at the shock of the news ; and verging on a hundred years as he was at the time, he could not be restored to consciousness, but quietly passed away at the sacred spot of Radhākunda in Vṛndāvana. The manner of his death as described in the Premavilāsa is believed by the Vaiṣṇavas, and the late Pundit Harādhana Bhaktinidhi, a devout Vaiṣṇava scholar, used to say referring to the death of the veteran writer "That tragic event should not be mentioned, it breaks my heart to recollect it."[1] But Karṇānanda by Jadunandan Dās, an almost equally authoritative work and written shortly after the Premavilāsa refutes the story as given in the latter book. Jadunandana says that it was true that Kṛsna Dās Kavirāja lay unconscious for a long time at the shock of the bad news, but he revived shortly after and his death did not occur immediately. Jadunandana says that he heard this from Hemlatā Devī, whose authority was Rāmachandra Kavirāj. We shall speak of this Ramachandra later on. He was certainly a great authority and commanded the respect of all by his learning and character. But Nityānanda Dās, the author of the Premavilāsa, was a contemporary of Kṛṣṇadās Kavirāja and his account cannot be pronounced unfounded until a confirmation of the contrary statement is obtained from some other authentic source. On the whole, however, it makes but little difference. There is no doubt that Kṛṣṇadās received the shock which greatly prostrated him. The only point in doubt is whether he did die immediately after, or lingered for a few days more. And he has been long dead !

[1] The Navya Bhārata Bhādra 1300 B.S., p. 262.

The manuscript was lost in about 1598 A. D. and Kṛṣṇa Dās, as I have stated, must have been very old at the time. While compiling the Chaitanya Charitāmṛta, he frequently referred to his old age and infirmities. As he lived 16 years longer after 1582, very little of life must have remained in him to enable him to bear the shock of such a calamity as the loss of the result of his great labours of so many years.

---o---

IV. *The works written in Bengal immediately before the middle period of Vaiṣṇava Literature.*

We have now given an account of the Vaiṣṇavas of Bengal and their great work at Vṛndāvana. So long as Chaitanya lived the holiest shrine of the Bengali Vaiṣṇavas was of course Puri where the Master spent the latter part of his life. We find that year after year a great crowd of pilgrims went to visit Puri headed by Çivānanda Sen of Çrikhanda who was not only their guide, but being a renowned physician himself, was more fit to give them help in every way than others. The Bengali Vaiṣṇavas had Chaitanya's permission to stay at Puri for four months every year, and we frequently come across passages in these biographical works describing the great pathos of the parting scene. Çrivāsa and Narahari showed themselves disconsolate every time and could not be easily persuaded to leave the presence of the Master. He was the adored one, their dearest friend and leader; and fain would they, if required, give up all they

Puri—the most important Vaiṣṇava centre, when Chaitanya was alive.

had for his beloved society. Chaitanya on such occasions would say to Çrivasa by way of cheering up his old friend :—"Though bodily I shall not be in your courtyard Çrivāsa, I shall be present there in spirit and you will see me with your mind's eyes."[1]

The thought that on the return of the pilgrims to Nadia, it would break the heart of poor Sachi, his mother, to see them back without him, weighed upon his soul every time and on such occasions he used to say to Narahari, "Tell my mother that when she prepares her meal, I shall be present in spirit to taste it, for nothing in the world did I taste as delicious as her cooking."[2]

The Bengali pilgrims returned every year to Nadia from Puri and longed for the time when they might be permitted to go again. There the scholars, the pious souls, the gentry of Bengal joined in the pilgrimage all yearning for that vision of heaven which they found in Chaitanya's ecstasies of devotion.

The *tirodhāna* of Chaitanya and the stupor of Vaiṣṇava community.

In 1533 Chaitanya passed away from the world. The Vaiṣnavas refuse to speak of his departure as death. They call it his *tirodhāna*, the passing away. Out of regard for their sentiments the writer of the present treatise must speak also in their words.

[1] "শ্রীবাস পণ্ডিতে প্রভু করি আলিঙ্গন।
কণ্ঠে ধরি কহে তারে মধুর বচন।
তোমার ঘরে কীর্ত্তনে আমি নিত্য নাচিব।
তুমি দেখা পাবে আর কেহ না দেখিব॥"

Chaitanya Charitamṛta.
Madhya Khanda, 15th Chapter.

[2] The Nityānanda Vaṁsa Vistāra.

"The passing away of Chaitanya" caused a deep grief in Bengal. His adopting the vow of an ascetic had created pathetic sense of grief, which found expression in a thousand songs. The saddest tales some times supply the highest poetic inspiration. And that portion of Rādhā Kṛṣṇa songs—the Mathur—or Çri Kṛṣṇa's desertion of Vṛindāvana, received a poetic—a pathetic impetus by the event of Chaitanya's *Sannyās*. The legend became real, as it were,—a fact in their living history, and therefore appealed so strongly to them. If, however, the *sannyās* of Chaitanya could be borne, and poetically expressed, his final passing away from the world was unbearable. The Vaiṣṇava biographers are all silent on the point, except one only recently discovered by the research of scholars and not yet recognised by the Vaiṣṇavas as an author of any status. The poets have not sung of the final episode, though every minute point in the life of the Master has been touched in detail, and worked into beautiful songs by them. A deep silence sealed their lips which had never stopped before in relating the Chaitanya theme—a silence which only shows the benumbing of their energies—their unspeakable and profound grief at the final separation from the Master. They believed that God had come to them in the human flesh and He had left them after a too short stay with them. Every eye was tearful but no mouth could speak. The Chaitanya Charitāmṛta and the Chaitanya Bhāgavata, the standard biographies of Chaitanya, say nothing as to the manner of his passing away. The earlier Sanskrit works Chaitanya Chandrodaya, Chaitanya Charita, and Murari Gupta's Kaḍchā also say nothing on this subject. Lochana Dās's Chaitanya Mongala closes with a bare hint. The biographers of the succeeding age who wrote huge works like the Premavilās, the Bhaktiratnākara, the Karṇānanda, the Narottamcharita and Baṁçiçikṣā, have all joined in the general conspiracy of silence.

In fact from 1533 to 1590 the Vaiṣṇava community of Bengal lay enervated by an overpowering feeling of forlornness. The *sankīrtana* parties lost all heart, and their great music which had taken the country by surprise and flooded it with poetry, broke in the midst of their enthusiastic performances, and sounded no more on the banks of the Ganges. The companions of Chaitanya, mute and striken with a sense of their great loss, one by one departed from the world. And the history of this period shows no striking feature of the Vaiṣṇava movement and no activity of any noteworthy nature. Rājā Pratāpa Rudra of Orissa had no heart to visit his capital—the deserted scene of the Master's work—and died in the seclusion of his retirement at Pratāpapur. Raghunātha Dās left Purī, and settled at Vṛndāvana. The Moslem convert Haridās had died shortly before Chaitanya left the world. What became of Çachī, Chaitanya's mother, no biographer had stated. The silence on this point also suggests a most affecting tale of death. At Vṛndāvana Rūpa, Sanātana, Lokanāth, Bhugarva, Gopāla Bhatta, Raghunātha Dās and Raghunātha Bhatta patiently worked, considering it their sacred duty to do what was bidden them by the Master. Rūpa and Sanātana wrote continually on the lines suggested by him. Under the allegorical form of the legend of Rādhā-Kṛṣṇa, they had found a deep seated substratum of truth in the glorious life of the Master, which they now detailed with all the powers of their gifted pens.

Their renewed activities.

When the Vaiṣṇava community rose once more from their stupor—from the Lethe Wharf of their grief in which they were plunged headlong, the last vestige of their historical glory had passed away from Bengal. The great lives inspired the people no more. Nityānanda was dead. Advaita had also shared the inevitable fate of man. Narahari ligered for a short time longer and then he too died. Raghunandana, his brother, stood, so to speak, with one foot in the grave. The eyes of the Vaiṣṇava pilgrims diverted from Purī fell on Vṛndāvana which had risen to a new fame. Great works were written and many authors were busy there in collating the materials for compiling canons for the Vaiṣṇava creed. The Vaiṣṇava community, paralysed for a time, recovered from their torpor, half a century later, and their pent up energies once more found an immense outlet in fresh movements which developed about the year 1590. The medieval school of the Bengali Vaiṣṇavas according to my classification arose from these movements which will be described in the course of these lectures. Not only were sacrifices of the highest order again made for the sake of religion, but a poetical literature which matched in excellence the achievements of the previous age as represented by Chandi Dās and Vidyāpati was produced and popularised amongst the masses to an extent not previously known.

Before we enter upon this epoch of our literature we should remember that Vṛndāvana had now attained a special sanctity above that of any other shrine in the estimation of the Bengali Vaiṣṇavas. No pilgrim who had not touched the sacred dust of that shrine was honoured by their community. No book that had not secured the approval of the Vṛindāvana masters was recognised by the lay Vaiṣṇavas dwelling in Bengal. Their lives were absolutely guided by the rules framed in the holy city. We have shown that enormous activity marked the literary attempts of some of the distinguished followers of Chaitanya. The Chaitanya Charitāmṛta says that Rūpa, Sanātana and Jīva worte a lakh of Granthas in Vṛindāvana. One might suppose that this is an absurd number and marks the extent of exaggeration in the accounts of Kṛṣṇa Dās Kavirāja. But there is no reason for such a supposition inasmuch as the word 'Grantha' means here a couplet, a Çloka, and not a book, as the ordinary people understand the term.

Vaiṣṇava works written in Bengal.

In Bengal a certain number of books, which could hold their own with the works of the hermits of Vṛindāvana, in point of learning and quality, were written, though the number of these books is much fewer than those written in the holy city. These few books are recognised as standard works by the Vaiṣṇava community, because they were written by authors who were either Chaitanya's personal friends or were inspired by those who enjoyed his confidence.

Murāri Gupta's Chaitanya Charita.

Foremost amongst these books should be mentioned the Chaitanya Charita of Murāri Gupta. The author was a constant companion of Chaitanya's childhood. I have already said that the desertion of Nadia by Chaitanya made him all the more dear to the people there. The great love and admiration in which he was held served to establish his divinity the sooner among these who were his early companions ; every inspired act of his assumed an exaggerated importance in their eyes, and the legends and historical facts were embodied together by Murāri Gupta in his work without discrimination in the enthusiasm of his admiration. The work is written in elegant Sanskrit and has its undoubted value from many points of view. The proprietors of the Patrikā Press, Bagbazar, Calcutta, have published an edition of this work.

Kaḍchā by Swarupa Dāmodara.

We have found mention of a Kaḍchā by Swarupa Dāmodara in many of the historical works of the Vaiṣṇavas. It was written in Sanskrit and its author Swarupa Dāmodara was a great favourite and constant companion of Chaitanya. So far as we have ascertained, this work has not been fully recovered. Passages are found quoted in some of the standard works on Chaitanya.

Kavikarṇapura and his works.

By far the greatest books written in Bengal about Chaitanya came from the pen of the distinguished poet Kavikarṇapura. His name was Paramānanda Sen and Kavikarṇapura or "the ear ornament of poets" was his literary title. He belonged to the Vaidya caste and to its Narahatta sub-section. We have had frequent occasions in course of these lectures to mention the poet's father Çivānanda Sen who was a respected friend of Chaitanya and his elder by many years. Çivānanda Sen was a native of the village Kanchḍāpārā, a few miles to the north of Calcutta, and was a great physician. He was a rich man and I have already stated that he was appointed the leader of the Bengali pilgrims who annually paid a visit to Purī to meet Chaitanya. If any enquiry in regard to the welfare of the pilgrims, among whom there were many honoured and noted names, had to be made, Çivānanda was communicated with. In another place we have described how Govardhana Dās, the Governor of Saptagrām approached him for information as regards the whereabouts of Raghunātha Dās when the latter had fled from the Saptagrām palace.[1]

Çivānanda was a poet himself, and some of his beautiful Bengali songs are found in the anthological work—the Padakalpataru. He had three sons, Chaitanya Dās, Ramadās and Paramānanda or Kavikarṇapura. Paramānanda was born in 1527 A.D. It is said that when he was yet a young child Chaitanya foretold his future success as a writer.

While on a visit to Purī in the company of his father, the young prodigy took the scholars there by surprise by composing the following verse in Sanskrit, when only seven years old :—

"श्रवसो: कुवलयमक्ष्णोरञ्जनमुरसोमाहेन्द्रमणिदाम वृन्दावनरमणीणां-मण्डनमखिलं हरिर्जयति ।"

"Victory be to Kṛṣṇa, who is like the lotus that adorns the ear, like the collyrium *anjana* to the eyes, like the great diamond Mahendra of the breast and the sole treasure of the gopies of Vṛndāvana."

The tradition has it that as a baby Kavikarṇapura once kissed Chaitanya's toe when the latter sat near him, and as a result was endowed with extraordinary poetical powers.

It is said that when a mere child he composed also the following verse which is now to

[1] See my lectures in connection with R. T. Lahiri fellowship.

be found in his celebrated drama the Chaitanya Chandrodaya :—

"विद्युद्दामद्युतिरतिशयोत्कण्ठकण्ठीरवेन्द्र क्रीड़ागामीकनकपरिघद्राघिमोद्दाम-बाहु: । सिंहग्रीवो नवदिनकरद्योतविद्योतिवासा: श्रीगौराङ्ग: स्फुरति पुरतो वन्द्यतां वन्द्यतां भो: ॥

"Look there Chaitanya approaches as a brilliant flash of lightning, with steps slow but steady, like those of a lion—in one of his thoughtful moods ; look at his arms like golden bars and his shoulders which match a lion's, his ochre-coloured cloth spreading a halo like the rays of the young sun ; bow to him ye that are present here, bow to him."

The poem Chaitanya Charita and the drama Chaitanya Chandrodaya were both completed in the year 1572 A.D. They are both characterised by great poetic beauty, the drama specially. It contains dialogues among personified virtues, while the powers of vice are also represented as human characters coming on the stage and acting like men. This book unfolds some of the vicious tendencies of the age and shows how Chaitanya came as a redeemer of men. The author dwells on his high subject in a sustained poetical language. Vaidhi Bhakti or Faith as defined in the Scriptures asked her sister Rāgānugā or faith which cares not for Scriptures but follows her own impulse :—"If a man leaves the established path, how may he attain his destination ?" The sister replies "It is like what takes place during the flood, dear sister. In the dry season one goes by the zigzag course of the river ; it is a sure and well defined path, no doubt. But when the fields are covered with flood, the river and the land become one sheet of water and there is no fixed course for the boat, yet it reaches its destination more quickly." This refers to the Chaitanya religion, which often discards time-honoured conventional ways and follows the natural path of faith.

Gaurganadveçadīpikā or "The light for those who want to know of the followers of Chaitanya"—was written by Kavikarṇapura in 1576 A.D. This is his last work. His other works are Ananda Vṛndāvanachampu, Chaitanya-çataka, Stavāvalī, Kṛṣṇaganadveçadīpikā, and Alankāra Kaustava. All these works are written in Sanskrit and the last one, as its name implies, is a work on Sanskrit poetics. Kṛṣṇadās Kavirāja quotes many verses from these works in his Chaitanya Charitāmṛta. Kavikarṇapura is also the author of some beautiful Bengali songs to be found in the Padakalpataru.

The descendants of Kavikarṇapura still live at Kanchḍā-pārā, one of them Babu Amṛtalāl Sen is a clerk in the Postal Department at Nagpur. The village Kanchḍāpārā is now almost deserted by its inhabitants on account of malaria. It is one of the stations of the Eastern Bengal State Railway.

Vṛndāvana Dās, his life and works.

Vṛndāvana Dās, the illustrious author of Chaitanya Bhāgavata in Bengali was a contemporary of Kavikarṇa-purā. The date of Vṛndāvana Dās's birth is generally believed to be Çaka 1429 (1507 A.D.). For obvious reason this date is untenable, as Vṛndāvana Dās was surely present and took active part in the Vaiṣṇava festivities at Kheturi which took place in the earlier part of the 17th century. We shall with difficulty accept the fact of a man, a century old, taking a vigorous part in those functions. Besides Vṛndāvana Dās himself has told us more than once in his Chaitanya Bhāgavata that he was not born when Chaitanya was alive.[1] The year of his birth Çaka 1459 (1537 A.D.) as given by Babu Kṣirodchandra Rāychaudhuri and obtained from reliable sources should be accepted.

Vṛndāvana was the son of Nārāyaṇī, a daughter of Nalin Āchārya, brother of Çrīvāsa whose historic courtyard was the favourite resort of the *kīrtana* party organised by Chaitanya at Nadia. Nārāyaṇī was married to one Baikuntha Chakravarti of the village Kumārhatta, who died in November, 1535 A.D. and 18 months after his death, Vṛndāvana was born in May, 1537. This gave rise to scandal, and Nārāyanī had to appear before the Mahomedan Magistrate of Nadia to vindicate her character.[2] The Vaiṣṇavas believe that Vṛndāvana Dās came to the world as a result of the blessings of Nityānanda and of Chaitanya. They mention a story in this connection which can only be believed by the devouter men amongst the Vaiṣṇavas. Even without assailing the legend, it is certain that the warmest advocates of Nārāyanī do not recognise Baikuntha Chakravarti, her husband, as the father of Vṛndāvana Dās. They imply this tacitly by calling Vṛndāvana Dās, the sage "Vyāsa" of their age. Vyāsa, the author of the epic poem Mahāvārata and of the Purāṇas was born of a mother who was not the legal wife of Parāçara, his father.

Whatever explanation the orthodox Vaiṣṇavas gave of the affair, it got but little credence from the people ; and Çrīvāsa, though in affluent circumstances and possessed a considerable influence, dared not keep his niece with her baby in his house at Nadia, where the tongue of scandal sounded its loudest note. Nārāyanī had to depart

[1] "হইল পাপিষ্ঠ জন্ম না হৈল তখন।" Chaitanya Bhāgavata.

[2] See Introduction to গৌরপদতরঙ্গিণী by Jagatbandhu Bhadra.

from her uncle's house in October, 1538, when Vṛndāvana Dās was only a year old, and live at the village Māmgachi near Nadia in an almost forlorn condition. It was Vāsudeva Datta, a Vaidya, who finally gave shelter to her. His boldness in this respect is much to be praised; not only did he allow Nārāyanī to live at his house but he gave a sound education to her child. Vṛndāvana Dās thus lived in a congenial atmosphere, where the scandal of his birth was silenced by compassion, nay turned into a legend that glorified him, and in which he himself believed more than any one else. He wrote his celebrated work Chaitanya Bhāgavata in the year 1573 A.D. at the behest of Nityānanda who had already taken pity on our author when an orphan and rendered active help in his education. In the latter years of his life, Vṛndāvana Dās settled at Denur, a village in the district of Burdwan in the police station of Mantreçvara and 16 miles to the west of Nadia. There is a temple of Kṛṣṇa founded by him in this village whith now ranks as a shrine of the Vaiṣṇavas. At Denur he led a pious life devoted to religious pursuits, and commanded the respect of all by his high character and attainments.

The Chaitanya Bhāgavata.

I have dwelt upon the Chaitanya Bhāgavata by Vṛndāvana Dās at some length in my History of Bengali Language and Literature. Making allowance for the legends and exaggerated stories about Chaitanya which Vṛndāvana Dās believed and incorporated in his book, it possesses great historical value as a faithful record of many incidents of Chaitanya's life and of those of his contemporaries. Belief in supernatural stories was a characteristic of the age in which Vṛndāvana Dās lived and we cannot condemn him for sharing contemporary beliefs. His descriptions are always brief and to the point and often he tells his story with a religious fervour which strongly appeals to the reader. When Vṛndāvana Dās wrote his great work, scandal was still rife and people annoyed him by referring to his birth. Our author occasionally betrays temper writing in the unrestrained language of the vulgar. Thus :— "Those who inspite of all that I have said still spread scandal should be kicked at the head for maligning us."[1]

But the merit of the book is great even if its author betrays his indignation against malacious scandal-mongers. It is now held to be the standard biography of Chaitanya, and Kṛṣṇadās Kavirāja whose humility was as great as his faith and scholarship, referred to this earlier biography of Chaitanya with high respect in his own Chaitanya Charitāmṛta which in his meekness he calls a mere supplement to the Chaitanya Bhāgavata.

The name of Chaitanya Bhāgavata was Chaitanya Mangala, and we have it on the authority of the Prema-vilāsa that the book was sent for approval of the six Gosvāmis of Vṛndāvana, and they are said to have been so highly pleased with it that they changed its name from Chaitanya Mangala to Chaitanya Bhāgavata.[2] The Bhāgavata, it is well known to you all, is a description of Kṛṣṇa's life and this work of Vṛndāvana Dās was held to be of equal merit, Chaitanya's life being described in it in a manner which shewed striking coincidences with that

[1] "এত পরিহারেও যে পাপী নিন্দা করে।
তবে লাথি মারি তার মাথার উপরে ॥"

Chaitanya Bhāgavata.

[2] See the Prema Vilāsa, 19th Vilāsa.

of Kṛṣṇa; hence the six Gosvāmis chose to call it the Chaitanya Bhāgavata.

The Chaitanya Bhāgavata is divided into three parts, called the Ādi, the Madhya, and the Anta Khaṇdas. In this classification it has served as the model for the Chaitanya Charitāmṛta.

The first part or the Ādi Khaṇda contains 12 chapters, the contents of which may be thus summed up:—

1. The texts giving interpretations of Chaitanya's life; an index of the book. 2. The birth of Chaitanya. 3. The incidents of babyhood. 4. Childhood. 5. The adoption of Sannyās or the ascetic life by his brother Viçvarūpa. 6. Chaitanya takes the sacred thread and begins his studies. 7. Meeting with Içvara Puri. 8. Chaitanya's conduct towards the people of the city (Nadia). 9. Defeat of the great scholar Keçava Kāçmirī. 10. Marriage with Viṣṇupriyā. 11. An account of Hari Dās. 12. Chaitanya's visit to Gayā.

The second part or the Madhya Khanda contains 26 chapters. 1. The beginning of the *kīrtana* processions. 2. Hostility of the people and the Kaziz's attitude. 3. Meeting with Nityānanda. 4. The mutual affection of Chaitanya and Nityānanda towards each other. 5. The worshipping of Vyāsa—the poet and the sage of ancient India. 6. Meeting with Advaita. 7. Meeting with Pundarika and Gadādhara. 8. Chaitanya's manifestation of divinity. 9. Meeting with Çrīdhara. 10. Further manifestation of divinity of Chaitanya. 11 and 12. Accounts of Nityānanda. 13. The reformation of two ruffians, Jagāi and Mādhāi. 14. The influence of the *kīrtana*-singing on the people. 15. The characters of Jagāi and Mādhāi described. 16. The eating of rice from the begging bowl of Çuklāmvara. 17. The glory of faith. 18. Chaitanya playing a part in the Kṛṣṇa-drama organised by him. 19. Stay at the house of Advaita. 20. An account of Murāri Gupta. 21. Devānanda taken to task. 22. Some incidents about Çachī Devī. 23. Anecdotes relating to Chaitanya and Çrīdhara. 24. Some miracles. 25. Sorrows of the friends at the news of Chaitanya's resolution to turn a Sannyāsi. 26. The taking of Sannyās.

The third part, the Anta Khaṇda contains, eleven chapters headed as follows: 1. The meeting of Chaitanya with Advaita at Sāntipur after the latter's adoption of Sannyās. 2. Meeting with Sārvabhauma at Puri. 3. Some incidents of Chaitanya's life at Puri. 4. Chaitanya's second visit to Puri. 5. Miracles performed by Nityānanda. 6 and 7. Further accounts about Nityānanda. 9. Chaitanya at the house of Gadhādhara. 10. Further accounts of Advaita. 11. Further accounts of Pundarīka Vidyānidhi.

Chaitanya Bhāgavata does not give an elaborate account of the last part of Chaitanya's life. The author shows a greater enthusiasm for writing the particulars of Nityānanda's life. This was the reason which made the scholarly recluses of Vṛndāvana approach the venerable Kṛṣṇadās Kavirāja with the request to compile a fuller biographical treatise about the Master.

Besides the Chaitanya Bhāgavata, Vṛndāvana Dās is said to have written the following works: Tattvavilāsa, Dadhikhaṇda, Vaiṣṇava Vandanā, Bhaktichintāmaṇi and Nityānanda Vaṁça Vistāra.

Other particulars about Vṛndāvana Dās are to be found in my History of Bengali Language and Literature on pp. 464-471.

Chaitanya Maṅgala by Jayānanda.

The next biographer of Chaitanya Deva is Jayānanda who has mentioned the work of Vṛndāvana Dās in his treatise. Jayānanda was a disciple of Gadādhara Dās. But he seems to have written his work without the permission of any recognised authority of the Vaiṣṇava community. Hence it has not met with adequate appreciation from them. But it is for this very reason that we find the work valuable and interesting in some respects. The dictatorial voice of the later Vaiṣṇava society, which had grown dogmatic in course of time, occasionally eliminated or changed earlier historical accounts to suit the purpose of more modern developments ; and "authoritative works" are those which were written in conformity with the censorship established to regulate all publications. It is therefore that we often obtain better lights from sources other than the orthodox ones, in regard to obscure points. The value of Chaitanya Maṅgala by Jayānanda rests on such occasional rays of historical light that illuminate some of the dark paths of the early Vaiṣṇava period. For instance we have an account in it as to how Chaitanya passed away from this world—a point on which all authoritative works have conspired to be silent. For particulars about Jayānanda's Chaitanya Maṅgala the reader is referred to pp. 471-477 of my History of the Bengali Language and Literature. Jayānanda's Chaitanya Maṅgala was written shortly after 1573, when Vṛndāvana Dās wrote his Chaitanya Bhāgavata. Jayānanda was much advanced in years when he wrote the book.

It was about this time also that Lochana Dās wrote his Chaitanya Maṅgala. Lochana Dās was a native of

Kogrām, a village in the district of Burdwan. His mother was Sadānandī Devī and his father was Kamala Kar who belonged to the physician caste. His grandfather on the mother side was Puruṣottama Gupta who is said to have been a distinguished man and his grandmother was Ananda Devī who gave the boy every indulgence so that he spent his early youth in play and amusement without minding his studies. The grand-father however was a strict man who taught him, when he was fully grown up, the alphabets "with the help of his rod." [1] His Guru was Narahari Sarkār of Çrīkhanda at whose command he wrote his Chaitanya Maṅgala about the year 1575.

Lochana Dās and his Chaitanya Mangala.

Lochana Dās married in the village of Kakut near Amodapur and the wife is said to have been an exceptionally virtuous and accomplished woman. Lochana Dās's poetical powers were great; in fact his biography of Chaitanya Deva is rather a lyrical poem than a historical work. The earlier portion of the work is a free translation of Murārī Gupta's Sanskrit work the Chaitanya Charita. Many of Lochana Dās's songs are to be found in the Padakalpataru and other anthologies and are justly admired for their elegance and intrinsic poetic worth. Our author, besides, freely translated the Sanskrit drama, Jagannathavallabha by Rāmānanda Rāy into sweet Bengali verse, and wrote the following works in Bengali: The Durllavasāra, Rāgānugālaharī, Vastutattvasāra, Ānandalatikā, Chaitanya Premavilāsa, Dehanirupaṇa, and Prārthanā. Some of these works as we find them to-day elucidate the

[1] "মারিয়া ধরিয়া মোরে শিখাল অক্ষর।"

Chaitanya Mangala.

Sahajia principles and contain, it is said, a good deal of later interpolations.

The original copy of Chaitanya Maṅgala in Lochana Dās's own handwriting is said to be preserved in the house of Prānkṛṣṇa Chakravarti in the village of Kankra, near Kogram. Further details about Lochana Dās will be found on pp. 489-495 of my History of the Bengali Language and Literature.

Besides these works, we find mention of the following biographical treatises in the Chaitanya Maṅgala by Jayānanda. These works have not yet been recovered. 1. Poems on Chaitanya by Gaurī Dās. 2. Do by Gopāl Vasu. 3. Do by Paramānanda Gupta.

Other works.

CHAPTER II

Historical Literature

I. Early careers of the three great Vaiṣṇava worthies—Crīnivāsa Narottama and Cyāmānanda.

II. Events in their lives after 1600 A. D.

(*a*) The robbery that changed the life of a great robber.

(*b*) Narottama at Kheturi.

(*c*) The great robber-chief Chānd Rāy.

(*d*) Rāma Chandra Kavirāja.

(*e*) An encounter with the scholars of the opposite school.

(*f*) Various centres of Vaiṣṇava activity. Vīrachandra's work. Legends about him.

III. The Works that describe the above narratives.

(*a*) Nityānanda Dās and his Prema Vilāsa.

(*b*) Jadunandana Dās—his Karṇānanda and other works.

(*c*) Narahari Chakravarti and his works.

(*d*) Miscellenious works.

I. Early careers of the three great Vaiṣṇava worthies—Crīnivāsa, Narotama and Cyāmānanda.

This extensive literature about Chaitanya serves as the background of the medieval period. Most of the books mentioned above were held as standard and authoritative works from which extracts were freely quoted by the writers of the medieval period to establish their views and justify them before the Vaiṣṇava public. Without a knowledge of the contents of the earlier works, the later ones will not be rightly understood. And in fact they will supply the keys to the succeeding age of Vaiṣṇava history. It is for this that we have taken pains to dwell upon the earlier chapter of Vaiṣṇava literature at some length.

A considerable portion of the history of the medieval period of the Vaiṣṇava literature, as I have defined and named it, relate to the description of the three great worthies whose names I have already mentioned, *viz.* Çrīnivās Achārya, Narottama Datta and Çyāmānanda Dās.

These three men helped the further development of the Vaiṣṇava creed in Bengal. Their great sacrifices, asceticism, scholarship and faith made them the central figures of the age that succeeded that of darkness and stupor caused by the *tirodhāna*—the passing away of Chaitanya from this world. Their mystic visions, the romance of their lives which cast a spell ever the wicked and innocent alike and their zeal and enthusiasm in propagating the creed of faith have been the subject of many illustrious memoirs and poetical songs which once more sprang like a rich harvest in the field of the Vaiṣṇava literature.

In the former age the vision of Kṛṣṇa was beheld by the apostles of faith—by Mādhavendra Purī first and then by Chaitanya and his followers. The dark-blue colour of Kṛṣṇa had become the symbol of all tender and sacred associations to the Vaiṣṇava philosophers and poets. In the succeeding age the fair colour of Chaitanya, bright as the Champaka flower, became as significant as the dark-blue; and whenever this colour was met, it constantly supplied the seer and the poet with visions beatific. The poets sang of him who for the whole day and night spoke of Kṛṣṇa with tearful eyes, seeing Him in the cloud and in the river and in the tree, following Him like a mad man through forests and fields as one follows an angel unseen by others and dedicating to Him his life which

The vision of Chaitanya.

blossomed as it received the ray of His divine love. The vision of Chaitanya came to the apostles of the succeeding age in their trances as that of Kṛṣṇa had come to those of previous times.

According to the Bhaktiratnākara, Çrīnivāsa Āchārya paid a visit to Puri when he was a lad of 12 or 13, imme-

The date of Crīnivāsa's birth

diately after Chaitanya had quitted his mortal frame. This is quite untenable. Narottama quotes some *clokas* said to have been written by Kavikarṇapura, in which he writes that Çrīnivāsa heard on his way to Puri that Chaitanya had disappeared. But it is well known that the writings of Narottama in which the Sahajiyā elements seem to predomoinate in their present shape, have been largely tampered with, by later writers.

The author of the Prema Vilāsa was a companion of Çrīnivāsa and we are bound to give a greater credence to the facts as described by him. The last portion of the printed Prema Vīlāsa may have been grafted on the original book by some later writer, but up to the 20th Chapter, its account is quite authentic. I have compared several MSS. of the Prem Vilāsa between 200 to 150 years old, and have been struck with the agreement in their readings, a circumstance which is not very frequently observed in other works of this class. Nityānanda Dās, the auther, writes a prosaic Bengali very unlike the finished poetic style of Narahari Chakravarti, author of the Bhaktiratnākara ; but the former has a greater power of mastering facts and observing with closer accuracy the sequence of events. The Prema Vīlāsa refers to the birth of Çrīnivāsa as having taken place long after Chaitanya had departed from this world. Gopāl Bhatta, one of the six masters at Vṛndāvana, is said to have dreamt of Çrīnivāsa birth, long after Chaitanya's *tirodhāna* ; [1] I need scarcely say that the dreams and prophesies mentioned in works like these always indicate what really happened. So there is no doubt that Çrīnivāsa was born exactly when Gopāl Bhatta is said to have dreamt of his birth. Besides the author of the Prema Vilāsa distinctly puts it in the mouth of Çrīnivāsa that he regretted the fact of his not being born while Chaitanya was alive. [2] This statement is supported by other facts which are of an unassailable character. We find in the Prema Vilāsa that Çrīnivāsa in his youth visited Vṛndāvana and found the temples of Govindaji complete. The inscription on the temple shows that it was built by Man Sinha in 1590. So the story of his arriving at Puri on his way to Vṛndāvana a few days after the Master departed from the world is not correct, for that melancholy event took place in 1533. Çrīnivāsa came to Viṣṇupur about the year 1600 A.D. when he was yet a young man. Vīra Hāmvīra was the reigning king there and ascended the throne in 1596. If we sift all these evidences we shall be bound to discredit the story of the Bhaktiratnākara which says that Çrīnivāsa paid a visit to Puri immediately after Chaitanya's passing away in 1533. Çrīnivāsa came to Vṛndāvana three days after the death of Sanātana in 1591. He must have been about 20 years of age at the time. So we may take the date of his birth to be about the year 1561. There is also other evidence which corroborates this, but we need not dwell upon its testimony here.

[1] The Prema Vilāsa, The first Vilāsa.

[2] "ভক্তগণ সহিত না শুনিল সংকীর্ত্তন।
হইল পাপিষ্ঠে জন্ম না হইল তথন॥"

The Prema Vilāsa, the 4th Vilāsa.

Not very far from the town of Nadia, there is a village on the bank of the Ganges named Chākhandi. Here lived one Gaṅgādhara Bhattāchārya who was an ardent admirer of Chāitanya. When the latter took the vow of Sannyās, Gaṅgādhara is said to have been so highly overpowered with grief that he cried like a child and behaved like a mad man. The people gave him the name of Chaitanya Dās or servant of Chaitanya on account of his great devotion to the Master.

Çrīnivāsa's early life

Chaitanya Dās married Lakṣmīpriyā, a daughter of Valarāma Chakravarti of Jajigram near Kātwa, and their only child Çrīnivāsa was born about the year 1561, when, says the Bhaktiratnākara, the courtyard of the Brahmin couple resounded with *kirtan* songs, one of them —that famous song of Vidyāpati which so often Chaitanya himself sang "কি কহব রে সখি আনন্দ ওর। চিরদিন মাধব মন্দিরে মোর" having been sung on the occasion. [1] It is said that Chaitanya once foretold that a great person should be born in the near future at Chākhandi, and the Vaiṣṇava community took the boy to be the very child mentioned in the prophecy of the Master.

Chaitanya Dās placed the young child under the tuition of Dhananjaya Vidyānivāsa, but it was at home that young Çrīnivāsa received a sound spiritual training. With a voice full of impressive eloquence and emotion Chaitanya Dās related the events of the life of the Master to his young son. He took him to Nadia and pointed out the spots made sacred by the Master's presence. There he showed him the courtyard of Çrīvāsa, the place where Chaitanya in course of his trances had so often fallen unconscious on the bare

The Courtyard of Crivāsa.

[1] The Prema Vilāsa, the first Vilāsa.

earth while poor Çachī, his mother, prayed to God with joined hands that her darling son might not be hurt by his fall. [1] Chaitanya Dās related to the boy the story of the defeat of the great scholar Keçava Kaçmiri by Chaitanya and of the marvellous change that came over his life on his return from Gayā. When Chaitanya cried 'Kṛṣṇa' 'Kṛṣṇa' with tears in his eyes, the world cried with him; as if the world also caught a glimpse of what he beheld in his trances. Then the topic turned to that which supplied never ceasing pathos—the event of his Sannyāsa. And when young Çrīnivāsa heard all this he could contain his grief no more. He burst into tears and could not cease from weeping for hours together. The very name of Chaitanya uttered, would bring tears to his eyes, and for days he spoke of nothing but of Chaitanya, so that the beauty of the Mastar's life and its pathos completely possessed the boy. By this time he had made a rapid advance in his studies, and his teacher was surprised to find that all that he could teach the boy was mastered by him when barely 14.

Çrīnivāsa was a handsome lad and all who came in contact with him liked him. One day the boy happened to meet Narahari Sarkār at Jajigram, and as he saw the noble poet and scholar of Çrīkhanda—one of the dearest of Chaitanya's companions, Çrīnivās's imagination clothed him with the sacredness of heaven itself. His heart went forth in love and gratitude to the veteran at whose feet he fell and asked him to teach him the Bhāgavata. Narahari felt a liking for his young admirer, and was anxious

[1] "যে কালে নিমাই পড়ে ধরণী উপরে।
ব্যাথা যেন নাহি লাগে নিমাই শরীরে ॥"
Chaitanya Charitāmṛta, Madhya Khanda, Chapter III.

that he should have a sound education. He accordingly advised him to go to Vṛndāvana and meet Sanātana and Rūpa who still lived there. But to make him fit to receive education at their hands, he suggested that young Çrīnivāsa might go to Puri first, and read the Bhāgavata with Gadādhara, the constant associate of Chaitanya and a master of Bhāgavata lore.

Crīnivāsa's tour.

Çrīnivāsa went to Puri. It should be remembered that journeys from one place to another were not safe in those days. And it was even more difficult for a boy of 15 who had no companion or guide. By the time Chaitanya Dās had died of fever, after an illness of only seven days, and Çrīnivās took his mother to Jajigram where his maternal uncles lived and placed her in their custody.

Çrinivāsa came to Puri about the year 1581, and met Gadādhara. The boy showed ecstasies of joy and devotion for Kṛṣṇa even as the great Master had done; so that already a report spread in the adjoining countries that Chaitanya Deva was reborn in Çrīnivāsa. Gadadhara was very old. He received young Çrīnivāsa with every mark of affection delighting in his devotion and scholarship. He promised to teach him the Bhāgavata, but the copy that was with him he produced to Çrīnivās, showing that the letters there were mostly effaced by Chaitanya's tears. Çrīnivāsa touched the sacred MSS. and his tears began to flow. He was here in one of those trances wherein the Master appeared before him and exhorted him to follow the path of faith. When he came to himself he was asked to bring a copy of the Bhagāvata from Bengal as there was no good MS. of that sacred book available at Purī. Çrīnivāsa had thus to return to Bengal for the copy required. But when he came back to Purī with it, Gadādhara, the great authority of the Bhāgavata lore, had died. In deep disappointment Çrīnivāsa had to plod his way back to Bengal. He came to Çrīkhanda and lived upon one *chattak* of rice every day; he cooked it himself on the banks of the Ganges, where one day he happened to meet Içana, the servant of Chaitanya's house. "The wonderful lad," as he was called by every body, was introduced to Viṣṇupriāyā who was then very old and lived a life of austerity and spiritual devotion worthy of the wife of the Master. She instructed Çrīnivāsa to go to Vṛndāvana and complete his education there. Çrīnivās next paid a visit to Sāntipur; But Advait, the venerable head of the Vaiṣṇava community there, had died three years before, and Çrīnivāsa met Sītā, the wife of the departed leader. All advised him to go as quickly as possible to Vṛndāvana lest he should fail to meet Rūpa and Sanātana, both of them being very old and not likely to live long. Çrīnivāsa next came to Kharda and met Jāhnavi, Nityānanda's wife. He received, in the temple of Kharda, strokes from the Jaymangala rod. This was to purge the body of all sin. He stayed here for a short time and then went to Jājigram to take farewell of his old mother who was mourning the death of her husband. Laksmipriyā was at the time ailing from fever and the Premavilāsa says that her disease was aggravated by the resolution of Çrīnivāsa to go to Vṛndāvana. Nor were his mother's fears ungrounded for the way was not safe in that troubled age.

It took Çrīnivāsa five days to reach Rājmahāl from Jājigram (near Kātwa). He came to Patna *via* Gauridwar.

He fasted for some days, and other times had but scanty meals. He crossed the Ganges and came to Benares. His ecstasies of joy were great as he visited the landing Ghat of the river where Chaitanya used to bathe. On the north of the Ghat lay the house of Chandra Çekhara Achārya and on the south a pleasant spot where Sanātana had, disguised as a Mahomedan Darvesh, met Chaitanya. An elevated place surrounded by Tulsi plants was there, and Çrīnivāsa wept to recollect the associations of Chaitanya with it. He next visited Allahabad and bathed at the confluence of the three holy streams, known as the Trīvenī. A pious pilgrim offered four pice to Çrīnivāsa for his food, and the young ascetic accepted the offer because of the earnestness of the giver. Then he came to a place from where it required him four days to reach Vṛndāvana. Here he met five citizens who told him that Sanātana had died four months ago, and later on as he proceeded he heard that Rūpa had also died three days before.

The route

His grief was great, for he had come all this way to meet the reputed apostles. He said "Such is my lot. I wanted to read the Bhāgavata with Gadādhara Pundit. He asked me to get a copy of the book and this I procured travelling to Bengal for the purpose; and when I returned he, my would-be teacher, was no more, and I have come to Vṛndāvana to become versed in the scriptures with the aid of Sanātana and Rūpa. The venerable Narahari Sarkār sent me here for this purpose, and, as I arrive, I learn that they are no more in the world."

He paid a visit to the temple of Madana Mohana and, stricken with grief and having none to look after him, the youth lay at the doorway of the temple, beholding the glorious image installed on the throne, from a corner. Though Çrīnivāsa was strikingly handsome, he was emaciated by fasting and every by-stander marked in his domeanour the shadow of a great grief. Jīva Goswāmi, the illustrious nephew of Sanātana and Rūpa, was interested in the young man and made enquiries as to the object of his coming to Vṛndāvana. No greater scholar lived in Upper India than Jīva at the time, and when the veteran scholar, who was himself advanced in years and distressed by the death of his uncles, sopke to young Çrīnivāsa kindly, the youth threw himself at his feet surrendering himself completely to his will.

Jīva takes charge of him.

Jīva marked in young Çrīnivāsa talents of a very high order and himself instructed him in Vaiṣṇava philosophy. The old scholar began to entertain a sincere respect for the young man's capacity as he came in close contact with one whose faith as well as progress in study were marvellous. Gopāla Bhatta became his spiritual Guru and both he and Jīva were delighted to observe in their pupil great capabilities which boded well for the cause of the propagation of the Vaiṣṇava faith.

Here Çrīnivāsa joined two fellow students both of whom came to the holy city shortly after him. These two young men also were as remarkable as he ; and the friendship of the three, founded on the unision of spiritual ideals, under the clear sky of the sacred Vṛndā groves, developed into life-long intimacy and helped the cause of Vaiṣṇavism in Bengal in a remarkable manner. But before we launch upon the period of their activity and actual work in the spiritual field, some account should be given of the other two young men.

Narottama, a second Budhha.

In my Ram Tanu Fellowship lectures, I have given in detail some account of Raghunātha Dās—that princely ascetic, who like the Buddha, renounced worldly pleasures to seek joys of a higher plane. The Buddha, though one of the greatest of India's sons, rose to his eminent height by steps which have not been altogether inaccessible to others. 'The enlightened one' is no solitary example—no unapproachable ideal in the region of renunciation and spiritual culture in India. The history of the Buddha has been repeated here times without number. Sons of Rājās and Princes have renounced their palaces from age to age and passed through great hardships taking the ascetic's vows in quest of higher truths, even as did the Buddha two thousand years ago. Even in very recent times—less than a century ago—Lālā Babu of Pāikpara in Bengal left his princely fortune, turned Fakir and begged from door to door in Vṛndāvana, while a considerable portion of his fabulous wealth was given to charity and to the building of temples.

I have had occasions frequently to refer to the sorrows caused to others by a man's taking the vow of Sannyāsa. The pathos of the situation, I am afraid, is not likely to be rightly understood by my foreign readers. It is not the joining a monastery as a monk, much less should it be confounded with the avocation of a missionery. In India Sannyāsa means practically the cutting off of all domestic ties—the death of one's family-life and the beginning of the spiritual one unconnected with home. In a country where domestic ideas have such a prevailing force the Sannyāsa of a child is a calamity which is almost as great to the family as his death. The Sannyāsi will not name his parents nor own his relations or have any connection with his home. He will not visit his native place in life, and will besides have to practise austerities denying himself the pettiest pleasure of the material world. He will sleep under a tree and live on whatever chance may bring him. In this world of ours he may be taken as one dead, owning no home, no kith or kin, no concern with the ordinary affairs of men. Thus a man's taking of the vow of Sannyāsa is indeed a great calamity and naturally viewed with horror by his relations and friends.

The Vaiṣṇava Sannyāsi, however, devotes himself to the well-being of the whole of humanity. The home loses, but the world gains him. Far away from his own native district, he may live in the recesses of a mountain or in a temple of a holy city, where hundreds of people gather every day to receive instructions from him, and if he be a real and genuine Sannyasi, he is revered as a god; his words have the power of assuaging grief and quelling passions by which the human soul is rent in its worldly struggles.

We are coming now to a great Vaiṣṇava Sannyāsi who like the Buddha, like Raghunātha Dās, Rūpa and Sanātana, showed by his life the example of the highest renunciation in the pursuit of a great spiritual ideal.

He was Narottama Datta of Kheturi—a place situated in the old Perg of Gopalpur in the district of Rājshahi. Kheturi is 12 miles to the north west of Boalia and one mile to the north east of a village named Premtali on the Padmā. His father Kṛsnānanda Datta was the Rājā of the adjacent country and held, besides, extensive lands leased out to him by a powerful Jāgirdar appointed by the Emperor of Gauḍa. Narottama was born about the year 1565 A.D. He was therefore junior to Çrīnivāsa Āchārya by a few years. When Narottama was born, he being the only son of the Rājā, the music of the sweet *nahabat* orchestra announced the glad event for eight days and nights, and every man in the town of Kheturi was happy beyond description that at last a son and heir to the Rājā was vouchsafed by God's gracious providence. But God did not mean the boy for riches, nor for the palace of his parents. A higher ideal was set before him by his tutor Kṛṣṇa Dās. The country was at the time moved by the great pain of Chaitanya's *tirodhāna*. And as young Narottama heard the story of his life from Kṛṣṇa Dās he resolved to turn an ascetic and sing the praises of God even as the Master had done all his life. When only 12 years old, he one day came to see the great Padmā—that vast sheet of sparkling water which is almost as boudless as the sea to the eye and whose transparence reflects in an unspeakable manner the beauty of the infinite. On the bank of the Padmā the young prince stood and beheld a vision, as if some one called him to a higher life, as if some one whose voice was very sweet cast a spell to win his soul, and there and then was he entrapped. The voice said "come unto me, child, home and its cares are not for you." The child wept as he heard it; for he really heard the call and it was no fancy to him; he was overpowered by the summons, and fell unconscious on the ground.

His early career.

His parents, indeed the whole town, saught him anxiously and found him lying unconscious on the banks of the Padmā, and when they had restored him to consiousness by their care, the child looked changed in aspect and said "This palace is not a fit place for me." It is said that Chaitanya frequently appeared to him in his visions, and the boy used to cry out "Wait, wait, oh lord, I am coming to thee to surrender myself body and soul to thy service."

Kṛṣṇānanda Datta did what all worldy men would do in a similar case. The physician was called and was bidden to cure his malady. The good man prescribed, '*Civādi ghrita*' a medicine which was to be prepared with the flesh of a fox. Narottama said to his father "If you kill an animal to cure my disease I will not take that medicine. I would rather die than see an animal killed for my life." So other medicine was given; But the vision came continually and made him restless; he sometimes wept for joy and at others became sad as he thought of the impediments to spiritual life. He had, however, made considerable progress in his studies. At this time the Jāgirdār of Gaur expressed a wish to see him and sent for him; the father thought that a visit to the capital of the province might possibly have some inflence in diverting his mind to the world, and, with the consent of his wife Nārāyani, sent the boy, then only 16, to Gaur accompanied by a large number of horsemen and other attendants. On the way Narottama made his escape. He fled, as his predecessors in asceticism had fled, and following paths not frequented by pilgrims came to Rajghat near Beneras after some day's travel. His foot was blistered so that he could not walk, lying helpless under a tree; for two days he had no food, and no one came to offer him any help. On the 3rd day the vision returned and he saw that a bright complexioned lovely boy, no other than the

The renunciation.

child Gaurānga himself, appeared before him and said "You are fatigued my child, you are stricken with illness, you are in pain and footsore, and all for me, child. You have saught me forsaking the world and its pleasures, I will not forsake you. Here is a cup full of sweet milk, take this and you will regain your strength". When Narottama arose, he saw near him the cup of milk just as he had seen it in his vision, and he took the milk and was fresh and strong once more. By this time five pilgrims bound for Vṛndāvana had come up and in their company he went without disclosing his name or other particulars about himself. He spoke to them of Chaitanya and as he uttered the name of the Master, a thrill passed into the hearts of the pilgrims bringing tears of joy to their eyes. They came to Allahabad and reached Muthrā where the pilgrims left Narottama.

Unknown to every one save to his Creator, he come to Vṛndāvana and visited the temple of Govindaji. There he lived on the meal supplied *gratis* by the temple and paid a visit to Lokanātha Goswāmi—that prince of ascetics and early friend of Chaitanya. While supplying materials of Chaitanya's life to Kṛṣṇa Dās Kavirāja, Lokanātha had prohibited him to make any reference to his life in his book. No worldliness spotted his pure life; yet he was devoted to the good of this world by silently yet most effectively influencing all who came in contact with him.

Every night Narottama cleansed and washed the place adjoining the hut where the venerable hermit lived and did other menial service for him without his knowledge.[1]

[1] "রাত্রি দিন সেই স্থানে অলক্ষিতে যেয়ে।
বাহিরে টহল ক'রে সাশ্রু নেত্র হয়ে॥"

The Anurāgvallī.

The latter was surprised in the morning to find the court-yard of his hut neat and in order, wondering as to who did all this for him with so great a care. One day the saint resolved to watch and saw a young and attractive lad sweeping the court-yard with his broom. At intervals of work the boy stood holding the broom to his breast, while tears freely flowed from his eyes. Then wiping them away, he again continued doing the sweeper's menial work.[1] This was the prince Narottama, the pet child of the palace, which was mourning his loss in deep grief.

The Princely Sweeper.

Lokanātha strode forward and seizing the boy said in a gentle voice: "Who art thou, my young friend? I do not need these services from thee." Narottama threw himself at his feet and wept like a bashful maiden. He had not the power to speak much; but on repeated questioning said, "I am but a poor child, will you, Master, take me as your disciple"? Lokanātha was so moved by compassion that although he had not yet taken a single disciple lest the vanity of being a Guru should possess him, he made an exception in favour of Narottama and admitted him to his discipleship.

Narottama soon became known to all; his family status, his great meekness and his progress in study made him to be respected by the residents of Vṛndāvana, and Lokanātha initiated him into the mystic faith of which the ceremony was a very simple one. He was taken to a neighbouring

[1] "আপনারে ধন্যমানে শরীর সকল।
প্রভুর চরণ প্রাপ্তি এই মোর বল॥
কহিতে কহিতে কাঁদে ঝাঁটা বুকে দিয়া।
পাঁচ সাত ধারা বহে বুক মুখ বেয়া॥"

The Prema Vilāsa, the 11th Vilāsa,

temple where the image of Kṛṣṇa and Rādhikā where worshipped. There the venerable saint asked Narottama to take a *tulasi* leaf in his hand and said " Throw the leaf at the feet of the god there " which done, he said " With that I take the burden of all your sin on me. Whatever fault may you have committed in life, let the punishment of it be visited on me. Oh Lavanga Latikā, the *gopi* of Vṛndāvana, take charge of the young boy. Oh Gunachuḍā, the maid of Rādhā, make the boy pure, full of love and piety; let not any sin spot his character or the fairness of his soul." Thus the simple initiation took place. Then came advices as to the ways of Sādhanā which lifts the soul above passions and makes the vision of Kṛṣṇa clearer to the mind's eye.

His initiation and spiritual progress.

Narottama continued to do all kinds of menial work for his Guru inspite of his remonstrances, only meekly saying " My master, when one is forced to do something against his will, it is mean. But when we recognise in every little act that we voluntarily do, the glory of serving the Lord, the humble deed ranks as a great work. These little things feed my soul and elevate it." We find that his hand was once burnt when cooking a meal, and he was on a sick bed for some time. But young Narottama did not mind his physical pain in his earnestness to serve his Guru. And the vision of God frequently came to him, calling up those sweet trances in which like the great Master himself he became filled with tears and saw sights which belonged not to this world.

A year passed and the young Sannyāsi advanced in those mystic paths which reveal to the human eyes the sight of a higher world. He had arrived at Vṛndāvana in

April, 1593, A. D. Another April passed away and the fame of his devotion spread in the Vṛndā groves. It was in August, 1594, that Jīva Goswami introduced him to Çrīnivāsa. It was the 5th day of the waning moon when the two met. Both of them made rapid progress in various branches of Sanskrit learning, especially in the Bhakti Çastras under Jīva Goswāmi—now their common teacher.

On many occasions did the two remarkable youths visit the places made sacred by memories of Kṛṣṇa and Chaitanya. Both of them had visions which only the chosen few are privileged to see. They again and again dwelt upon the incidents of Chaitanya's life in their conversations, and wept for joy, and found their friendship established on the firm ground of unity of purpose and a common ideal based on absolute resignation to the will of Kṛṣṇa. The Narottama Vilāsa mentions that their friendship began from the very day when Narottama came to Vṛndāvana, but the earlier and more authentic record of the Premavilāsa mentions that occurrence to be full one year and four months after Narottama arrived at the holy city. The Bhaktiratnākara mentions the various shrines visited by the friends together and in this connection gives a topography of Mathurā and Vṛndāvana at the period. It is possible to study the details of this description, and compare them with the minute account of the places given by Mr. Growse in his History of Muthrā, we may note the improvements made in the city by the millionaires among the Jāt and Rājput merchants in latter times.

Cyāmānanda's early carrier.

We now come to the third man of the illustrious trio whose lot was cast with these two, one who co-operated with them for the rest of his life in the propagation of the Faith. Çrīnivāsa was a Brahmin and Narottama a Kāyastha, but Çyāmānanda's social status was much lower. He belonged to the Satgopa caste, whose profession is to tend cows and sell milk.

Çyāmānanda's ancestors were inhabitants of Bengal, but the family had removed to Orissa a few generations before. Çyāmānanda's father had settled in the village Dharenda Bahadurpur in the district of Dandakeçwara in Orissa. Kṛṣṇa Mandala was the name of his father, and his mother was named Durikā. The couple had many sons, all of whom died when young; so that when Çyāmānanda was born, they called him 'Duhkī' or "the sorrowful one." The people of this country often give such names to their pet children in their superstitious belief that death may not notice one called by so humble an appellation. Çyāmānanda, inspite of the great difficulties experienced by one belonging to the humble classes in his attempts to pursue higher studies, learned Sanskrit in his youth and being naturally of a spiritual bent of mind, resolved to devote himself to religion. He thus left home one night and reached a place named Naraden; thence he proceeded to Cheuwa, and then reached Ambikā near Kālnā. He stayed at the temple of Chaitanya and Nityānanda founded by Gauridas Pundit in 1510 A.D. The latter had died sometime before, and Hriday Chaitanya, one of his disciples, was in charge of the temple. He took great compassion at the forlorn condition of the lad, and though Çyāmānanda was of humble birth, he admitted him as his disciple. Dukhī's name was changed, and he was called Kṛṣṇa Dās by his Guru. He was instructed in the mystic ways of the Vaiṣṇavas, and made great progress in his studies receiving a full course of spiritual instruction imparted to him by his kind Guru who took a fatherly interest in him.

He left Ambikā in order to visit the various shrines of India, and a work named Rasikamaṁgala gives details of the places visited by him. Amongst the places mentioned, we find the following : Vakreçwara, Vaidyanātha, Gayā, Benares, Allahābad, Mathurā, Hastinapur (Delhi), Dwārakā, the shrine of Kapila on the Indus, Matsatīrtha, Çivakānchi, Viṣṇukānchi (modern Kanjivaram), Tritkuptpayana Ajodhyā, Hardwar, Draviḍa, Benkata, Tamraparṇī, Rangadhāma Payoṣṇi, Rāmeçwara, Trimalya and Purī. But the Premavilāsa does not mention these. It says that from Ambika Dukhi came direct to Vṛndāvana for the purpose of completing his education. This omission may be due to the fact that while Premavilāsa only incidentally mentions the fact of his life, the Rasikamaṁgala undertakes to give a fuller account of his doings and travels. But the names of the same shrines are so often mentioned in connection with the pilgrimage of Vaiṣṇavā worthies that biographers may often be led to repeat the list without much investigation, saying the same thing over again in every particular case. At the same time it must be admitted that every Vaiṣṇava pilgrim must have visited most of the same shrines that had some repute in these days. Leaving aside this disputed point, however, we come to surer ground and know for certain that Dukhi now called Kṛṣṇa Dās came to Vṛndāvana to complete his education under the instruction of his Guru. Jīva Goswāmī was struck with his great intelligence and taught him various Çāstras with great labour and attention. Kṛṣṇa Dās first finished Sanskrit grammar here which offer great difficulties in the way of mastering that wonderful tongue, it being a most abstruse and comprehensive subject, taking six or seven years of a scholar's life to acquire. Dukhi read the huge Sanskrit work, the Bhaktirāṣamṛta Sindhu, with annotations and also studied the Ujjalnīlamaṇi by Rūpa Goswāmī. The intricate and minute details of the Bhakti Çāstras were mastered by him very quickly, and his comprehension of its system was of a thorough character. The Premavilāsa refers to many questions that Jīva put to him by way of testing his acquirements in the subject. The faith which follows the ordinances of the scriptures—the *Vaidhi Bhakti*, and that which transcends them—the *Raganuga* offered points for frequent queries on the part of the illustrious teacher; and Çyāmānanda was always found up to the mark—nay more, giving him satisfaction by answering to the point and with interpretations which not only proved his mastery of the subject, but something strikingly original of his own. Jīva gave him the key to the mystic philosophy, and said " Before you preach the doctrines you must know what sort of man your hearer is. Most men of the world are materialistic. Do not disclose the secret doctrines to them. Find out those who are prepared to accept the truth, and to them alone you must speak in confidence." Then the master gave his pupil instructions showing the superiority of the Parakiyā over the Svakiyā. The fundamental teaching of the creed is " be saved yourself first, before you try to save others. Teach good deeds by practising good deeds yourself and not by speaking words merely. The man who preaches to others but does not follow his own precept, is not a true teacher ". In regard to how a man should save himself, the first lesson pointed out was " to repeat the name of God." But the doctrinal sides of the Vaiṣṇava scriptures, I shall discuss in a future lecture.

I shall here describe a legend about Kṛṣṇa Dās which has been repeated in each of the accounts of his career.

Dukhi stayed one evening in a temple and beheld the images of Rādhā-Kṛṣṇa, there. He was so overpowered by his mystic reveries, that he forgot the hour and stood silent in a corner of the courtyard, till the five-lights that were waved by the priest before the figures went out, the blower of the conch desisted, and the drummer retired, the cymbals played no more, and the sacred offerings were shared among the crowd who gradually dispersed. But Dukhi, transported to another region by his reveries, forgot time and place, and the vision of Rādhā-Kṛṣṇa appeared vividly before his senses. And he was so fascinated by the celestial sight that he lay transfixed to the spot and did not know how time had passed. A strange vision here revealed itself to his eyes; he saw in the courtyard Rādhā dancing before Kṛṣṇa. She was in the height of her delight and every movement of her arms and feet indicated the joy which belonged to the paradise of love in which she was the dweller. The morning dawned and the dance did not end—the fair dancer waving her arms and swiftly whirling round and round with her feet—with a delirious joy which bespoke the dedication of herself to the beloved deity before whom she danced. Hours passed away like seconds; the dancer knew not how they fled, nor did her mortal spectator, who with silent tears in his eyes beheld this wonderful spectacle. When the rays of the morning sun first

The legend about him.

burst on the gold-cupped pinnacle of the temple, the goddess who came to her senses and was ashamed of her long stay on the earth, disappeared with all swiftness; but in the quickness of her movement left behind her a golden *nupura* which had adorned one of her feet. Dhukhī found it, and he offered it to the temple. The story at once believed; for a sweet fragrance came out of the ornament from which it was apparent to all that the precious thing was not of the earth. When Dukhī with great reverence and devotional feeling presented the sacred ornament to Jīva and related the story, the latter embraced his pupil and said "Though of humble birth you are more favoured of Kṛṣṇa than any of us. Hence forward you will not be called 'Dukhī' or even Kṛṣṇadās. I give you the name of Çyāmānanda." Dukhī Kṛṣṇadās was known from this time as Çyāmānanda Dās.

We shall now enter upon an epoch of great activity in the life of these youths and relate events which gave a mighty impetus to the cause of Vaiṣṇavism in Bengal as a result of the united efforts of the trio.

II. Events in their lives after 1600 A.D.

In the month of November, probably in the year 1600 A.D. all Vaiṣṇavas of the vicinity met at Vṛndāvana. Çrīnivāsa and Narottama who had by this time completed their education, and whose faith in Kṛṣṇa elicited the admiration of all, received from Jīva Goswāmi the titles of Achārya and Thākura respectively. Jīva Goswāmi gave a feast to the Vaiṣṇavas on this occasion, all men who were anxious for the propagation of the faith in Bengal. The works of Sanātana and Rūpa, the Chaitanya Charitāmṛta by Kṛṣna Dās Kavirāj and Haribhaktivilāsa and the commentaries on the Bhāgavata by the masters contained the cream of Chaitanya's teachings; and how could these works, which were the results of the uninterrupted and whole-hearted devotion and of life-long labour of their authors, be made available to the readers of Bengal? True, they could be sent by men. But unless some one who had a regular course of training and were thoroughly versed in them should visit the dear land of Bengal and interpret the works in their true light, it would be of no use to send the manuscripts for the use of Bengali readers.

Çrīnivāsa and Narottama were called by the Vaiṣṇava assembly and asked to return with the manuscripts to Bengal. Another man was also called upon to join them. This was Çyāmānanda. They expressed their reluctance to leave the Holy city. Jīva said "You three are fit to do this great work. The propagation of faith is a noble object and you cannot avoid the call of this high duty."[1] Gopāla Bhatta and Lokanātha also joined in pressing the request and the three had accordingly to prepare for a trip to their mother-land with the sacred books, and though they had taken the vows of Sannyās and had no right to visit their homes, they did so by the order of their Gurus.

(a) The robbery that changed the life of a great robber.

A rich merchant of Mathurā, a disciple of Jīva Goswāmi supplied a spacious cart, four strong bullocks and ten armed men. The manuscripts were placed carefully in a large wooden chest which was locked and wrapped in wax-cloth.

[1] "বড় ধর্ম্ম রক্ষা হয় ধর্ম্ম প্রচারণে"—The Prema Vilāsa, the 12th Vilāsa.

Now were they ready for starting. Jīva Goswāmi was greatly moved when bidding adieu to Çrīnivāsa and Narottama "I may not live again to see you, lads, I have finished my duty of teaching and must now wait for death only" he said. He gave full instructions as to how his pupils should work on reaching Bengal, what books should be first taught to the youngmen of the country, and what books should be reserved for the chosen few. To Narottama he said "You have begun a great career, stick to it, my boy, and when any religious problems offer any difficulty, Çrīnivāsa will help you as brother helps brother." He recommended Çyāmānanda to their care, and said that they should send him to his home paying him the expenses of his trip.

The Journey.

They set out, deeply affected by the parting with their noble *Gurus*, the holiness of whose lives had cast a dream-like beauty over their imaginative souls, and for a long time they could speak of nothing else but of Jīva Goswāmi, of Raghunātha Das, of Lokanātha, Gopāla Bhatta and of the sacred shrine where so often the vision of Kṛṣṇa had come to them. They had a pass-port with them from the Rājā of Jaipur which they produced in the several cities through which they marched. They spent one night in Agra and came to a place named Itā along a well-metalled spacious road; but changed their course and now adopted a path through the jungles of Chota-Nāgpur. On their left lay the "Magha" country; "The wooded country" says the Premavilāsa "was delightful to the eyes and their topics turned to God whose beauty they saw mirrored everywhere." Crossing the forest they arrived at Tamluk. "The birds

—the kōkila and peacock—were in great numbers there, and the former with its gay notes, and the latter with its dance reminded them of Vṛndāvana, the sacred shrine they had left. And they recollected that Chaitanya had wandered like a mad man through the amphitheatre of the woodlands of Jhārikhanda once in ecstasies of spiritual joy. The dust trodden by the Master was sacred and they touched it with reverence. A great mishap however overtook them here, but before we describe it we must give an account of Vanaviṣṇupur or shortly Viṣṇupur, a principality held by an independent chief who was also a notorious robber.

A brief survey of the history of Vana Viṣṇupur.

The kingdom of Vanaviṣṇupur is in the district of Birbhum. It was once bounded on the north by the Santhal Pergannahs and on the south by Midnapur; portions of the district of Burdwan and of Chota Nagpur were also within its territorial jurisdiction. Leāgram was once the capital of Adimalla, born in 715 A.D. The non-Aryan tribes known as the *Bagdis* were very powerful there and had carried on depredations in the neighbouring Hindu kingdom and latterly founded a kingdom themselves under Adimalla—"The first Malla"—(Malla means a hero)—which was a title, the name of the king being Raghunātha Siṁha. Tradition says that Raghunātha was a Kṣatriya by birth but was brought up by the Bagdi chief, who installed him on the throne. I do not know how far this tradition can be believed. The kingdom was independent and powerful. A record of the kings of Viṣṇupur with dates is to be found in Oldham's Historical and Ethnological aspects of the Burdwan District. Adimalla's son Jaymalla extended his dominions by conquering Padampur, the whole family of the Rājā there committing suicide by drowning themselves in the tank Kānai Sara, after the latter's defeat in order to escape a capture by Jaimalla. The 48th king of Viṣṇupur from its founder, was Vana Malla whose son Hām vīra (lit. "I am a hero") ascended the throne in 1596 A. D. Hām vira is generally known as Vīra Hāmvīra. He was a daring chief who even dreamt of conquering the whole of Bengal, and had led an expedition against the Mahomedan Emperor of Gaur. In fact during the early period of his reign, the Pathan throne had become unsteady and until the Moghul rule was firmly established early in the 17th century, the warlike chiefs living in the outskirts of the province of Bengal not only a serted their independence, but openly set the Emperor of Gaur at defiance, whenever they found an opportunity to do so. In latter times Vīra Hamvīra was obliged to submit to the suzerain power and promise to pay Rs. 1,67,000 as annual revenue to the Emperor. Vīra Hamvīra had 15 forts; and the twelve feudetory chiefs under him had, besides, 12 forts. The Pathan Emperor to whom Vīra Hamvīra is said to have submitted was Katlu Khan. But Vana-Viṣṇupur remained practically independent, till the reign of Murshidkuli Khan. Its status was equal to that of Tipperah and Panchakota.

Vīra Hamvīra was the leader of a strong body of bandits who were the terror of the adjoining countries. He had employed a large number of thugs and assasins who infested the highways and killed and robbed the wayfarers. The astrologers of the court were ever ready to submit to him confidential reports as to what fortunes the stars would grant him if he carried on robberies in particular localities.

The cart containing the valuable manuscripts passed through the highway leading to the province of Bengal, and the robbers followed it, but did not dare take any violent step till it had reached the jurisdiction of their own Rājā. A spy had brought information to the robber king, and he learned that there were altogether fifteen men who accompanied the cart,—ten soldiers with arms, three holy men and two cart-men. The Rājā employed two hundred men, and the astrologers prophesied the acquisition of a really valuable treasure, and the spies inflamed the imagination of the chief by say'ng that it was possibly something more valuable than gold with which the cart was loaded. It might be diamonds and precious stones, since the men guarded it with great care and the load, every body said, contained immense riches.

"A great treasure."

The robbers employed by Vīra Hamvīra, secretly worshipped Chandi before embarking on their wicked errand, and overtook the loaded cart at a village named Tamar. "They had", says the Bhaktiratnākara, "planned to commit the robbery there, but could not find any opportunity." They followed it secretly through the village of Raghunāthpur; on the left of the way lay the village Panchavati. In the village of Maliārā the owners of the carts with their escorts stopped for a night in the house of the Zemindar of the place who gave them a warm reception. The three youths left Māliārā in the evening and came to a village named Gopālpur. The two hundred men employed by the Rājā, some of whom were armed with guns and the others with arrows, now mustered strong, and in the night fell upon

The pursuit.

the sleeping guards who fled leaving their assailants masters of the cart.

The cart carried away with its contents.

The Bhaktirasāmṛtasindhu of Rūpa, the Ujjalnīlamani, the Bidagdhamādhava, the Haribhaktivilāsa, the Chaitanya Charitāmṛta, the Lalitamādhava and the Bhāgavata-commentaries were all there, and no copies of these works were left at Vṛndāvana. Fair copies had been ordered to be made of them in Bengal, and thence circulated all over India. What a dire misfortune it was to the three friends—the custodians of a treasure, which far exceeded in their eyes their weight in gold or precious stones! The tradition prevalent in the district of Bankura is that there were altogether 121 books in the chest.

Çrīnivāsa, however, collected himself and controlling the first impulse of grief, to which all the three had yielded, went to a neighbouring village and with a pen and a bit of paper obtained from a villager communicated the tidings to the Goswāmis of Vṛndāvana. The ten guards were entrusted with the letter and sent back to the holy city. Jīva received the letter and read it out to Lokanātha; and Gopāla Bhatta heard of its contents. Raghunātha Dās and Kṛṣnadās Kavirāja were already very old. The last named scholar, who was about 100 years old at the time, could not stand the shock. The fruit of his devoted labour was lost with the Chaitanya Charitāmṛta; he fell unconscious at the shock the news gave him, and died then and there. This is the account given in the Premavilāsa, the earliest of the histories describing this episode. The Karṇānanda, however, written a few years after, corrects this statement by saying that

The news causes the death of Kṛṣṇa Dās Kavirāja.

Kṛṣnadās, though "taken to be dead did not actually die as the Premavilāsa says" but slowly recovered consciousness and lived for a few weeks more. I have already referred to this point in a previous lecture. The authority of Karṇānanda was Hemlatā Devi, a daughter of Çrīnivāsa, from whom the author personally heard it. The Goswāmis of Vṛndāvana felt the profoundest grief, but submitted to the inscrutable ways of the providence for which they could not divine any reason.

Çrīnivāsa said to Narottama, "it is no wonder that the miscreants should take our manuscripts to be a treasure; what treasure could be more valuable than that in which the fascinating discourses of Chaitanya with Rāma Ray were described? What more valuable than the works of Rupā, every word of which breathed the loftiest truths of the spiritual world?"[1] And here he stopped with a sigh—his sentiments being shared by his two comrades.

[1] "ধন বলি গ্রন্থ সব চুরি করি লইল।
অপ্রমাণ নহে সেই ধন মাত্র সার।
গণিতা গণিল কিবা দোষ আছে তার॥
প্রভু রামানন্দ সঙ্গে যত প্রত্যুত্তর।
লিখিলেন কবিরাজ আনন্দ অন্তর॥
রস ভক্তি কৃষ্ণ তত্ত্ব প্রেমের আখ্যান।
কতেক লিখিব তার যতেক প্রমাণ॥
সেই তত্ত্ববেত্তা যেই মনে তাহা জানে।
আমি যে লিখিয়ে তার বুঝিবে কারণে॥
ধন মধ্যে কহ হায় কোন ধন গণি।
রাধাকৃষ্ণে প্রেম যার সেই মহা ধনী॥
শ্রীরূপের গ্রন্থে যত লীলার প্রসঙ্গ।
কত প্রেম ধন আছে তাহায় তরঙ্গ॥
প্রেমধন গাঁথিয়াছে অক্ষরে অক্ষরে।
স্পর্শমণি বলি তারে গনিল অন্তরে॥"

The Premavilāsa, the 13th Vilāsa.

Çrīnivāsa asked Narottama to carry out the orders of Jīva and go to Bengal. Çyāmananda should accompany him. "But I stay here to try if even at the risk of my life I can recover the manuscripts, I shall not leave this spot before I try my best to recover what we have lost."

The friends part in deep sorrow.

The two friends took leave of him in silent grief and he with a poor coarse outer mantle and a strip of cloth, four and half feet long, with which he covered his loins, a solitary grief-stricken wanderer,—went from village to village making enquiries and heard the report that the Rājā himself was a great robber.

Vira Hamvīra's disappointment.

We now come to the robber chief. It is stated in the Bhaktiratnākara that at the advent of the chest containing the manuscripts the city of Viṣṇupur assumed altogether a new aspect. The hearts of the people became pure; the very atmosphere of the place changed; the air gladdened the hearts of all; wickedness ceased and mercy, love and other higher qualities of the soul manifested themselves and predominated in all human action.

Vira Hamvīra kept awoke till a late hour of the night in order to receive the treasure, and when the robbers brought the chest he gave them rewards even before they had opened it, so confident was he of the value of its contents. But said he :—"The very sight of the chest makes my heart throb with a strange delight—not like what I am accustomed to, what can be in it?" And as he said this he had the chest opened and to his astonishment discovered the manuscripts; he turned a leaf and saw the handwriting of Rūpa which Chaitanya had so often admired and said "His handwriting is a delight to the eyes—the lines are like stringed pearls."[1] As the king pored over the cover of the sacred books, his mind became pure, and again and again he glanced at them, and then said to the astrologer who was present "How is it that you calculated that there were gold and precious stones in the cart?" The astrologer was silent, and the Rājā continued "No matter, your prophesy is true, for are not these a really valuable treasure?" To the robbers he turned and asked again and again in great repentence "Tell me, have you killed any one?" They said "None did we hurt, we carried out your Majesty's order to the letter. If life can be spared while securing our own interest, we do not wilfully do any violence to any body. The guards were all sleeping and we did the act as covertly and as much without violence as we could." Then the Rājā said "Many a wicked act have I done and this is the crowning one of them all; for I have certainly given pain to pious souls, and it may be that their sighs may burn my palace." Saying so he had the chest closed and deposited it in his treasury, and did not talk with any one for some hours.

Crīnivāsa at Dewāli.

Çrīnivāsa after having wandered about Viṣṇupur and its vicinity in vain in quest of information, on the 10th day stopped near a village called Dewāli one mile from Viṣṇupur, on the other side of the river Jaçoda. Here he met a young scholar named Kṛṣṇavallabha and had a talk with him about the Rājā. Kṛṣṇavallabha said that the Rājā was a wicked man and

[1] "রূপের অক্ষর যেন মুকুতার পাঁতি।"

Chaitanya Charitāmṛta.

committed robberies on strangers. "It is only the other day," he continued, "that he had a cart-load of treasure pillaged and brought to his palace." But Çrīnivāsa was not sure that the manuscripts were the treasure that he spoke of, though a faint doubt crossed his mind.

Kṛṣṇavallabha, the young scholar.

Kṛṣṇavallabha observed that the people of Viṣṇupur were very sorry at the conduct of the Rājā; but there was no help. He heard that the Rājā had some respect for the Bhāgavata. "That is the only door open by which God may approach his soul if He would do so to save it from perdition and save the people of Viṣṇupur from his oppressions."

The young scholar Kṛṣṇavallabha felt a great admiration for Çrīnivāsa, for the moment the latter talked on learned subjects, his words breathed inspiration into his soul. They showed a great command over various branches of learning and Kṛṣṇavallabha was soon on his knees asking the remarkable scholar to teach him Grammar and Rhetoric—subjects which the former was already studying. Çrīnivāsa consented to do so. Kṛṣṇavallabha offered him a meal, but his teacher said "I prepare my own meal. It is very simple, only a little vegetable boiled in water with rice."

The young scholar studied with Çrīnivāsa that day, and in the evening went to the court of the Rājā to hear discourses on the Bhāgavata delivered by Vyāsāchārya—his court Pandit. He came back after a few hours and Çrīnivāsa asked him "What did you see and hear in the court?" His pupil said "Revered sir, my mind longed for a sight of you, and I could not stay long in the court. The matters went on as usual, the Rājā heard the

Bhāgavata explained for sometime and then retired to his apartment."

The custom of hearing the interpretations of Bhāgavata during some fixed time in the day seems to have been a fashion with the Hindu Rājās, prevalent in their courts from the 10th or the 11th century A.D. onwards. The Dharmamangala poems which give vivid pictures of the courts of the Hindu Rājās mention this, every time when a Rājā's court is described. It was a favourite point with the poets to mention the chapter and verse of the Bhāgavata which was read on particular occasions. Before introducing an incident connected with the court, the poets used to anticipate it by referring to some episodes of the sacred book corresponding to the event going to be described in the chapter.

Çrīnivāsa asked his pupil if the latter could ake him to the court next day to hear the Bhāgavata as explained by the court Pandit, and to this Kṛṣṇavallabha readily ascented.

Accordingly they went to the court together the next day. Çrīnivāsa was disappointed to hear the interpretations of the Bhāgavata from the court Pandit. But he said nothing, and on the day following paid a visit to the court again. When Vyāsāchārya explained the scriptures that day, Çrīnivāsa said "You do not, sir, follow the text, and the standard commentary of Çrīdhara, in your eagerness to say something original. This is not what it should be." The Pandit did not mind his remarks but went on. The king however glanced at Çrīnivāsa frequently. Nothing further transpired that day. On the next day the Pandit explained the Rāsapanchāddhāya—a very abstruse

In the Court of the King.

and at the same time interesting chapter of the Bhāgavata. Çrīnivāsa interrupted the Pandit that day also, and said "Sir, how can it be possible for you to interpret the book without following the commentary of Çrīdhara with which you are presumably unacquainted ?" The Pandit became angry at this interruption from a stranger. But the Rājā said "How is it that this Brahmin scholar finds fault with your explanations ? Are you not interpreting the text aright ?" Whereupon the Pandit replied arrogantly "Where is there a scholar who can interpret the texts better than I ? This Brahmin is a conceited fellow and dares interrupt me in your Majesty's presence." Then looking at Çrīnivāsa he indignantly added "Now come here and let us see what a prodigy you are, explain the text yourself" So the Pandit vacated his seat and Çrīnivāsa occupied it. Each *Cloka* he explained in several ways on the basis of *Bhakti*. The Rājā was highly gratified and his Pundit frightened. At the request of the king Çrīnivāsa continued his discourses for some hours and drew a shower of tears from the Court Pandit's eyes and indeed from those of all others present there. As he entered deeper into the subject, his audience was amazed by his wonderful scholarship and power of appealing to the heart. The Rājā was beside himself with joy. All asked "Who is this Brahmin, whence has he come ?" They heard him with rapt attention till a late hour in the evening, when Çrīnivāsa fastened the book with twine, and closed his lecture. All bowed to him and especially the court Pandit whose admiration was so great that he forgot the sting of his own humiliation and now approached the stranger with

The Court Pandit takes umbrage.

The wonderful discourses on the texts of the Bhāgavata.

these words "You have brought out the hidden meanings of the scripture in such a remarkable manner and so impressively and thrown such new light on the texts that I do not remember to have heard anything of the kind since I began my studies." The Rājā who also was greatly moved, said reverentially "whence do you come Brahmin, and what is your name?" And he replied "My name is Çrīnivāsa and I am a native of this country (Bengal). I came here to see your court." The Rājā ordered for him the best quarters available in his palace, and the Pandit had a further talk with him in which he again paid the tribute of his regards to Çrīnivāsa and then departed.

At night the king called on Çrīnivāsa again and entreated him to take his meal in the palace. Çrīnivāsa said "I take my meal only once a day." "What harm" said the Rājā "if you take light refreshments though you may not take cooked food." And Çrīnivāsa agreed to do so to please his Majesty. Good clarified butter, sugar, fried rice and fruits were brought there and the Rājā himself sat by the side of Çrīnivāsa when the latter partook of a small quantity of them.

During the whole night Çrīnivāsa repeated the name of Kṛṣṇa and inwardly felt that there would be some mark of divine grace shown to the people of that country at no distant future.

In the morning the Rājā saw Çrīnivāsa again who said "The sight of a king in the morning bodes well for the whole day, so glad am I to see your Majesty." But the king replied in a tone of humility "A sight of such a holy man as you cleanses the soul and brings it nearer to divine grace."

Çrīnivāsa, as was his wont, bathed in the morning, and the king himself waited upon him all the while like a mute admirer and requested him to attend the court after his meal. His Majesty then went to his room and asked Vyāsachārya, the court Pandit what he thought of Çrīnivāsa's lectures. The Pandit said that they were wonderful.

A second discourse and its marvellous effect.

Then after meal Çrīnivāsa went to the court and unfastened the twine of the manuscript of the Bhāgavata and began his speech before an eager and large audience. Such were the ecstasies of joy created by his discourses that "even the very stone walls of the hall seemed to melt at the pathos." The Rājā who sat near him looked at him through his tears. He appeared to His Majesty as bringing a divine message to his soul.

Then when the lecturer stopped, a murmur of wonder and sobbings were heard in the big hall, and the king called Çrīnivāsa to his private chamber and said "I hear that you have come to Viṣṇupur on a certain private mission, may I hear what it is, so that I may serve you with all my power?" This raised a point too delicate for Çrīnivāsa and he naturally felt hesitation in stating the facts which sorely troubled him. He controlled himself and said briefly "I came from the holy city of Vṛndāvana with a mission from Gopāla Bhatta and Jīva for the propagation of the faith in Bengal. The sacred books written by the great masters—the result of their life-long devotion,—the only copies they had, were entrusted to me; but as ill luck will have it, I have been robbed of this treasure in the way. My comrades—one a prince who has taken the ascetic's vows and another a talented scholar, have gone to their homes stricken with grief. I am here to inquire for the lost treasure. If I do not get it back, the loss will be worse than death to me. May I not claim your Majesty's help in the matter?"

The remorseful king and the recovery of the Manuscripts.

Then the remorseful Rājā, whose heart was full, could not control his emotions and burst into tears. He confessed his crime and added "A poor worm am I, lost hopelessly in the world. Had I not stolen the manuscripts, no god would have knocked at my doors to redeem my soul. The cart is exactly in the same condition here as it was when stolen. Punish me, sir, and do not spare me because I am a king. It is to reclaim an abject sinner like me that you are here to-day. What criminal in my kingdom is worse than he who calls himself the ruler of the land?" So saying he fell on the bare earth and wept, careless of his royal robe, which was soiled with dust.

His initiation.

Çrīnivāsa was led to where the manuscripts were kept, and as he saw the chest he was filled with great joy. The Rājā who reverentially bowed before the sacred books was garlanded by Çrīnivāsa. In July, 1600, the Rājā was thus initiated, and the name Haricharan Dās—a servant of the feet of Kṛṣṇa was given him by Çrīnivāsa on the occasion. The court Pandit Vyāsachārya was also initiated in the Vaiṣṇava faith by Çrīnivāsa on the same day. So great was the esteem in which Çrīnivāsa was held by the Rājā, that the latter placed his kingdom at his disposal, and said that he was a mere regent holding the helm of the state under the direction of his *Guru*.

The account of the conversion as given by the Bhaktiratnākara is slightly different. The description given above has been mainly taken from the Premavilāsa

—a contemporary historical work, the author's knowledge being taken at first hand in regard to all points he has stated. The account enters into minute details, as may be expected from one who heard them himself from the parties concerned. The Bhaktiratnākara, a much later work, has taken the view of affairs natural in a poet writing at a distance of time. The details are scamped and the incidents are more artistically represented. Çrīnivāsa, at the time of Narahari Chakravartī—the author of the work, was already surrounded with a halo of glory in the eyes of pious Vaiṣṇavas; and his admirers had ceased to think of him as a man; they had begun to regard him as an incarnation of Chaitaṇya. So whenever the author speaks of him, he uses the coloured language of a poet, and in narrating the incidents of his life cannot free himself from pre-conceived notions about the deified subject of his memoir.

The discrepancies in the different accounts.

Thus for instance it is stated in the Bhaktiratnākara that when Çrīnivāsa first goes to the court of Vīra Hāmvīra, the monarch is struck by the beauty of his person and his noble demeanour. The whole court feels the influence of his inspiring presence. The Rājā asks him what may be the object which brings him to his court and which he may be honoured by fulfilling. Çrīnivāsa does not take his seat though requested to do so, nor does he say anything beyond these simple words "Your Court-Pandit is reading the sacred scriptures, I cannot take my seat so long as they are read, and there need not be any interruption by introduction of worldly topics when the sacred book is read." He stood silently hearing the interpretations of the texts with great reverence, a circumstance

11

which only enhanced the respect of the whole court for him. Do not such descriptions show that the author wrote from preconceived notions about the greatness of Çrīnivāsa? There is also a slight difference between the accounts given in the two books in regard to small details. The Premavilāsa states that it was the Rāsapanchādhāya of the Bhāgavata on which Çrīnivāsa gave his first discourse in the Rājā's court, the Bhaktiratnākara says that it was the Bhramara Gītā. On such points, however, I am always inclined to accept the earlier and more reliable statements of the Premavilāsa. When a great man dies in India, it always happens that his admirers relish poetical and exaggerated descriptions about him rather than plain and simple facts which prove his kinship with ordinary mortals. Hence the Bhaktiratnākara is held in higher esteem than the Premavilāsa by the orthodox Vaiṣṇava community. Whatever the details of the case may be, it is certain that from after the conversion of Vīra Hamvīra, a new life began in Vanaviṣṇupur which became one of the most important centres of Vaiṣṇavism in Bengal. The impetus which that religion gave to its art and sculpture will be seen in the excellence of the architectural designs and the artistic decorations of the temples erected by Vīra Hāmvīra and his successors. There are inscriptions on the doorways of many of these temples. Çrīnivāsa Āchārya worked from here for the most part changing the very tide of the lives of the people, and the prince of robbers now became known as the Royal Monk whose extensive endowments and charities in the cause of the Vaiṣṇava religion became the chief feature of his subsequent administration. It is said that he enacted laws by which it was

Viṣṇupur turns into a Vaiṣṇava centre.

made obligatory on his subject to repeat the name of God a certain number of times every day. Vīra Hāmvīra's Queen Sulakṣaṇā became one of the devoutest followers of Çrīnivāsa. From the material point of view this episode in the history of Vaiṣṇavism in Bengal is full of striking results and meant a great advancement in its spreading abroad. Vīra Hāmvīra reigned from 1596 A.D. to 1622 A.D. He composed many Bengali songs some of which are to be found in the Padakalpataru and others in the Bhaktiratnākara. Some of these breathe a spirit of remorse for his past sins and his devotion to Çrīnivāsa Āchārya for creating in him a taste for spiritual life. (*a*)

(*a*) One of these songs runs thus :—

প্রভু মোর শ্রীনিবাস পুরাইলা মোর আশ
তুয়া বিনা গতি নাহি আর।
আছিনু বিষয় কীট বড়ই লাগিল মিট
ঘুচাইলা রাজ-অহঙ্কার॥
করতু গরল পান সে পথে হানিল বাণ
দেখাইল অমৃতের ধার।
পিব পিব করে মন সব লাগে উচাটন
এমতি প্রেমের ব্যবহার॥
রাধা পদ সুধা রাশি সে পদে করিলা দাসী
গোরাপদে বাঁধি দিলা চিত।
শ্রীরাধার পদ সহ দেখাইলা কুঞ্জ গেহ
জানাইলা দুঁহু প্রেম-প্রীত॥
যমুনার কুলে যাই তীরে সখী ধাওয়াধাই
রাধা কানু বিলাসয়ে রূপ।
এ বীর হাম্বীর হিয়া ব্রজপুর সদা ধিয়া
পদ্মে যেন বিহরে মধুপ॥

Typical Selections Vol. II, p. 1121.

(b) *Narottama at Kheturi.*

Parting from Çrīnivāsa in profound sorrow for the loss of the books, Narottama by the orders of his Guru came back to his native town of Kheturi accompanied by Çyāmānanda. Many years had elasped since he had left home as a Sannyāsi, and his bereaved father Rājā Kṛṣṇānanda no longer found himself capable of holding the helm of the Rāj, but retired, making the kingdom over to his beloved nephew Santoṣa Ray. They frequently talked of Narottama, their "Naru" as they used to call him, in deep sorrow; and never suspected that the lost one would ever be found again. But the report now spread that Narottama had come back. Hundreds of men went to see him. They beheld the princely youth dressed in the ochre-coloured cloth of a Yogi and changed into a quite different man. He uttered the name of God and wept like a child; and in reply to a thousand enquiries said only 'yes' or 'no' communing only with his companion now and then. His father and mother came to see him with all the passionate eagerness of their soul; but just as the waves of the sea are retarded by its own beach, so the emotions of their heart met a check at the sight of Naru. So reverend did he look that he seemed to belong to another world and they dared not bless him though he was their child.[1] They asked him, however, to return to the palace; he, however, said meekly but in a firm tone "My revered parents, I will live in this Kṛṣṇa temple of Kheturi. Far from going to the palace I shall not touch any present from it, but shall share the simple meal of the priest here for which there is an endowment of the State. If you

[1] See Narottama Vilāsa by Narahari Chakravarti.

ever urge me to return to a wordly life I shall leave Kheturi once more."

They were therefore content to see him back in his native city, and did not venture to do anything against his will.

Meantime a messenger came from Çrīnivāsa with a letter communicating the news of the recovery of the books and of the conversion of the Rājā Vīra Hāmvīra. Narottama was glad beyond description. And his parents and Santoṣa Rāy were glad also. The latter appointed trumpeters and musicians to proclaim the news to the citizens and there were general signs of joy all over the city.

Narottama's high character, scholarship and spiritual life became the subject of admiring talk throughout the country, and Valarāma Miçra, a scho.ar, became his first Brahmin disciple. This was a great step, for Narottama was a Kāyastha, reckoned as a Çudra, and the news of a Brahmin accepting such a one as Guru created a great commotion in society. The position of a Guru to his disciple is a unique one. He is held as a god, and there is no service, however mean, which the disciple can refuse to do for him; while the ordinary duty of the former requires him to eat the latter's leavings, to drink the water touched by his toe, and touch the dust of his feet with reverence morn and even. That a Kāyastha, whom the Brahmins considered a Çudra, should place himself in the exalted position of a Guru in regard to a Brahmin, was an indignity which the Hindu community could not patiently bear; and there were many plots formed by them against Narottama to which I shall have to refer hereafter.

The next Brahmin disciples of Narottama were Rāmakṛṣṇa and Haricharana, natives of Gayespur in the district of Jessore. Narottama did not tolerate a feeling of undue humility towards him in his disciples. He was far above worldly vanity; it was his sweet spiritual discourses which made an impression on the people and led them to surrender themselves body and soul to his service.

In the village of Gāmvīlā on the Ganges, lived a haughty Brahmin named Gangānārāyaṇa Chakravartī—a rich man and one who was versed in the Çāstras to such an extent that few could be found to rival him in the adjacent country. He had a big *tol*—a boarding college—at his house at Gāmvīlā, where he taught Logic, Rhetoric and Poetry to 500 Brahmin students who were lodged and fed by him.[1]

This man once met Rāmakṛṣṇa and Haricharana, two brothers who had given themselves up to Narottama and become his disciples. Indignant at the humiliation of the whole Brahmin race by the two brothers' 'unworthy conduct,' he held a learned disputation with them for some hours. The quotations from scriptural authorities were as copious as were the reasons adduced by the contending parties in support of their respective views, and Gangānārāyaṇa could not hold his position for long in

[1] "আর শাখা গঙ্গানারায়ণ চক্রবর্ত্তী ।
গঙ্গাতীরে গাম্ভীলা গ্রামেতে যার স্থিতি ॥
কৃষ্ণপ্রেমে সদা মগ্ন করেন ভজন ।
ঠাকুর চক্রবর্ত্তী বলি সবে তারে কন ॥
বারেন্দ্র ব্রাহ্মণ তিঁহো পণ্ডিত প্রধান ।
পাঁচশত পড়ুয়ার নিত্য অন্ন দান ॥

The Prema Vilāsa, the 20th Vilāsa.

the debate. The brothers, though unassuming in their conduct and apparently humble, were illuminated by the new light; and the influence of the noble life and the sacrifices of their master had animated them with faith in their cause; so they advocated it with a warmth and eloquence which made a deep impression on the proud scholar of Gāmvīlā whom orthodoxy had not blinded, and who inspite of his pride was open to conviction.

Gaṅgānārāyaṇa now yearned for a sight of the great Kāyastha Guru and accompanied the brothers to Kheturi. There he saw the princely youth who had sacrificed all pleasures of life for the religion of love. He was far from having any shadow of that conceit attributed to him by malice, and which the scholar of Gāmvīlā had, like others, heard and believed. He was meek, heroic, absolutely given to God and superb in learning as in faith. The proud scholar was charmed by his presence and instinctively bowed to him and touching his feet accepted him as his Guru.

Narottama declared that he would be glad if a temple were erected at Kheturi—dedicated to Chaitaṇya. It was not in 1582, as some have said, but in some year between 1602 and 1606, when the great festivity of the Vaiṣṇavas took place on the occasion of the foundation of the new fane. It was in the month of March on the full moon day.

Rājā Kṛṣṇānanda Datta and Santoṣa Rāy, his nephew, declared that if the income of their whole State for a number of years needed to be spent on the occasion for the success of the function, they would be prepared to spend it, as "Naru" had expressed a wish to hold the ceremony at Kheturi. In the list of the invited the first name was of

Jānhavi Devī, wife of Nityānanda, the second of Vīrachandra his son, third of Gopāla Miçra,—the eldest son of Advaita Āchārya and so forth. A very large number of Vaiṣṇavas, in fact all who were known as such in Bengal,

The great Vaiṣṇava festivity at Kheturi.

were invited, and the invitation-letter added : "We cannot invite all, because we do not know all, but bring all who may be willing to come and join the festivity."[1] Temporary sheds and camps were erected which covered the villages adjacent to the town of Kheturi, and vast arrangements were made to give hearty reception to the guests. Unexpectedly, however, Viṣṇupriyā Devī, herself—wife of Chaitaṇya—now grown very old, graced the occasion with her presence; for she was very happy that Narottama was going to found a temple in honour of Chaitaṇya. She saw the image of her Lord in the temple through happy tears and could not speak for hours together. The occasion created indescribable sympathy as each Vaiṣṇava beheld the venerable lady bowing to the image of her lord, who was now the god of millions, with joint hands and weeping.

Çrīnivāsa Āchārya and Vīra Hāmvīra came to Kheturi to join the festivity. Each guest wore a silken cloth—the present of the Rājā of Kheturi—was garlanded and welcomed with a sacred Tulasī leaf as he approached the triumphal gate built on the occasion, and for ten days each night the *kīrtaṇ* chorus song and played. On the first night the gifted Devī Dās Kīrtaniyā sang assisted by the

[1] For a full account of this festivity see. (I) Narattoma Vilāsa by Narahari Chakravartī, (II) Bhakti Ratnākara by the same author, (III) the Prema Vilāsa by Nityānanda Dās and (IV) Narottama Charita by Shishir Kumar Ghosh.

chorus, and Gaurānga Vallabha headed those who played on the Mṛdanga. Narottama who had a sweet voice joined the chorus. The vast courtyard of the palace presented a sea of human heads, and all silently heard the singers, their sighs and sobs indicating the appreciation of the songs in praise of Chaitanya and Rādhā-Kṛṣṇa

They sang the *padas* of the great masters, Chandidās, Vidyāpati and of Narahari, one of which ran thus:

The *padas* sung.

"In this bower I leave my golden necklace, tell him (for I shall not live to tell him myself) that he may wear it on his breast for my sake. The Mallikā plants are there, my maids, I planted them with my own hands; the season of their flowers has not come (when it comes, I shall not live). Do you, my maids, weave a garland with the flowers for him and hang it on his breast. When I am dead and gone, put my body on the Tamāla tree (the tree charms me because of its colour dark as that of Kṛṣṇa). Ask him, dear maids, to come to this bower once, and when he does so, whisper to me, though dead, that he has come; perchance my senses will revive at the news. Narahari, will you not then kindly recite Kṛṣṇa's name to my ears!"[1]

[1] নিকুঞ্জে রহিল এই আমার হিয়ার হেম-হার।
পিয়া যেন গলায় পরয়ে একবার॥
রোপিনু মল্লিকা নিজ করে।
গাঁথিয়া ফুলের মালা পরাইও তারে।
সখি প্রাণ যদি দেহছাড়ে,
বাঁধিয়া রেখো সখি তমালের ডালে
এ বনে বারেক আসিতে তারে ক'ও
নরহরি করো এই কাম।
সে সময় কাণে শুনাইও কৃষ্ণ নাম।

The soul in its eternal separation from the Beloved One pines away for Him; it yearns to offer its necklace of love, its garland of tender emotions for the service of the Adored One. Alas, it seeks Him in vain and dies of a broken heart. The singer's interpretations give a mystic charm to the songs. The occasion became a solemn one, and every one was reminded of that love which is presented to the eyes of all in the gift of flowers, to the child's lips in mother's milk and to life in the air which covers us like the arms of the mother. Pilgrims are we all, over plodding on our way in quest of the Beloved One; and the songs of the Vaiṣṇava masters continually remind us of the divine love, though they use the language of human emotions.

Mystic visions came to Narottama often during this concert of music and he was so everpowered by them that at one time he swooned away. For sometime the songs had to be stopped and all were busy trying to restore him to his senses, and when this was done, he looked divineby inspired as though just returned from the presence of God. Even his father Rājā Kṛṣṇānanda Datta forgot that Narottama was his son and looked on him as a being of a higher world and did reverence to him.

The next day, the famous Kīrtaniyā Gokula Dās sang of Rādhā-Kṛṣṇa. He sang this celebrated song of Vidyāpati:

1. Oh lucky night that I spent, I beheld the moonlike face of my love! My youth, my life, became blessed and every thing around assumed an air of joy. My home has become a true home to-day and my body a worthy one indeed. Providence has favoured me to-night and all my doubts are removed. May the cuckoo sing a lakh

of times, and instead of one may a lakh of moons arise in the sky; the five floral arrows of Cupid, may they be a lakh in number; I have no fear of them now! May the air blow sweetly, and when I shall meet him again I shall feel that my body has attained its goal. Says Vidyāpati, oh fortunate one, blessed is your love."[1]

2. "When my beloved shall come to my house, all the rites of reception shall I perform in my body. My breasts will be like golden jars,[3] my eyes will be like his mirror. My heart will be his throne and my hair the broom to dust his path."[2]

The words referred to that union with Kṛṣṇa, the living example of which was beheld in Chaitanya; which made Raghunātha Dās, Rūpa and Sanātana, give up

[1] আজু রজনী হাম ভাগে পোহাইঁলু, পেখুঁলু পিয়া মুখ চন্দা।
জীবন যৌবন সকল করি মানিনু, দশদিশ ভেল নিরদ্বন্দা।
আজু মঝু গেহ, গেহ করি মানুলু, আজু মঝু দেহ ভেল দেহা।
আজু বিধি মোহে অনুকুল হোয়ল, টুটল সবহুঁ সন্দেহা।
সোহি কোকিল অব লাখ ডাক ডাকুউ, লাখ উদয় করু চন্দা।
পাঁচ বাণ অব লাখ বাণ হুউ মলয় পবন বহু মন্দা।
অব মঝু যবহুঁ পিয়া সঙ্গ হোয়ব, তবহুঁ মানব নিজ দেহা
বিদ্যাপতি কহ অল্পভাগী নহ ধনি ধনি তুয়া নব লেহা।

[2] One of the auspicious signs with which a visitor is welcomed in an Indian house is to keep jars filled with water at the door-way.

[3] পিয়া যব আওব ই মঝু গেহে।
মঙ্গল যতহুঁ করব নিজ দেহে॥
কনয়া কুম্ভ করি কুচ যুগ রাখি।
দরপন ধরব কাজর দেই আঁখি॥
বেদী বনাওব হাম আপন অঙ্গমে।
ঝাড় করব তাহে চিকুর বিছানে॥—*Vidyāpati.*

their worldly glories to live the lives of the poor in the holy city of Kṛṣṇa, it was this love that had inspired the great renunciation of Narottama himself.

Çyāmānanda, one of the trio, of whom I have already spoken, composed many songs of Rādhā-Kṛṣṇa-love. One of them runs as follows. Rādhā says:

"To the bank of the Jamunā did I go one evening, oh my maids. There I saw Kṛṣṇa with the flute in his hand standing under a Kadamva tree.

"To be sure he was a hunter,—a hunter of human souls. His smile acted as a charm, and the loveliness of his person was like the trap; and my eyes like poor birds were captured by them.

"Oh my maids, on the great golden hall of my patience on the high gate of my noble lineage, the sweet sound of the flute fell like a thunder-bolt. Alas! they were at once demolished. In the stable of my soul I had kept the great elephant of my vanity chained; but maddened was the animal by the goad of his glance. The huge animal left the region of my soul and long has it departed. Alas maid, all vestige of worldly glory is gone, I have only my life left and it is for him"[1]

[1] শুনোলো পরাণ সই, আমি মরম কথা তোরে কই
আমি গিয়াছিলাম যমুনারই জলে।
দেখ্‌লেম নন্দেরই নন্দন কানু, করেতে মোহন বেণু
ব্যাধছলে কদম্বেরই তলে।
দিয়া হাস্য সুধা চার, অঙ্গ ছটা আঁটা তার
(আমার) আঁখি পাখী তাহাতে পড়িল।
আমার মন মৃগ্‌ সেই কালে, পড়িল ব্যাধের জালে,
বদ্ধ হৈয়া সেখানে রহিল।

The song, sung by Devī Dās, with his poetical comments, drew the eyes of the large assembly to Narottama, though too obvious a reference was not given in the text. Had he too not heard the sound of the divine musician's flute and abandoned his golden palace, all claims on honour due to noble parentage and the vanity of wealth as huge as the elephant? Was he not too captivated by the flute of Kṛṣṇa and by his sweet glances, which were the perpetual fount of joy from which his soul drank? An ascetic was he, not, however, a stern or a self-torturing one, but ever-joyful himself and diffusing joy into others. The life of the poor, which he had embraced, and his humility indicated only the great spiritual wealth that he had acquired. The song said "I have only my life left and that for his service." Indeed Narottama's physical life, the success of which in popular notion lay in the acquisition of material comforts and glory, was now nearly extinct, and the spirit only remained to serve the Beloved One. Another song of Chandidāṣ says:

আমার ধৈর্য্যশালা হেমাগার গুরুগৌরব সিংহদ্বার
ধরম কপাট ছিল তায়।
বংশীরব বজ্রাঘাত, পড়ে গেল অকস্মাৎ
সমভূম করল আমায়।
দম্ভ শালে মত্ত হাতি বাঁধা ছিল দিবা রাতি
ক্ষিপ্ত কৈল কটাক্ষ অঙ্কুশে।
দম্ভের শিকল কাটি, আবেশে পলাল ছুটি
লুকাইয়া গেল কোন দেশে॥
আছে শুধু প্রাণ বাকী তাও বুঝি যায় সখি
[কি করব কি হবে উপায়।
শ্যামানন্দ দাসে কয়, শ্যামত ছাড়িবার নয়
পার যদি ধর গিয়া পায়॥]

"Here do I offer my body to thee, beloved, with sessamum and leaf of Tulasi plant."[1] The last two offers prove the completion of the conditions of a legal gift according to the Hindu idea. It makes the gift absolute in every way. The body is thus made an absolute gift to the Deity. The devotee means that he has abandoned all right to act for his self-gratification: his body is entirely dedicated to the service of Kṛṣṇa.

The reader will see that the mystic songs of the Vaiṣṇavas, though occasionally expressed in the language of sensual poetry assume a quite different aspect in the presence of their living commentaries—the lives of the masters. Narottama, Çrīnivāsa and Çyāmānanda were there in the assembly, men who had abandoned all personal desires and devoted themselves absolutely to God loving Him with all their might. How could the songs be interpreted in any other light than the spiritual by the crowd when the poetry of the Vaiṣṇavas continually hinted at their great renunciation.

The cost of the function.

The Vaiṣṇavas dispersed after the great procession and festivities which took place at Kheturi for several days together. The cost of the function was enormous. For many thousand people had assembled, and Rājā Kṛṣṇānanda Datta and Santoṣa Ray, his nephew, gave each of them the costs of his journey and besides made presents to them according to their rank. Çrinivāsa Achārya was given two gold *mohurs* and two silken cloths. Vyāsacharya, the court Pundit of Viṣṇupur, Rs. 5 and a cloth. Viṣṇupriyā Devi, Chaitanya's wife, was about to

[1] "তিল তুলসী দিয়া এ দেহ সমর্পিলু।"

start for Vṛndāvana, and the Rājā privately gave Rs. 100 to Içāṇa, her servant, for expenses of the intended pilgrimage. And there were, besides, contributions, small and great to others numbering many thousands, suitable to their status in Vaiṣṇava society and personal qualifications.

Narottama's fame now spread far and wide over the whole country. For the vast crowd had all witnessed his life which appeared like a living poem to them in which the highest sacrifice mingled with highest love was manifest in the most impressive and unmistakable manner. People forgot that he was a Kāyastha. Many Brahmins became his disciples, as I have already stated, though this served to irritate the orthodox community the more, and led them again and again to make determined attempts to overthrow his influence. I shall here narrate how the life of a great robber-chief changed its course by Narottama's influence.

(c) *The great robber-chief Chānd Ray*

Rāghavendra Ray, a chief of Gauradvār, near Rājmahal had two sons, Chānd Ray and Santoṣa Ray, the former of whom was a great warrior. The father was an old man, and Chānd Ray and Santoṣa were the masters of the State. They were Brahmins by caste, and their landed property alone yielded an annual income of Rs. 84,000. This was but one of the sources of their income for they were robber-chieftains as well, and every year gathered large amounts of money by pillaging the neighbouring countries.

This was the period when Daud Khan, the Pathan king of Bengal, had revolted against the Emperor Akbar, and the administration of Bengal was on the eve of a great transition. The Pathan king was making vast preparations to meet the expedition sent against him from Delhi. The king could not think of maintaining the internal peace of his country as his mind was busy solving the great problem as to how to face his perilous situation.

Taking advantage of this state of affairs, some of the chiefs under him set all order at defiance and tried to assert their independence. Chānd Rāy had become the Faujdar or Magistrate of Gaurdvār and occupied the military station of Rajmahal. He now stopped paying revenue to the king, and carried on depredations throughout the neighbouring lands. His army at first had consisted of 5000 cavalry and a large number of foot-soldiers. Their number was gradually increased. He invaded and plundered the adjacent provinces and was now the master of a formidable force. The Pathan king dared not send an expedition against him, not venturing on a civil war when a mighty foe knocked at his doors from outside.

A terror to the people.

Chānd Rāy was physically a very strong man and had become the terror of the people. He killed men, looted their property and seized their wives and daughters, so that at the mere report of his approach, poeple of a town or village fled with their families and treasures.

The ceremony of Durgā Pujā, says the Premavilāsa, was performed at the palace of Chānd Rāy with great pomp, and innumerable goats and buffaloes were sacrificed at the altar of the goddess every year; for Chānd was a great Çākta. The two brothers, says this historian, were worse than Jāgāi and Mādhāi whom Chainya had reformed at Nadia.

But a great change came over the spirit of the robber-chief about the year 1605 A.D. He was attacked with the desease known as hysteria; fits of unconsciousness and delirium came frequently on him and the people said that the ghost of a murdered Brahmin had possessed him.

The ghost of a murdered Brahmin.

The strong man became bed-ridden and after trying various remedies despaired of his life. Rāghavendra Rāy, the father of Chānd, had by this time heard of the marvellous tale of Narottama's great renunciation and spirituality. People thronged to his palace to tell him that there was none who could heal the maladies of the soul so effectually as Narottama, the very sight of him brought peace to the mind and cured it of all trouble. The notion that Chānd did not suffer from any physical disease but had a mind disturbed by the influence of an evil spirit, was strong in the thoughts of Rāghavendra Rāy and indeed of all near relations and friends of Chānd.

Rājā Rāghavendra Rāy accordingly sent a man with a letter to Rājā Kṛṣṇānanda Datta, describing the circumstances and asking him to send his son Narottama to his palace for a few days. Narottama said that he did not know any charm or miraculous cure and declined to go.

The refusal caused a great disappointment to Chānd, for on his sick bed he had begun to repent his wickedness and feel an aversion for his ill-gotten wealth. He yearned for the sight of the holy man who was a prince but had abandoned his earthly riches in order to attain to a higher life. While his mind was in a state of great agitation, he dreamt one night, that some one whose voice was sweet whispered to him advising him to surrender himself to Narottama.

The repentent soul.

He awoke and could hardly suppress his tears. He was a proud Brahmin—an aristrocrat and a great warrior, who had never submitted even to the Pathan king. And what was Narottama now but a Kāyastha and a beggar dressed in rags? Yet the voice called him to offer himself to the beggar, and the voice was so commanding that it demolished all his pride. His soul panted with thirsty eagerness for an interview with the ascetic youth. He sent two Brahmins with a letter written in an imploring strain, begging him to come if only to save a sinner steeped in vice. Though there were men to tell Narottama that the wicked chief should not be believed, the princely ascetic was touched by his letter and felt compassion for the repenting soul. The letter showed that it was written to the dictation of a sincere heart. Accompanied by the great physician and scholar Rāmachandra—his dearest friend—he came to the great city of Chānd Rāy. The people thought that their saviour had come, for the wickedness of Chānd Rāy had made them offer constant prayer to God so that a change might come over his life, saving him from hell and themselves from his oppression. The Premavilās thus records the reception which the people of Gauradvār gave to Narottama.

The visit of Narottama to Rājmahal and his reception there.

"When they (Narottama and Rāmachandra,) entered the city, the people were all attention to them. They were greeted with a warm reception. Jars filled with water were placed with cocoanut fruits over them at various points of the main road as auspicious signs. Hundreds of plantain trees adorned the doorways of the houses which were decorated with wreaths of flowers and banners. Thousands had assembled to have a sight of them, and even women of the Zenana greeted the holy men from the windows and terraces of their houses. People from distant villages had come to see the great ascetic who had left his palace for the temple, and looked like the poorest of the poor for the sake of God's love. As they caught a glimpse of Narottama's face, some of the crowd wept for joy."[1]

Chānd Rāy was restored to health after the advent of Narottama to his city. From the day of the holy men's arrival the chief improved steadily. It seemed that the load which had oppressed his soul was removed. Narottama, assisted by his friend, the physician, regulated the habits and diet of the patient, and this completely cured him within a few days. The two brothers one day bowed to Narottama in great humility and said "Master, here do we surrender ourselves to you absolutely, do as you like with us." Chānd added "the sins I have committed I need not mention. They are too many and too horrible to be mentioned. It is your unlimited grace which can alone redeem a soul oppressed with unlimited sins. They say that an evil spirit possessed my soul; but what evil spirit is more horrible than we two brothers are?" Rāghavendra Rāy,

[1] যখন গ্রামেতে যাই করিল প্রবেশ।
দর্শন করয়ে লোক আনন্দ আবেশ॥
পূর্ণ কুম্ভ রাখিয়াছে পথে স্থানে স্থানে।
কত শত কদলী বৃক্ষ করিল রোপণে॥
পুষ্পমালা গৃহে গৃহে রাজ পথে পথে।
কত সহস্র লোক হইয়াছে সাথে সাথে॥
মঙ্গল হুলাহুলী দেন যত নারীগণ।
আপনাকে ধন্য মানে সফল জীবন॥
নয়নে নিরখে রূপ ধারা বহি যায়।
শুনি অন্য গ্রামীলোক উভরায়ে ধায়॥

the old Rājā, came there and was greatly moved, and all of them became initiated into the Vaiṣṇava faith by Narottama. When the function of initiation took place, the proud Brahmin chiefs touched the feet of the Kāyastha ascetic with tears in their eyes, the scene was profoundly affecting and the Vaiṣṇavas present there thanked God for the great event of the day, and indeed the crowd were so moved that their voices were chocked with emotion.

The initiation.

The first step which Chānd Rāy took after his conversion was to send his pleader to the court of the Pathan king with the message that he submitted to His Majesty and that he was prepared to pay all outstanding Government revenue. But the Minister of the Finance said to the king that this outward submission was a mere trick played by that "prince of bandits" in order to further some wicked ends. The courtiers also believed this to be the case, so that no one was found willing to visit Chānd Rāy's city to collect the outstanding revenue from him. Even the soldiers of the king, says the Premavilāsa, would not approach the precincts of the capital of the proud rebel for fear of losing their lives.

The Nawab's distrust.

Narottama stayed at Gauradvār for ten days, and though Chānd and his people implored him to remain a few days more, he did not comply with their request, as the temple of Gaura Ray at Kheturi was the place of his liking and he could not long remain absent from the sight of the image.

Chānd himself accompanied Narottama to Kheturi which was 30 hours trip by boat from Gauradvār. The former took ten boats with him, two of which were laden with silver, gold and precious stones, and the remaining eight with various articles of food and clothes. These he presented to the temple of Gaura Rāy. It should be mentioned that Narottama had nothing to do with these riches. All endowments to the temple belonged to it and of these Kṛṣṇānanda Rāy and Santoṣa Rāy were the custodians.

A visit to Kheturi.

In the spacious courtyard of the temple that night Devī Dās Kīrtaniyā and his party sang Rādhā Kṛṣṇa songs composed by Vidyāpati and others. One of them began thus:

"His beauty passes all description. Night and day he loves me and tries to win my heart. His ways take me by present surprise; I cannot forget them for a moment."[1]

The audience felt with the singer that Kṛṣṇa, day and night, tried to win the human heart. His divine flute sang constantly calling all unto him. But "whilst this muddy vesture of decay doeth grossly close us in, cannot hear it." Chānd Rāy was so greatly moved that he made enormous gifts of money and of valuable *shawls* to Devi Dās.

Staying ten days at Kheturi he came back to his city in Rajmahal, a completely changed man. One day attended by 100 cavalry and 400 foot soldiers, he came to the bank of the Ganges to bathe in the holy waters. A spy of the Nawab gave him information, and he forthwith sent a strong army to capture Chānd Ray. This was easily done as the soldiers of the Nawab far outnumbered those

Chānd made a captive.

[1] "অপরূপ মাধুরী, পীরিতি চাতুরী
তিল আধ পাশরিতে নারি।"

of Chānd. The latter was bound in chains and brought before the king in close custody.

The Nawab glanced at him and indignantly said "What upstart art thou that daredst plunder my country?" Chānd bowed to him and said "Your Majesty, I have sinned against you and against the people of my country. A criminal am I of the worst type. Give me whatever punishment your Majesty may consider just." The quiet and fearless demeanour, his attitude of repentance and humility struck the Nawab, but he said "Take him to our subterranean dungeon. There let the miscreant rot for some time before I bring him to justice."

Thrown into prison.

In a small dark cell underground he was put, and there he passed his days and nights,—hardly permitted to see the face of any man. But Chānd breathed free from the troubles of the world and thanked God. He was all the time in one of those trances which are vouchsafed to the more favoured of the mystics. In the morning he thought he weaved garlands of fresh field-flowers for Kṛṣṇa; in the noon-tide he thought he fanned his god; in the evening he thought that he decorated his person with the perfumed red kūmkūm powder, and his lotus feet with the scarlet dye *āltā*. In the night he thought he saw his divine face lit up with the five lights waived by the priest. He thus drank the joy of his beatific vision, and that which sprang from his own humble service, all uninterrupted day and night. How time passed he knew not. Hours passed like minutes absorbed in the trance in which he rested. His small prison-house became, as it were, a

A great faith.

temple to him, and he was so occupied with rendering his service and worship to Kṛṣṇa, that he forgot everything else and thought that he had discovered a strange mine of joy—a perennial source of bliss. He exclaimed to himself in that solitude "Wherever I be, there can I offer my whole-hearted service to the Lord."[1]

His father Rāghavendra promised a large reward to one who assured him that he would rescue Chānd from the Emperor's prison. The man dug a subterranean passage and reached the room in which the prisoner lay, unconscious however of his physical surroundings—ever joyed because of his communion with Kṛṣṇa. The rescuer said

Declines to worship Kāli.

that he came there under orders of the old Rājā, his father, and would be able to effect his escape provided he performed certain rites in which the goddess Kāli was to be worshipped. Chānd said "I have tasted the sweets of physical life ever since my childhood; they have proved to be my bane, I have now discovered the true source of bliss and not for the world shall I forsake Kṛṣṇa and worship any other deity." The man did not help in the chief's escape as without the rites performed, he thought that his attempts would go in vain.

After some days the king ordered Chānd to be brought before him. His feet bound in chains, the prisoner stood before his Majesty who considered that it was not safe

The capital sentence.

to allow him to live. He accordingly ordered that Chānd should be trampled to death under the feet of an elephant. He was

[1] "ষেখানে যেখানে থাকি সেই সেবা মোর।"

The Premavilāsa, the 18th Vilāsa.

brought to the execution-ground where the king himself was present to behold the death of the miscreant.

An elephant was set to trample him under its feet and the animal charged him ferociously. He with his feet bound in chains stood for a moment with his mind fixed on the lotus feet of Kṛṣṇa and on those of his *guru* Narottama; and then seized the elephant by his trunk. It should be remembered that he possessed herculean strength which had made him the terror of the people of the surrounding country in his wicked days. This strength stood him in good stead at this critical hour and he pulled the trunk of the charging elephant with such force as to stay its onset. The astonished beast trumpeted and fled inspite of the goadings of the *Māhut*.

The elephant forced to retreat.

The king was filled with wonder at this proof of his captive's great strength and ordered his chains to be removed. He was brought to the royal presence again and His Majesty asked him as to how, living in the dungeon on the scanty food, he could retain so great a physical strength. Chānd first asked pardon for all from the king before he could relate the whole truth, and this granted, he related as follows:

"My father bribed the Jail Superintendent who gave me a better meal than falls to the lot of a prisoner. I was not miserable in the prison, rather I was happy, for I saw my god more vividly there than elsewhere and could serve him without interruption. My father sent a man who wanted me to worship Kāli in order to effect my escape. This I declined to do. Far beyond the turmoils of the world I had at last found a resting place for my soul and I could not give it up for all the fortunes of the world."

As he said this, his voice trembled in fervent faith and his eyes glistened. The king was so highly impressed with his truthfulness and faith that he at once ordered his release. He called the Munshi and granted Chānd a *farman* giving him the absolute right of all the land he had acquired by force. His Majesty embraced the prisoner, and the eyes of his courtiers were tearful at the sight. The assemblage bowed to Chānd with great respect.

The Nawab's favours.

Chānd's brother Santoṣa came to the capital of Gour with many presents to the King, and the brothers were happy to go home. But before he returned, Chānd paid a visit to Kheturi to see his *guru* first. When the chief stood before Narottama he could hardly help weeping, and he said with great humility: "I have now known through your kindness that a palace and a prison make no difference when the soul is fixed on the lotus feet of Kṛṣṇa." There were *kīrtans* for 10 days and the chief forgot his home and family in the overwhelming delight of that spiritual atmosphere. Rāghavendra Rāy, meanwhile, eager to see his son after his quite providential release, himself came to Kheturi and there was great joy at the meeting of the father and his sons.

On return to Gauradvār Chānd Rāy received an invitation from the Nawab to pay him a visit again. This he did forthwith and the king received him very kindly, saying "Last time I only saved your property from confiscation, but I have called you now in order to show you a favour. Here take this. And he presented the chief with a *farman* bestowing on him the valuable property of Pergannah Āhedi.

Thus lived Çhānd Ray the ordinary span of human life. Once a wicked zemindar and leader of bandits, he became a respected and trusted friend of the king and a pillar of the State; once an oppressor of the people, now beloved of them, by reason of his great faith in Kṛṣṇa and his extensive charities and benevolent acts.

(c) *Rāma Chandra Kavirāja.*

I have already stated that Narottama had found a great friend in Rāma Chandra Kavirāja. I shall relate here briefly the story of the latter, who was a remarkable man and in the forefront of the scholars of his age in Bengal. He was the son of Chiranjīva Sen, a Vaidya and a notable physician of Kumār Nagar on the Padmā river, and his mother Sunandā was the daughter of Dāmodara, one of the great Sanskrit poets of the 16th century[1] and an inhabitant of Çrīkhanda in the district of Burdwan. Rāma Chandra Kavirāja's brother Govinda Dās is well known to those who have any knowledge of the Bengali literature. He is one of the greatest of the lyrical poets of Bengal and stands next only to Chaṇḍi Dās. His language is most finished and elegant—a point in which he has even excelled Chaṇḍi Dās himself. Govinda Dās wrote several Sanskrit poems also, but we shall speak about him when

[1] পাতালে বাস্থকি বক্তা, স্বর্গে বক্তা বৃহস্পতিঃ।
গৌড়ে গোবর্দ্ধনো বক্তা, খণ্ডে দামোদরঃ কবিঃ॥"

The Sangīta Mādhava.

"দামোদর সেনের নিবাস শ্রীখণ্ডেতে।
যেঁহো মহাকবি নামে বিদিত জগতে॥"

The Bhakti Ratnākara.

we deal with the lyrical poems of the Vaiṣṇavas of the mediæval age.

Rāmchandra Kavirāja, at the point of time to which my narrative refers, was already renowned as a great Sanskrit scholar and had achieved a considerable reputation as a physician. We are to think of him on his marriage day, naturally handsome and to-day more than usually splendid in the auspicious purple bridegroom's dress, and crowned, as is the bridegroom's privilege, like a king. Çrīnivāsa Āchārya had come to Jājigram in the Burdwan District that day, taking leave for a short while from his great disciple Rājā Vīra Hāmvīra of Viṣṇupur. While he talked with his own people, Çrīnivās's attention was drawn to a handsome young man in the bridegroom's purple passing in a princely palanquin attended by a large crowd of singers and musicians.[1] He had heard of the great learning of the young man and of his professional success. Çrīnivāsa felt drawn to him though he was as yet a stranger. Two days after, the young man of his own accord paid a visit to Çrīnivāsa Āchārya, and both started a discussion of controversial points on Rhetoric, Grammar and other subjects. Çrīnivāsa had had a sound training under the Masters at Vṛndāvana and was a man of trained intellect. But as he proceeded in the discussion, he wondered at the learning and intellectual powers displayed by his opponent. Says the Premavilāsa "From morning to evening they discussed and the next day they resumed the discussion and

The meeting between Rāma Chandra and Crīnivāsa.

[1] For a graphic account of this incident, see Karṇānanda by Jadunandana Dās (Niryāsa I).

continued till 10 A.M.[1] Logic, literature and other kindred subjects they discussed." A great impression was created in the minds of all present by the learning of the young scholar, who though respectful to the veteran Vaiṣṇava, steadily maintained his points in opposition to him. Çrīnivāsa spoke of him publicly in high terms of praise, but added "All learning is of no avail, if a man does not know the literature of the Bhakti-cult which alone has the power to crown him with spiritual life." For one month Rāmachandra stayed with Çrīnivāsa and studied the works of Sanātana, Rūpa and other Goswāmīs till he obtained the key to Vaiṣṇavism as taught by Chaitanya; and Karṇānanda, written in 1607 A.D., devotes two long chapters to a detailed account of the instructions on the doctrines of Vaiṣṇava creed, which Rāma Chandra gave to Rājā Vīra Hamvīra by the wish of Çrīnivāsa.

Rāma Chandra accepted Çrīnivāsa as his *guru*, and in point of learning at least, the former was the greatest of Rāma Chandra's disciples.

The meeting between Rāmachandra and Narottama, to whom the former was introduced by Çrīnivāsa, was an important event in the life of both. Narottama found in his new acquaintance a friend whose devotion was unchangeable,—one who became his constant companion from the day he met him, and who admired him and loved him with an attachment based on spiritual unison of souls, the closest link known to humanity, while Rāma Chandra found in the princely ascetic a living example of the *bhakti* of which he had read in the Çāstras—one whose life was a triumph over passion, a living refutation

[1] I have reduced the "*dandas*" in the original to hours and found the time given above.

of the idea that the soul is a plaything of material forces, and a proof of the joy which cannot be described in this world's language, a joy far nobler and purer than the worldly pleasures of every day life.

Rāma Chandra's friendship with Narottama.

Rāma Chandra left home and his professional calling and lived in the temple at Kheturi with Narottama. Rāma Chandra's wife wrote many letters to him asking him to return home, but he refused to part from Narottama. His family was, however, in affluent circumstances and his earnings had not wholly ceased, though he seemed to have given up the profession in which he had already built himself name and fame. We find it mentioned in the Premavilāsa, that Chānd Rāy on his visit to Kheturi made a present of Rs. 100 and two silken robes to Rāma Chandra Kavirāja who also used to recieve similar gifts now and then from others who admired his learning and spiritual life. The Premavilāsa quotes the following anecdote showing how greatly Rāmachandra was devoted to Narottama. Rāma Chandra's wife having failed in her efforts to induce him to return to her, wrote a touching letter to Narottama begging him to help her in getting her husband back. Narottama prevailed upon him after continued persuation to leave Kheturi and start for home. He obeyed reluctantly and travelled homewards for half a day; but he could not bear the thought that he would not be permitted to see the *ārati* (the evening service) in the temple of Gaura Rāy at Kheturi. The five lights waved before the image of Chaitanya there seemed to illuminate the path to spiritual life. And the figure of the princely ascetic in the fervour of his devotion before the image came to his mind again and again, till he was so overpowered that he retraced his steps and came back to the temple just in time to witness the *ārati*. And when Narottama wondered at his return, Rāma Chandra tearfully explained that his regard and respect for his teacher had brought him back. Such absolute devotion could not but produce a lasting effect even on the mind of an ascetic who had severed all ties with the world. Hence we find that when Rāma Chandra Kavirāja died after some years, the grief of Narottama was profound. In many poems does Narottama lament his loss, and the pathos of these poems reminds us of the English poet's sorrow for his Lycidas. In some of these he deplores an irreparable loss which had stunted his energies and delayed his task of preaching the message of peace and love.

(*d*) *An encounter with the scholars of the opposite School.*

The orthodox community was now fully alive to the danger of the preaching of the Vaiṣṇava leaders. Caste-rules were neglected; and indeed what greater blow could it receive than a Brahmin's accepting a Kāyastha as his *Guru*? The rules as to eating so stringently observed by the orthodox community, also lost hold upon a number of people who now followed the tenets preached by Çrīnivāsa and Narottama. Çrīnivāsa, Rāma Chandra and Narottama used to eat from the same plate, and the man Jadunandana Dās, the celebrated author, who served them, was a Vaidya.[1] The number of Brahmins who accepted Narottama as their *Guru* increased daily. The orthodox community could no longer overlook a social reform contrary to their belief and practice. By means familiar to

[1] See Karṇānanda, Niryāsa III.

all who know India they persecuted Narottama and his followers. We find that Rāmachandra and his brother Govinda were obliged to leave their ancestral home at Kumārnagar and to settle at Teliabudhari, because of the hostility of their former friends and neighbours.

Among the Brahmins whose names we find on the list of Narottama's disciples are many who had been robbers but had repented owing to the influence of Narottama's holy life. Men who had been notorious bandits in the gang of Chānd Rāy (mostly Brahmins) accepted Narottama as their Guru. We come across the following names of the more noted of them in several Vaiṣṇava works: Govinda Banerjee, Lalit Ghoṣāl, Kālidās Chatto, Nivāraṇa Chakravarti, Rāmajaya Chakravarti, Harinātha Gānguli and Çiva Chakravarti. "They formerly belonged to the band of Chānd Rāy and were his friends and relations. In many tough skirmishes they had defeated the Mahomedans. They had plundered the adjoining countries, and the king of Gaur did not dare meet them in open field. They now turned to peaceful pursuits; they felt the healing of the example set by Narottama, who, perceiving their sincerity, admitted them as his disciples."[1]

[1] "পূর্ব্বে তারা চাঁদরায়ের সৈন্য যে আছিলা।
চাঁদরায়ের সনে বহু দস্যুবৃত্তি কৈলা॥
চাঁদরায়ের আত্মীয় বান্ধব এরা হয়।
যুদ্ধ করি যবনেরে কৈলা পরাজয়॥
নানা দেশ লুটে রাজ্য করয়ে বিস্তার।
ভয়েতে যবন রাজ নহে আগুসার॥
*　　*　　*
ঠাকুর মহাশয়ের প্রভা জানি তার মর্ম্ম।
সবে হইলেন শিষ্য ছাড়ি পূর্ব্ব ধর্ম্ম॥

The Prema Vilāsa, the 19th Vilāsa.

A Brahmin robber might in those days be tolerated in society but not a Brahmin violating the rules of caste. Those were rough and cruel days when the central Government was powerless. Learned Pandits met and discussed what steps should be taken to remedy the new evil and punish that leader of ill-doers—the upstart Narottama.

Six Pandits, well versed in the Hindu scriptures and stout advocates of the orthodox views, resolved to see Rājā Narasiṁha Rāy of Pakkapalli. The Rājā belonged to the same family as Narottama, and was famous for the respect he paid to the Brahminic claims, and for his strict observance of caste rules. The names of the six Pandits are mentioned in the records. They are Jadunātha Vidyābhuṣaṇa, Kaçinātha Tarkabhuṣaṇa, Haridas Çiromaṇi, Chandrakānta Nyāyapanchānana, Çivacharana Vidyāvagīça and Durgadāsa Vidyāratna. The title Vidyābhuṣaṇa means "ornament of learning", Tarkabhuṣaṇa—" ornament of logical debates"; Çiromaṇi—'the jewel of the head'; Nyāyapanchānana—'the five-faced god (Çiva) of Logic.' Vidyāvagīça—'the lord of learning and speech.' Vidyaratna—'The jewel of learning.' These six heads charged with wisdom and learning, and fiery with indignation, approached Narasiṁha Rāy, Rājā of Pakkapalli (the modern Pāikpāra on the eastern bank of the Ganges, three miles to the north of Calcutta). Their interview with the Rājā is thus described in the Premavilāsa :—

"The Brahmins came to the Rājā and exclaimed 'Alas, Your Highness, the country is ruined. The iron age has come. The Çudra is now the Guru of Brahmins; it staggers the mind to believe this. Whence have these upstarts brought the Vaiṣṇava creed? The worship of our gods and goddesses is abondoned. The sacrifice of animals at the altars of our temples is stopped. The sacred rites are abolished, and we are undone. They do not touch meat or fish and live on vegetable food. They form Kīrtana parties; they dance and cry like mad men. The rites enjoined by the Vedās and the Tantras are abandoned. They have charmed the people by their songs and music. Surely Narottama Dās uses some magical art. Many learned Brahmins have become his disciples. Your Hīghness is our protector at this crisis. Be pleased to lead us to him; in your presence we will vanquish him in a public debate, and we shall stipulate that if he be defeated he shall leave this country for ever."

The Rājā had a famous courtier, by name—Rūpa Nārāyaṇa. We have in a previous lecture already related the story of this scholar's early youth and acquisition of learning. The Rājā had great confidence in him and consulted him as to what he should say in reply to the request of the scholars. Rūpa Nārāyaṇa said "Let the matter be finally decided by a debate amongst the Pandits in a public meeting, but without disparaging the acquirements of these scholars which are certainly great, I must confess may suspicion that Narottama may not after all prove too strong even for these six heads put together."

The Rājā agreed to make a trip to Kheturi and started with a large number of men. The six scholars had a great number of pupils who also accompanied their teachers, and they took cart-loads of manuscripts with them to prove their points.

On the way to Kheturi they came near a village named Kumārpur. By the time the report had spread that Rājā Narsiṁha Rāy of Pakkapalli was on his way to Kheturi with a number of Brahmin scholars in order to have a public debate with Narottama regarding his procedure in contravention of the caste rules.

Gangānārayaṇa Chakravarti, as already stated, was one of the most scholarly disciples of Narottama. Rāmā Chandra Kavirāj and his brother Govinda Dās were his staunchest friends and invincible in learned discussions. These three and other numerous admirers were the constant companions of Narottama.

All said that they could not endure the indignity of seeing Narottama dragged to the field of a public defence of his conduct. They then hit upon a plan. Gangānārayaṇa, Rāma Chandra and Govinda at once started for Kumārpur near which the Rājā had encamped. One disguised himself as an oilman, another as a grocer and the third a betel-seller. They occupied three huts close to the camp, and when the Brahmin pupils of the proud scholars who accompanied the Rājā visited the shops to purchase the articles they professed to sell, the three spoke in Sanskrit to them. This amazed the pupils. For no shop-keeper had ever spoken in Sanskrit since the age of the Upanishadas. They had a conversation with the oilman, the grocer and the betel-seller in Sanskrit in course of which the Brahmin pupils were told "We belong, sirs, to Kheturi the capital of the Rājā of that land. The place is a centre of learning and many Çāstras are taught and discussed there. We have learnt a little from our contact with the scholars there." The pupils eagerly entered into learned topics and were defeated in argument. Disappointed and amazed they came back to their professors,—the six Brahmin scholars, with the startling news, and their teachers forthwith left the camp to meet the shopkeepers and the Rājā awaited the issue with anxiety.

The discussion was maintained with much force on either side, but the followers of Narottama were possessors of a new light for the interpretation of the Çāstras; the orthodox ideas could not be supported by the old texts when these were given a newer and more vigorous interpretation at the hands of the Vaiṣṇava scholars. The six men of learning were utterly vanquished. Rūpa Nārāyana who also accompanied the Rājā and had become convinced of the superiority of the Vaiṣṇava faith from contact with Jīva Goswami many years before, did not join the discussion, acting only as a judge. And when the Pandits lost their points he urged upon them and the Rājā to surrender themselves to Narottama whom he declared to be a true leader of men, a teacher of great powers, both by the example of his life and by his unique faith and scholarship. So all the Brahmins went to Kheturi with the Rājā and became disciples of Narottama. Rājā Narasiṁha was initiated into the Vaiṣṇava faith with his wife Rūpamāla.[1]

The grocer and the betel-seller.

(*e*) *Further details about the lives of the three apostles.*

A great meeting of the Vaiṣṇavas took place at Kheturi shortly after, in which Çrinivāsa, Vīrachandra (Nityananda's son) and other leaders of that community were assembled. Vīrachandra delivered a thrilling discourse on the text of the Haribhaktivilāsa by Sanātana.

Narottama, declared a Brahmin.

"যথা কঞ্চনতাং যাতি কাংস্যং রসবিধানতঃ।
তথা দীক্ষা বিধানেন দ্বিজত্বং যায়তে নৃনাং॥

[1] For graphic accounts of this episode see the Narottama Vilāsa by Narahari Chakravarty and the Prema Vilāsa by Nityānanda.

(As brass by alchemy may be transmuted into gold, so does initiation into spiritual life (Dikṣa) give Brahminhood to people of all castes). The Premavilāsa mentions these conclusions as being accepted unanimously by the Vaiṣṇavas on this occasion.

"হৃদে যার ব্রহ্ম আছে সেইত ব্রাহ্মণ।
বাহ্য পৈতা কেবল ব্রাহ্মণজাতির লক্ষণ॥"

(One who has faith in god is a true Brahmin, the sacred thread is a mere outward sign of the caste).

Vīrchandra proved to an appreciative audience at this meeting that though born in a Kāyastha family Narottama was a true Brahmin.

As a sequel to this important meeting, there was a great Kīrtana performance at Kheturi, and Rūpa Nārāyaṇa, himself, a great singer took the lead in the function, while Rājā Narasiṁha himself played on the Mridanga.

Narottama after this converted another robber-chief named Harichandra Rāy. This man belonged to a place called Jalāpantha in Eastern Bengal. He was a Brahmin and as ruthless a depredator as Chānd Rāy himself had been. A discussion with this chief, after his initiation, on various points of the Vaiṣṇava creed, led to the composition of the celebrated theological work of Narottama entitled the Premabhaktichandrikā.

Among the images worshipped by Narottama, the Radharamaṇa (lit. captor of Radha's heart, *i.e.* Kṛṣṇa), was given by Narottama to his favourite disciple Gangānārāyana Chakravarti. It is now worshipped at the house of Gokulānanda Goswāmi of Bāluchar in Murshidābād.

Çrīnivāsa Āchārya had by this time made himself the most conspicuous figure in the Kingdom of Viṣṇupur.

Rājā Vīra Hamvīra would not do anything without the advice of his Guru even in political matters. His voice prevailed alike in the court and in the domestic circles of Viṣṇupur. We find that repeating the name of God a fixed number of times was made compulsory by penal law in the State. Sacrifice of animals at the altar of the gods was also discountenanced, though not actually prohibited by law. Worldly dignity attended the Guru who had brought spiritual glory to the country. We find that on every occasion of Vaiṣṇava festivities of any importance, valuable presents were given to Çrīnivāsa, while Rājā Vīra Hamvīra was ever ready to minister to his physical comforts in every possible manner. But true to the traditions of a Brahmin scholar and saint, Çrīnivāsa contented himself with living in a straw-roofed hut though he might have built palaces with the help of the Rājā and other influential disciples. The money he received was mainly spent in feeding his disciples of whom there was always a large number residing at his house. He married two wives. In those days it was a very common practice for a Hindu to take a number of wives and he endured no loss of consideration in popular estimation by conforming to a prevailing custom. If a desirable party offered his daughter of his own accord to a man who had already a wife it was thought unbecoming and discourteous to reject the offer. Çrīnivāsa's first wife was Draupadī; afterwards known as Içwarī, a daughter of Gopal Dās of Jajigram, and his second wife Padmāvatī, afterwards known as Gouranga Priyā, a daughter of Raghu Chakravarty of Gopālpur.

Crīnivāsa's later career and a history of his family.

A few of the six masters at Vṛndāvana were still alive, and Chaitanya Dās, a native of Viṣṇupur, once paid a visit to Gopāl Bhatta, the Guru of Çrīnivāsa at Vṛndāvana and related the story of Rājā Vīra Hamvīra's conversion, and of the great influence which Çrīnivāsa had acquired in his kingdom. "An enormous sum of money and extensive endowments of land have been made by the Rājā to Çrīnivāsa Āchārya and in the last Falgun (March) he married." Gopāl Bhatta did not share in the enthusiasm of the speaker, but remained silent for a while and then said in Sanskrit "स्खलत्पाद, स्खलत्पाद" (alas for him; he has lost his step), again and again. When Chaitanya Dās on his return to Viṣṇupur communicated this to Çrīnivāsa, the latter refused his food and was downcast for the whole day, regretting that he was lowered in the estimation of his Guru.

But whatever feeling was created in the minds of those who actually retired from the world and lived in absolute seclusion, as to the conduct of Çrīnivāsa, it is sure that the latter did not lose that living faith in God which made him known as an incarnation of Chaitanya amongst the lay Vaiṣṇavas. He lived in the world like an ordinary man, but he was not as other men. He lived with men but he lived for Kṛṣṇa alone. Karṇānanda describes the touching story of the mystic vision which Çrīnivāsa saw, and this story has been repeated in many later biographical works of the Vaiṣṇavas. One evening with his soul fixed on the lotus feet of Kṛṣṇa, Çrīnivāsa passed into that world which is not beheld by others but only by the chosen few. He saw that Rādhā and Kṛṣṇa were bāthing in the holy Jumna. They were sporting in the dark blue waters, crested with the golden rays of the setting sun, when the *besaro*, or nose-ornament of Rādhā fell into the river. She asked one of her maids to seek for it. The maid Maṇimanjari by name, searched in the transparent water under which every grain of clear sand was visible, but the *besara* could not be found. For three days Çrīnivāsa lay unconscious enjoying this mystic vision, and Rājā Vīra Hamvīra called all the physicians of his kingdom to bring him back to life. None of the remedies prescribed was of any use and it was believed for a time that Çrīnivāsa was dying. Rāmchandra Kavirāj, the physician and the scholarly disciple of Çrīnivāsa at last arrived, and he restored the patient to his senses by the simplest means. Çrīnivāsa awoke with a start, and exclaimed. "It has at last been found, it lay stuck in the roots of a water weed but it is now recovered." Whether this trance was morbid or a healthy vision of a world not seen by ordinary mortal eyes, this is a problem which we need not attempt to solve here. He related the story of the missing ornament with a reverence which touched the heart of all who heard it from his lips.

The legend of the nose-ornament.

Such visions came to him at times, and when he returned to his senses he looked like one purified by immersion in the holy Ganges. In these lectures, which are purely literary and historical, we need not dwell upon the philosophy of mysticism, a subject which is now being handled by such eminent scholars as Miss Under Hill, Frof. James, Dean Inge and other Western scholars.

The Karnānanda mentions the routine of Çrīnivāsa's life in detail.

In the morning he used to read at least some of the following Sanskrit books, explaining and interpreting them to his disciples : 1. Bhakti Rasāmṛta Sindhu, Vidagdha Mādhava, 3. Lalita Mādhava, 4. Haribhaktivilāsa,

5. Haṁsaduta, 6. Gītāvali, 7. Ṣatsandarvato.inī, 8. Bhāgavata, 10th Skanda, 9. Brahma Saṁhitā.

The study of the sacred books occupied him till 10 A.M. From 10 A.M. till 12 A.M. he shut himself in a room and said his prayers. From 12 to 2 P.M. he worshipped Kṛṣṇa. From 4 P.M. to 6 P.M. he sang Kīrtana songs with his disciples. The songs were mainly selected from the poems of Jaydeva, Chandidās and Vidyāpati.

At night he used to instruct his disciples, and discuss religious subjects with them.

Çrīnivāsa had three sons ; 1. Vrindāvanācharya, 2. Rādhā-kṛṣṇa Āchārya and 3 Goviṅdagati Āchārya ; the last named one was lame of one leg. Çrīnivasa had three daughters : 1. Hemlatā Devī, 2. Kṛṣṇapriyā Devī and 3. Kanchanlatikā Devī.

Gopijanaballabha, son of Ramkṛṣṇa Chattarāj, married Hemlatā ; Chaitanya Chattarāj, son of Kumuda Chattarāj, married Kṛṣṇapriyā Devī. In the districts of Birbhum and Bankura, a very considerable number of Vaiṣṇava Brahmins are at the present day disciples of the descendants of Çrīnivāsa or of those of whom Çrīnivāsa Āchārya was the Guru.

The most unassuming of the trio was Çyāmānanda by reason of his humble birth. The fact of his holding a low status in society served to adorn his nature with a naive humility which made him receive all tokens of favour, however small they might be, with a gratitude and joy which aided the development of his spiritual life. He become a great scholar. This, however, would have been impossible but for the Vaiṣṇava catholicity which opened the portals of education to all, irrespective of creed and colour. A

Çyāmānanda's success at Orissa.

Sadgopa (milkman) would have no opportunity whatever to study Sanskrit, if Vaiṣṇava Goswāmis would not have taken him as their pupil and subsequently even as a disciple.

I have already stated, that Çyāmānanda came back to Kheturi with Narottama, when the sacred manuscripts were lost. From Kheturi he made a trip to Ambikā Kalnā where he met Hṛday Chaitanya his Guru. He stayed there for a short time, and then visited his own native village Dharendā in Parganā Dandakeçwar in Orissa. His scholarship and faith drew to him a large number of pupils, who accepted him as their Guru. Nature had stamped him with greatness and caste-prejudice could not obliterate his native nobility. At Dharendā he had a long disputation with Dāmodara, a non-dualist scholar whom Çyāmānānda converted to the Vaiṣṇava faith. A Mahomedan robber named Sher Khan, who was at first hostile to him, was also made a convert to the new creed by Çyāmānanda at Dharendā. The name of Sher Khan was changed into Chaitanya Dās. Some of the Rādhā-Kṛṣṇa songs composed by this man are to be found in the Padakalpataru. The details of the conversion of Sher Khan are to be found in the 15th Taraṅga of the Bhakti Ratnākara, and the Premavilāsa says that in Kīrtaṇa parties Sher Khan, now known as Chaitaṇya Dās, distinguished himself by his vehemence in singing Rādhā-Kṛṣṇa songs.

The river Suvarṇarekhā (*lit.* the golden streak) runs to the north of the village of Bharajit, close to Rayani. Here was a powerful Rājā, named Achyuta. His jurisdiction extended over a considerable portion of the country known as the Malla Bhūm. Bharajit, the capital of Rājā

Achyuta was bounded on one side by the river Dolonga. The Bhakti Ratnākar says that on the bank of this river there was a spot romantically beautiful and picturesque. Here was the temple of the god Çiva under the name of Vāṇeçwara. Achyuta, the king, spent many years with his wife Bhavānī in this place. Achyuta's eldest son was Rasika Murārī who succeeded his father at his death.

Rasika Murāri, the Rājā, once paid a visit to a village named Sāntaçilā in Orissa. He stayed here for sometime and met Çyāmānanda. The Rājā felt the beginning of a new life come to him as he lived with the Vaiṣṇava scholar, and though the latter was a Sadgopa and he a Kṣattriya Rājā, all barriers melted away under the irresistible influence of the Vaiṣṇava Master's piety. He accepted him as his Guru and his queens Īçānī and Mālatī followed his example.

The whole of Orissa lay at the time under the magnetic charm of Chaitaṇya's life. Chaitaṇya lived at Purī for 18 years. The beauty of Vaiṣṇava visions, the purity of Vaiṣṇava life, the devotion and religious fervour of Pratāp Rudra, the monarch of Orissa, were already the general topics there, and when Çyāmānanda came about half a century later, though a Sadgopa by caste, the spell of his living faith irresistably appealed to the multitudes. Among a very large number of the followers of Çyāmānanda, the Bhakti Ratnākara mentions these distinguished names: Uddhaba, Akrura, Madhuvana, Govinda, Jagannātha, Ānandānanda, and Rādhāmohana. But it was Rājā Rasika Murāri, whose influence was the greatest amongst the aristocracy of Orissa. The Mahārājā of Mayurbhanja and the chiefs of other feudatory States of Orissa acknowledge the disciples of Rasika Murārī as their

Guru to the present day. And thus Çyāmānanda is recognised by the aristocracy of Orissa as their great spiritual head.

There were now various centres of Vaiṣṇava activity in Bengal and Orissa. The most sacred of these places was of course Nadiyā where Chaitanya was born. Viṣṇupur, the capital of Rājā Vīra Hāmvīra, became now a favourite resort of of Vaiṣṇana leaders and their influence spread far in the interior of the Birbhum and Bankura districts.

The various centres of Vaiṣṇavism.

Kheturi in the Rajshahi district where Narottama was born and lived the greater part of his life, became another recognised centre of the new faith. We find that his disciples in their proselytizing zeal went up to the eastern borders of Bengal, to Tipperah and Manipur, where the ruling chiefs now accepted the Chaitaṇya-cult. Rupanārāyaṇa, the Court Paṇdit of Rājā Narasinha of Pakkapalli, the first among the Brahmin scholars there to accept the teachings of Narottama, spread the tenets of Vaiṣṇavism in the Dacca district, at Bhāgyakula, Jaymontāpa and other places where the Vaiṣṇavas shewed great activity in preaching their propaganda.

Çyāmānanda held the torch in Orissa and illuminated not only the palaces, but the humble huts and the straw-roofed cottages of the poor. So that Vaiṣṇavism covered a greater area and claimed by far a larger number of adherents now, than even in the time of Chaitaṇya himself.

(e) *Vīrachandra's work. Legends about him.*

We have but incidentally mentioned Vīrachandra, son of Nityānanda, in these lectures. He wielded great influence in the Vaiṣṇava community from Khaḍdaha, a village on the eastern bank of the Ganges—a few miles to the north of Calcutta. Here 1,200 hundred Buddhist Bhikṣus and 1,300 Bhikṣunīs surrendered themselves to Vīrachandra who admitted them to the Order of the Vaiṣṇavas.[1] After the decadence of Buddhism these people had been treated as outcastes by Hindu society, they were looked down upon as fallen and degraded in the eyes of the people. The ideal of chastity no longer worked among them, as they were cut off from the great Buddhist monasteries of Asia, whilst they were subjected to all the corrupt influences due to their degraded social status and to the contemptuous treatment of the victorious Brahminic school, which had succeeded in bringing about the fall of Buddhism. No wonder that sunk into depths of depravity they became despised of all. They were called the Neḍā-Neḍīs or the shaven men and women; for the Buddhist Bhikṣus and Bhikṣunīs used to have their heads shaven. The contemptuous name of Neḍā the shaven head—given to Mahomedans by bigotted Hindus is derived from the title of the degenerate Buddhist Bhikṣus many of whom now swelled the ranks of Islamite converts.

The Neḍa-Neḍis.

The Brahmins shut the portals of their society against these men and women. The new Brahmins like the venerable Nityānanda, Sanātana and Rüpa again opened them to receive the fallen and the lost. The Bhikṣus and Bhikṣunīs had taken the vows of celibacy, but sunk in degeneracy, they led grossly immoral lives. Vīrachandra enacted a law by which the Bhikṣus and Bhikṣunīs could marry when converted into the Vaiṣṇava faith. Thus what

[1] For particulars of this, see Nityānanda Vaṁsa Vistāra by Vṛndāvana Dās.

could not be checked was elevated. For promiscuity was substituted the permanent relation of wedlock. And if vice is still found to prevail in their ranks, it were wrong to impute it to the Vaiṣṇavism which reclaimed them rather than led to inevitable decay. The instances of immorality in their society are but remnants of the old latitude which once prevailed in their society. Vaiṣṇavism has undoubtedly elevated their society by legalising marriage amongst them.

Vīrachandra carried on all the noble works which were inaugurated by his venerable father. He laid the axe to the very root of caste distinction by publicly proclaiming Narottama to be one of the best of Brahmins. The 'Neḍā-Neḍīs,' who now became Vaiṣṇavas, annually held a fair at that particular spot at Khaḍdaha where they surrendered themselves to Vīrachandra, and their Guru stretched his compassionate arms to raise and elevate his depressed brethern covered with shame and despised and rejected of men. The fair which used to sit every year to indicate the gratitude of the 'Neḍā-Neḍīs' for their social promotion, was ceased six or seven years ago owing to lack of funds. It would be well if the Goswāmīs of Khaḍdaha could see their way to revive this historic fair, a living memorial of the compassion and love which actuated their great ancestor in receiving with open arms the fallen and the depressed in society. The Sahajiyās, as these "Neḍā-Neḍīs" are sometimes called, have a literature which possess a unique value in showing the transitional forms of their religious belief as it passed from Buddhism to Vaiṣṇavism. But of this we shall speak hereafter. The narrative of the conversion of the Neḍā-Neḍīs has been described in a book called the Nityānanda

Vañça-Vistāra by Vṛndāvana Dās. The book was written towards the end of the 16th century.

Many legends are related about Vīrachandra. A striking example is found in the Premavilāsa connected with the building of the stone image of Çyāmasundara Rāy (Kṛṣṇa) at Khaḍ-daha. Vīrchandra once went to Gaur and was introduced to the Moslem Emperor there as a Fakir of great psychic powers. The Emperor received him with great kindness but said that as he was a Sannyāsī he should have no caste prejudices. Vīrachandra said he has none. The Emperor was pleased with the reply, and ordered the Mahomedan cook of the Royal kitchen to serve Vīrachandra with a rich dish of meat. The genuine Vaiṣṇavas, like the Jains, have a dread and abhorence for meat-food of any kind, so the feeling of Vīra-chandra may be realised when he was served with such food by a Mahomedan cook. But he concealed his feeling. The cook brought a plate full of rich meat covered over with a milk-white piece of cloth. Vīrachandra ordered the cook to take away the cloth, which done, it was discovered to the wonder of all who witnessed the sight, that the plate contained nothing but a variety of beautiful fragrant flowers such as the rose, the jessamine, velā etc. The Emperor thought this was due to the complicity of his Hindu officers in order to save the Sannyāsī from his disagreeable ordeal, and ordered another plate, the contents of which he personally examined. But this time also the meat was converted into flowers as soon as the cloth was removed. Yet the Emperor tried a third dish, subjecting it to a still greater scrutiny. But when this time also

The reception at the hands of the Nowab.

Invitition to dinner.

the result was the same, the Emperor was struck with wonder, and promised the Sannyāsī whatever he might seek of him. Vīrachandra made two requests. One was for an order that the temple at Khaḍdaha, the native city of Vīrachandra, be for all future time free from the attacks of the Moslem iconoclasts, and the second was for the gift of a valuable black stone which was in the palace, wherewith to make image of Kṛṣṇa. Both the prayers were granted, and the sign known as Khunti—the well-known combination of the cresent-moon and the Hindu trident—was first erected over the temples of Khaḍdaha, thus proclaiming them free from all attacks by Mahomedan bigotry. Many temples now bear the sign, some with the sanction of the Moslem rulers and others without it, erected by the owners with the object of averting Mahomedan inroads. But the Khaḍdaha temples were the first in Bengal that were exempted by royal command from such attacks. The image built by the valuable stone was called Çyāmasundara Rāy (Kṛṣṇa). [1]

The Miracle.

The present of a black stone and the *khunti*.

The author of the Premavilāsa, Nityānanda Dās, repeatedly mentions in his book that he wrote an elaborate biography of Vīrachandra. This book which probably

[1] Three images were made by this piece of blackstone. The first and the most noted one was of course Cyāmasundara Rāy established in the Khaḍdaha temple by Vīrachandra's son Achyutānanda. The second one was called 'Nandadulāla' and established in at a place called "Swāmī Vana." The third "Ballavaji" is in the temple at Ballavapur. We have no hesitation in believing that the Gaur Emperor became an ardent admirer of Vīrachandra, whatever the cause might be, and made a gift of the blackstone to him. See the Premavilāsa, the 24th Vilāsa.

contained many historical information seems to have been lost, and yet it is curious that such a precious work should have been allowed to disappear. For the biographer was a contemporary of Vīrachandra, and was held in repute as a historian. Vīrachandra was undoubtedly at the head of the Vaiṣṇava community of his time, not only because of his high character and attainments, but particularly because he was a son of Nityānanda, the apostle whom Chaitaṇya himself revered as his elder brother. And it is much to be wondered that not a single copy of this important biography has been preserved by any of Vīrachanda's numerous descendants. Nityānanda Dās wrote the Premavilāsa by the order of Vīrachandra. Five hundred copies of this work, the author himself states, were made as soon as it was finished. [1] These were circulated in various centres of the Vaiṣṇava creed in Bengal. Is it not a very mysterious circumstance that when a general history of the Vaiṣṇavas like the Premavilāsa got a large circulation, obviously through Vīrachandra's powerful support,

The Vīra-chandra Charita not yet recovered.

the biography of the leader himself, a long and elaborate work, was allowed to pass into oblivion by his descendants though, they were the most influential people amongst the Vaiṣṇavas at that time as they are even now ? It has been whispered in some quarters that the genealogy of some of the Goswāmīs who call themselves direct descendants, of Nityānanda is a questionable one. The parentage claimed by them, now recognised by all, has

[1] "এক এক অধ্যায় রচি যবে সমাপ্ত করিত।
পাঁচ শত ভক্তে তাহা লিখিয়া লইত॥

The Prema-vilāsa, Index to the 16th Vilāsa

given them an undoubtedly enviable status in Vaiṣṇava society; and if the allegation of their enemies has any grain of truth in them, it must have caused them considerable expenditure and trouble to recast the old genealogical tables to make the revised pedigree acceptable to the members of Nityānanda's family. This may account for the deliberate extinction of so important an work as the Nityānanda Charita, whose testimony would have prevented all accretions of new matter other than really genuine ones in the pedigree of Nityānanda's line.

III. The Historical works that describe the above narratives.

(*a*) *Nityānanda Dās and his Premavilāsa.*

The historical works of the mediæval Vaiṣṇava period (according to our classification) are devoted to the narratives briefly summerised by me in the foregoing pages.

The most important of these works is the Premavilāsa by Nityānanda Dās. We have great doubts about the authenticity of the last four chapters of the work published by Babu Jasoādlāl Tālukdār of Kumārtuli. I have come across numerous old manuscripts of this historical work, but nowhere have I found these chapters in them. In the library of the University of Calcutta there are two copies of such manuscripts, and one of them announces on the last page that the Premavilāsa ended there.

The date of the Prema-vilāsa.

But though the texts tally almost *verbatim* as far as the first 18 chapters are concerned, the printed book shows large accretions of new materials, the authenticity of which seem to be of a doubtful character. Indeed the date of the work given in the supplementary portion of the work seems to be quite untenable. If the pedigree of the Viṣṇupur Rājās quoted in the Viçvakoṣa,[1] is reliable, the hitherto accepted date of the composition of Premavilāsa can by no means be supported. Vīrachandra according to that pedigree ascends the throne in the year 1597 and Çrīnivāsa came to his court when the Rājā was a full grown man and had already acquired notoriety by his tyrannical administration. This was certainly the case some years after 1597. The Premavilāsa not only records all these facts, but relates two marriages of Crīnivāsa which took place successively after the conversion of Vīra Hāmvīra into the new creed. There the author goes on to say that for a number of years Çrīnivāsa had no child which created some anxiety in his family. But his narrative does not stop here ; he gives us the names of the four sons and three daughters who were afterwards born to Crīnivāsa, and gives an account of the marriages of the daughters ! So if the date of the ascension of Vīra Hāmvīra to the throne of Viṣṇupur, as recorded in the court-records of the royal family, is reliable, the date of the composition of the Premavilāsa to be found in the printed book and that of Karṇānanda given in Rāmanārāyaṇa Vidyāratna's edition are incorrect. We have every reason to believe the testimony of the Viṣṇupur court-records. One reason is that it is related in all the biographical accounts of Çrīnivāsa that he paid a visit to Vṛndāvana after the temple of Govindajī was complete. The inscription in the temple says that it was built by Rājā Mānsinha by the direction of Rūpa and Sanātana in the year 1590. Now it is also mentioned in the old records that Çrīnivāsa came to Vrndāvana four

[1] See the word Vīrabhuma.

months after the death of Sanātana and three days after the death of Rūpa. This must have been in the year 1591. Çrīnivāsa stayed at Vṛndāvana for a number of years, and after having completed his education there paid his visit to Viṣṇupur at some time between 1606 and 1610 A.D. The date of the inscription and that of the ascension of Vīra Hamvīra to the throne according to the records of the Viṣṇupur court do not present any difficulty in reconciliug facts about Çrīnivasa's life. The narrative of the Premavilāsa, as I have stated, brings the events of Çrīnivāsa's life down to the marriage of his daughters; and yet the date of composition of the Premavilāsa in the printed book is given as 1600 and that of Karṇānanda, a later work, as 1607! The events narrated in the two books evidently cover a period between 1620 and 1640 A.D. So neither of these books could have been written earlier than the latter date. My recent researches in this field have made me lose all trust in the dates of these two books as given in their modern editions, from which I had unsuspectingly accepted the dates in my History of Bengali Language and Literature. If the first 16 chapters of the Premavilāsa are taken as genuine and the rest dismissed as later interpolations, the date of the compilation of the work may be earlier than what we have suggested.

An account of Nityānanda Dās.

Nityānanda Dās was, as I have already stated, a contemporary of Çrīnivāsa and other distinguished persons who formed the subjects of his biographical sketches. In fact he refers again and again to the fact that what he wrote he either observed with his own eyes or heard from the lips of his illustrious contemporaries. He belonged to the village of Çrīkhanda in the district of Burdwan. His father was Atmārāma Dās descended from Pāntha Dās, the famous general of Vallāla Sen (1100-1169 A.D.) Nityānanda's mother was Saudāminī. He was born in 1459 A.D.[1] and had a brother named Rāmachandra Dās. He was a good scholar in Sanskrit and read the Bhakti Çāstras with Vīrachandra, son of Nityānanda. He acquired a practical training in the processes of Yoga and studied the science of music with Rūpa Nārāyaṇa, the court Paṇdit of Rājā Narasiṁha. In the Premavilāsa we find some Sanskrit Çlokas that Nityānanda himself composed. We also find him accompanying Jāhnavī Devī, wife of Nityānanda, in her journey to Vṛndāvana as her guide. So it may be presumed that he held an important position in the Vaiṣṇava community, and indeed this is proved beyond doubt by the fact already stated that his disciples prepared 500 copies of the Premavilāsa immediately after it had been written. He tells this himself incidentally in the work.

In the supplementary portion of the Premavilāsa, the authenticity of which, as already stated, I have reasons to disbelieve, Nityānanda Dās is represented as declaring to his readers that he was very old at the time he wrote the book, so that those subjects which he had already treated, he touched again, in some cases because his memory had grown defective and in others because new materials were obtained which he could not put in their proper places owing to his physical and mental infirmities. The plea of old age may be advanced as an apology for the imperfect nature of the patch-work done by the writer of the

[1] See Introduction to Gaurapada Taranginī compiled by Jagatbandhu Bhadra and published by the Sāhitya Pariṣat of Calcutta.

supplement. It was not safe to interpolate passages or obliterate any, as numerous authenticated copies of the work were already current. It was safer to say that a portion was recovered which others had not found. Jasodā Babu, the editor of the book, should have carefully gone through the old manuscripts in the light of historical research. This would have given him a better comprehension of the quality of the materials with which he had to work. One of the most obvious points which should strike him in that case would be the absolute untrustworthiness of the elaborate accounts of the pedigrees of Kulīns given in the supplementary portion of the work. No Vaiṣṇava writer ever laid any stress on this point in Bengal. All Vaiṣṇava biographers have in fact deliberately avoided mentioning their own pedigre es as Kulīns,[1] and the genealogies of those who have been the subjects of their memoirs. The canons of Vaiṣṇavism enjoined upon the followers of that sect not to vaunt their lineage which they absolutely ignored by calling themselves Dās or servant in place of their family surnames. That an elaborate list of pedigrees should be introduced by an illustrious writer who had directly received religious instructions from Vīra Bhadra, Jāhnavī Devī and Çrīnivāsa, leaders who had altogether abandoned caste-prejudice seems to be absolutely incredible. The comparatively modern movements of different castes to establish their claims of superiority were undoubtedly at work in the supplementary portion.

[1] In many works of the Vaiṣṇavas, those "who take pride in marrying their children to Kulīn families" and "who boast of their pedigrees" (Premabhakti Chandrikā by Narattoma), are greatly condemned.

In my previous works I identified the author Nityānanda Dās whose other name was Valarāma Dās, with the lyrical poet Valarāma Dās, one of the most favoured Pada-kartās of this period. But I am now inclined to change my opinion. I find in the Karṇānanda that Pada-kartā Valarāma Dās was a native of Budhuipāḍā and not of Çrīkhanda, the native village of Nityānanda Dās. The former's title was Kavipati, and as Govinda Kavirāja also belonged to Budhuipāḍā, Valarām Dās, the lyric poet was no doubt a member of the gifted family, a fact which is confirmed by the following line of the Padakalpataru. "কবিনৃপতিবংশজ ভুবনবিদিত যশ জয় ঘনশ্যাম বলরাম।" So he cannot be the Nityānanda Dās, who was son of Atmārāma Dās and author of the Premavilāsa.

The Premavilāsa though written in verse is prosaic in its spirit and in its style. Nowhere in this work is there any touch of poetical sentiment. Facts are put forward in a simple and unassuming manner. The great merit of the book consists in its brevity and power of condensing and arranging facts. As the author gives his accounts mostly from first-hand knowledge, the descriptions are characterised by a vividness of detail, which excites curiosity and does not oppress the reader with that feeling of weariness which so often confronts him in perusing some of the laboured Vaiṣṇava biographies of a later period.

Life of Rūpa Nārāyaṇa.

Nityānanda Dās wrote an elaborate biography of Vīrachandra; but the work, as already stated, is now lost. The author of the Premavilāsa mentions that he had contemplated writing an elaborate life of Rūpa Nārāyaṇa, the court-paṇdit of Narasiṁha Rāy of Pukkapatti. Whether such a book was written at all is not known. If it was ever written,

pays in them his respects to several Vaiṣṇava worthies. In these verses he praises Çrīnivāsa in the following line:

"শ্রীনিবাসপ্রভুং বন্দে পরকীয়াসমর্থিনং"

(I bow to Çrīnivāsa, the supporter of Parakīyā); but of this I shall speak in course of my lecture dealing with the theological literature of the Vaiṣṇavas.

His other works.

Jadunandana Dās is, however, well known as a translator of some of the Sanskrit poems of the Vaiṣṇavas, such as the Govinda Līlāmṛta by Kṛṣṇadās Kavirāja, Vidagdha Mādhava by Rūpa and Kṛṣṇakarṇāmṛta by Vilvamangala. These translations are all metrical, and they have retained in their lucid and happy style the beauty of the originals to a remarkable extent. Jadunandana is indeed reputed as the best of all translators of the Sanskrit works of the Vaiṣṇavas. And his Govinda Līlāmṛta is really an excellent piece of work deservedly commanding a wide popularity. He is besides a writer of many Rādhā-Kṛṣṇa songs to be found in the Padakalpataru and other anthologies of Vaiṣṇava verse.

(c) *Narahari Chakravartī and his works.*

The next historian of the Vaiṣṇavas in Bengal was Narahari Chakravartī. He was the son of Jagannath Chakravartī, a disciple of Viçvanātha Chakravartī, the distinguished commentator of the Bhāgavata. The latter compiled the commentary in Çaka 1626 (1704 A.D.). And Narahari must have lived about this time or a short time after. The period of the latter's literary activity may be roughly taken to cover 1716 to 1740.

A short sketch.

Narahari Chakravartī held the post of cook in the famous temple of Govindajī in Bengal, a circumstance which accounts for his accurate description of the legends and other particulars relating to the shrine and its neighbourhood. A reliable topography of Mathurā and Vṛndāvana is to be found in his celebrated work, the Bhaktiratnākara. Narahari was a disciple of a Guru of the Order of Narottama and hence paid a tribute of honour to him by writing a biography of the great Kāyastha. Narahari wrote the following works:—

1. Gauracharita Chintāmaṇi, 2. Anurāga Vallī, 3. Bhakti Ratanākara, 4. Bahirmukha Prakāça, 5. Narottama Vilāsa.

The Bhaktiratnākara is the most important and elaborate of his works; it gives the history of the progress of the Vaiṣṇava cause from the time of Chaitaṇya's passing away to the end of the 17th century. Çrīnivāsa, Narottama and Çyāmānanda claim a most important mention in this voluminous memoir. The work contains about 18000 couplets or 36000 lines. The author has quoted a considerable number of Sanskrit texts in support of his descriptions, and many extracts from Chaitaṇya-charitāmṛta and Chaitaṇya Bhāgavata are also given a prominent place among the authorities quoted by him. Bengali poems for the first time received recognition equal to the famous Sanskrit sacred books in this great work. The Bhaktiratnākara (lit. sea of spiritual emotion) is divided into 15 *tarangas* (waves) and for the details of the contents of each chapter, the reader is referred to p. 373 of my Vangabhāṣā O Sāhitya (3rd edition) and p. 511. of my History of Bengali Language and Literature.

The Narottama Vilāsa or the life of Narottama contains 12 chapters. It was written after the Bhaktiratnākara, and though a smaller work, shows a better command over Bengali style and an abler treatment of the subject. The Gauracharita Chintāmaṇi is a collection of lyrics devoted to a description of the incidents of Chaitaṇya's life. Of the other two works the one is a historical and the other a theological treatise.

Narahari is also known by his another name Ghanaçyāma (Bhaktiratnākara, 15th *taranga*). And is the author of many songs of Rādhā-Kṛṣṇa.

Narahari gives an account of his life at the end of his Narottama Vilāsa. He speaks of his father's Guru Viçvanāth Chakravartī at considerable length in this account. Narahari was born at the village of Reāpur near Pāniçālā in the district of Murshidabad. This Pānicāla is not very far from Nasipur, the present seat of the Mahārājā of that locality. In a supplementary account of his life written in 1855 A.D. by Anandanārāyaṇa Maitra Bhāgavatabhūṣana of Giāspur in the district of Maldaha, we find that Narahari was a disciple of Nṛsinha Chakravarti who was a member of the spiritual family of whom Vīrchandra is the head.

Narahari was a bachelor all his life. In early youth he visited Navadwipa, and the sight of Chaitanya's birth place filled his mind with overpowering emotion. He prayed to him, whom all his community now knew as God himself, that he might be permitted to dedicate his life to the Master's service. Returning home he acquired a thorough mastery of the Vaiṣṇava scriptures, and left home for Vṛndāvana. There he attracted the attention of all the Vaiṣṇavas by his scholarship and faith. He talked sparingly and often he was seen shedding tears as he fixed his gaze on the image of Govinda in the temple.

God's cook and musician.

Sometimes he would be discovered waving the Chamara over the image—at others washing the temple with his own hands. Sometimes he fanned the image while tears rolled down his cheeks. The priest respected him for his faith and for his character. Seldom did he talk with any one, but always lay absorbed in the study of scriptures or in these dreamlike visions which mystics alone are privileged to behold. In one of these he heard the voice of the God Govindaji calling him in sweet familiarity, saying "Narahari you know how to cook well, won't you cook food for me ?" The memory came back to Narahari that in his early youth he was known to be a good cook amongst his friends, whom he often served with dainties prepared by his own hands for the sake of friendship. "The Lord wants food cooked by me, may my hands be ever blessed" said Narahari, and that day he took permission of the temple-cook to do his task himself. When the food was prepared, it was so delicious that the Rājā of Jaipur, who was the custodian of the temple, employed him permanently as the cook there. It is said that the Rājā did so by the order of the deity himself who appeared to him in a dream and told him how greatly he relished the offering of food cooked by Narahari. Narahari of course did not accept any pay for this work. He was an ascetic and as every day he brought the meal with care and love before the image, he could not restrain the tears which gathered in his eyes.

He was also a great singer and musician and thought within himself "Here are my hands employed in his service but he has also given me a good voice, of what use may it be if I do not sing praises unto him ?" And there all night long he would perambulate the temple and sing and dance and declare to all that he was blessed by this other service. He repeated the name of God night and day, and people as they saw him forgot their cares and realised what the blessings of faith and God's grace are. So many bad lives were reformed by his example. Surely a mystic's simple happiness in God and goodness may be as useful to humanity as the toil of the artizan or the chattering of the tradesman !

Narahari did service as a cook for some years in the temple of Govindaji but became a wandering monk and beggar during his last years. He sang God's name to all and wrote works which show his wonderful scholarship and great poetical talents.

(*d*) *Other works.*

There are other works of a historical and biographical nature more or less important in this period of Vaiṣṇava literature and amongst these we may mention the Rasika Mangala by Gopivallabha Dās. Rasikānanda was the eldest son of Rājā Achyuta, a disciple of Çyāmānanda. This we have already noticed. Rasikānanda was born in 1590, and Gopivallabha was his contemporary. The latter gives a faithful account of the proselytising effected by the latter and particularly how Vaidyanātha Bhanja of Mayurbhanga and other chiefs were converted to the Vaiṣṇava faith by Rasikānanda. The Vaiṣṇava festivals that took place at Berakuli and Alamganj in Midnāpur are vividly described in this poem.

Rasika Mangala.

Another important work of this class is the Baṁçī Çikṣā by Puruṣottama Siddhāntavagīça. It was written in the year 1710 A.D. It narrates some of the incidents of Chaitanya's life, but its main object is to give an account of the life of Baṁçī Dās, a companion and follower of Chaitanya. Baṁçī Dās's father Chhakari Chatto had a beautiful house on the banks of the Ganges at Nadia ; his mother Bhāgyavati was known for the piety of her life and high character. Prof. Bhāgavatakumāra Çastri of the Hughli College is a direct descendant of Baṁçī Dās. Baṁçī Dās's songs on Rādhā-Kṛṣṇa, inserted in the Padakalpataru, are admired for their poetical excellence and their spiritual fervour.

Baṁçī Cikṣa and other historical treatises.

Regarding the other biographical and historical works of the Vaiṣṇavas in Bengal, the reader is referred to pp. 511-515 of the History of Bengali Language and Literature and to pp. 367-385 of my Vanga Bhāṣa O Sāhitya.

CHAPTER III

(*a*) The spiritual philosophy underlying the songs.
(*b*) Govinda Dās.
(*c*) The peculiar excellence of the Vaiṣṇava Songs.
(*d*) Jnānadās.
(*e*) Valarāma Das.
(*f*) Song by a Mahomedan poet.

(*a*) *The spiritual philosophy underlying the songs.*

We now come to the literature of the Padas in which the Vaiṣṇava poets have excelled. The Rādhā-Kṛṣṇa songs form the bulk of this literature which also contains songs on Chaitanya and Nityananda, some of these being of great beauty. I cannot undertake to give even a superficial idea of the merits of this extensive literature. These songs represent the highest culture of the Vaiṣṇavas and are due to a variety of social and local causes which make it extremely difficult to convey an idea of their beauty and intrinsic worth to foreign scholars. The songs seem occasionally sensual in language, yet they are not so. It is not the commentator's labour which invests them with a mystic interpretation. The poets wrote under mystic influences, and what may seem to superficial readers to be a sensuous garb is the mere language of human love without taking recourse to which the spiritual joy cannot be conveyed to ordinary people. Yet the diamond is a diamond and should not be confounded with the clay and dross with which it is found covered when Nature hands it to the jeweller.

We have seen a number of ascetics, some of them princes and most of them nursed in the environment of ease and of world's affection in their early years. They severed the ties and abandoned the comforts of home for God's love. This love was a definite point of realization with them. Joy intoxicated and maddened them, so that it made them totally unconscious of all physical pain and discomfort. We find Chānd Ray thrown into a noisome prison by the Emperor of Gaur. There we find him occupied with his mystic visions and blessed. In fact he told the Emperor that cut off from worldly care he was happier within the dark walls of the dungeon than ever, since he could there devote himself to God undisturbed. There were the lives of Narottama and of Raghunātha Dās, who like Galahad in Europe pursued a holy vision all their lives, and were happy and contended inspite of their renunciation of all worldly pleasures. They were not only merged in joy themselves but imparted it to all who beheld their trances. Asceticism did not isolate them as it did some of the Yogis of old. The joy they tasted was shared by hundreds of men who came in contact with them, and were sanctified by their influence. Nor did it extinguish their moral lives as some positive-minded critics may suppose. Until and unless the highest point of moral life is reached, mystic visions are impossible to the soul. We find Çrīnivāsa for three days and nights merged in the vision of a search for Radha's ear-ring lying unconscious but happy. Whether it be the Holy Grail or Radhā's ear-ring, whether it be the sight of a crucified Christ[1] or Kṛṣṇa playing on his flute or the Bridal ring of Christ worn by Catherine

The idea of asceticism according to the Vaiṣṇavas.

[1] St. Teresa used to behold visions of Crucified Christ: see *Life of St. Teresa translated from the Original Spanish by I. Dalton (1851).*

of Siena,[1] it does not matter; the vision is a truth, it comes to the chosen few, and when it comes it is a strange experience of joy to the soul; it sanctifies even those who behold the mystic-trance. This holy influence cannot be spread by a diseased soul. If it be a disease, it is like the pearl which is said to be a disease of the pearl-oyster. To its owner it is a pearl beyond all price. It may be called a disease by the scientific observer, cold and practical. But the pearl of the oyster is the crowning point of its life-history. It may be painful; it may even cause its death; yet is its culmination, and its destiny. The vision of the mystics is also his highest joy and the highest reward and success of his life. When he gets it, well may he hold it forth to the Emperor and say in ecstasy of pride and delight, "This is far more precious than your kingdom."

We need not refer again and again to Chaitanya. Even his followers showed to the world the living beauty of the realization of a joy superior to anything which the world calls pleasure. The sight of these mystics impress the poets more than others; for the poets are nearer to the mystics than are ordinary folk. The *padas* of the Vaiṣṇavas record the beauty of the visions of the mystics.

The Purva Rāga.

The soul marches in its search for God. It has first heard the sound "Come unto me ye that are weary and heavy-laden." The sound beeomes more and more distinct. Worldly pleasures lose their charm and through and beyond all the

[1] "Catherine of Siena was betrothed to Christ with a ring which remained always on her finger though visible to herself alone. Christian Mysticism by William Ralph Inge D.D. p. 371 (1913).

sounds heard around, the call of the winner of the soul comes floating in the air with its irrestible music. The soul knows not from what direction the call comes, nor from whom it comes—but it comes with an irresistible force. The Purva-Rāga songs describe this awakening of the holy passion in the human soul for God. One of the songs runs thus: "The wonderful beauty of the Being have I seen. It has grown impossible for me to stay at home, but yet I knew not who He is nor do I know His name."[1] The illimitable is beyond comprehension but nevertheless it attracts the soul, which awakes to this sense of first love and with it to the pain of separation from Him. The world has long veiled Him from the sight by many enticements. His great love first comes personified as the mother having no sleep in her eyes as she watches her babe, who protects the baby from the gnat and the fly fanning it through long nights and then in the march of life she continually follows her child, some times scolding, some times speaking in the voice of love. The voice of Him who speaks in love we do not hear in this noisy world of self and all on a sudden the first sound is caught from a higher world; it says "Up, up, Oh maiden soul, work as I bid. Be in the world and work in it, but yield thyself unto me. Just as a maiden in love works all day in her household, but yearns with her whole soul for the night of union, so do thou work in this world but do all for the sake of my love".[2] The soul engaged in its

[1] "যে দেখিলাম রূপ তার, ঘরে থাকা হোলো ভার
নাম নাহি জানি তার"। &c., Old song.

[2] Chaitanya's teachings to Sanātana :—
"পরব্যসনিনী নারী ব্যগ্রাপি গৃহকর্ম্মস্থ।
তদেবাস্বাদয়ত্যন্তনবসঙ্গমরসায়ণম্"॥

weary work of the day feels that the quality of the work done, does not always satisfies its hopes. Inspite of its best attempts it is not always the gold that is produced. There is alloy in the result of its labour. Critics find fault, and enemies are ever ready with the crown of thorns for the devoted head ; and in despair the soul threws itself at the lotus feet of Kṛṣṇa and weeping says "Whether I am chaste or not you know best, I do not know even what is good or bad for me. Says Chandi Dās, what is vice and virtue I do not know. Your lotus feet are all to me."[1] The very name of God creates a pure flame in the soul at this stage. As Chandi Dās says "Lo, I have not seen Him yet, the very Name has such a power to win the soul, that I wonder what I shall be if I am so fortunate as to have a touch of Him."[2]

The Padas or songs of Rādhā-Kṛṣṇa were often sung by Kīrtaniyas or the head-singers, aided by a chorus, before such men as Narottama and Raghunātha Dās. Rādhā is the type of the soul craving for God ; she, a princess, has given up all for the sake of Kṛṣṇa. And did not these Vaiṣṇava apostles, before whom these songs were sung, also do the same for the sake of Kṛṣṇa? Kṛṣṇa is always before their eyes too. The dark blue colour of the Jumna brings a vision of Him to their eyes ; the sky, the tree, the flower and its fragrance all remind

[1] "সতী বা অসতী, তোমাতে বিদিত
ভাল মন্দ নাহি জানি।
কহে চণ্ডীদাস পাপ পুণ্য সম
যুগল চরণ মানি"॥
Chandidās.

[2] "নাম পরতাপে যার, ঐছন করলগো,
অঙ্গের পরশে কিবা হয়"।

these devotees of One from whom flow all beauty, all music, and all fragrance. They have risen to a plane where the eye is not that of the dreamer but of the actual seer of strange sights. The abstract symbol of love becomes a tangible reality illustrated by the lives of the Masters. The '*Rūpa*,' or a description of God as imaged in the soul of the devotee, combines in its conception the highest poetry that the human soul is capable of realising with the highest spiritual elevation. The Padas are mere commentaries, interpreting these lives vividly to the people.

The Goṣṭha songs.

The song begins with the measure of the cowpen—Goṣṭha. The great Being plays with the cow-herds. The Christian scripture says:—"Where two or three are gathered together in my name, there am I in the midst of them." He plays with us too, though we know it not. The cow-herds knew not that he was the great Being but they loved Him with their whole soul. It is by love alone that He may be approached. Yogis have tried to approach Him by penances, austerities and physical mortifications. They have got but a glimpse. Thinkers have tried to solve the problem of the Being's existence by philosophical reasoning. Alas, the problem has proved too knotty for them. But these cow-herds of the Vṛndā-groves loved him with their whole soul; and the Being is with them, playing with them. Says one of the cow-herds "When we sleep, we dream of you Kṛṣṇa and utter your name. Mother says 'what a fool are you; where is Kṛṣṇa now in your house?' then am I ashamed of myself." When the play is played without Him, danger comes in the shape of the Demon Vaka or Tṛṇāvarta. The poisoned lake is a peril to the life, or death approaches riding on the hurricane or in the hailstones let loose by the God of the skies. Lo, the cow-herds are overwhelmed with despair and pray into Him with their whole soul's might. The mighty Being comes to their rescue, and is with them even in the body of a child, when the child's soul, full of simplicity and love, clings unto Him with unswerving devotion. This is the commentary of the 'Goṣṭha' play. One of the most fascinating points of the Goṣṭha Padas is the decorating of child-Kṛṣṇa by his mother Jasodā. The very language of the poetry here seems to be resonant with that music played in a temple on the occasion of putting the right ornament in the right place. It reminds one powerfully of the morning service in a Hindu temple, when the image is dressed with its morning robes by the priest. The deity is the babe here and Jasodā, the type of divine motherhood. She displays every sentiment of worship and devotion while she dresses her son for his day in happy life of the fields. The Deva Goṣṭha describes the wonderful spectacle of the gods paying their respects to the cow-herd who is the greatest of gods. The god of Thunder, Indra, the God of the Vedas, Bramha, the civil-head of the gods—Ganeça, and the Hermit-god Çiva, all come to the grove and bow before Kṛṣṇa, the god of divine love. This is but a symbol of the great fact that love is mightier than the sword; it humilates the pride of learning and makes it way to the heavenly region at whose gate asceticism vainly knocks. It is as though Bonaparte or Cromwell or the monk king Charles V were bowing before the child Christ,—the Divine Babe adored by poet and sage as well as by priests and rulers. It is love that subdues the proud Emperor's haughty eyes and it is love that employs the greatest forces of the world to protect the weakness of women and frail children. It is on this love that the Goṣṭha-songs dwell; they lead us besides to grassy meadows and the occupations of the pasture and the simple pleasures of the country—to a region of joy in which the awful might of the Lord is kept in the background; the cowherds are almost unconscious of it; it is his love that thrills so sweetly that they forget its awe; and if He leaves them, they throw themselves on the ground and feel themselves listless and sad—too forlorn to tend their herds and do their simple pastoral tasks. In the Uttara Goṣṭha-songs, when the Queen waves her lamp to welcome Kṛṣṇa back from the fields to home, we see his face brighten in response to the gleam, giving unspeakable joy to the mother. The scene reminds us of the evening service where the priest makes a wave-offering of light to his deity. The temple and the home become one in these accounts, because home and temple alike are mystically the abode of the loving God we love. He is indeed the Terror of the terrible as the Mahānirvāṇa Tantra has it, but still he is soft as a babe, and his voice is sweeter than the sound of the lute as the Vaiṣṇavas say. The mysterious power that loves yet terrifies, that attracts with smiles and repels with frown,—that watches like a mother and yet pursues as an enemy and spy, this mighty Power gives the key to His Paradise to him who cries, "Beat me if you will, look at me with frowning brow and angry eyes, but I shall not leave thee." It is as the child clasping the mother with his arms and crying "Oh mother, mother" when she beats him. And so also the divine heart melts into compassion and love, and He showes himself as the Upanishads have said "as our father—as the guide of our lives and as our only friend".

The Padas of the Goṣhṭha through pastoral scenes, bring us to the very gate of heaven, as the distant landscape often seems to the eye to dissolve into the horizon. In the language of the world, thy speak of the world beyond. They raise the soul to that harbour of safety which may be called its true landing place, leading it to what is unfamiliar and strange, through the familiar and the old. The song with which a Kīrtaniyā first begins the Goṣṭha Kīrtana is often that the first line of which is "আইল শ্রীদামচন্দ্র রঙ্গিয়া পাগড়ী মাথে।" (Here comes the cowherd Çridāma with a striped turban on his head). The picture becomes gradually more and more vivid. Çṛdāma has gold rings on his ears and a jewelled necklace on his broad chest. He clothes himself in picturesque robes which show a mingling of many colours. But though his costume is rich, he carries on his shoulders a stout rope for tethering the cattle; the cord almost touches his golden earrings and hangs carelessly with his gold necklace down his breast. As he comes he reels like a madman for joy of the expected meeting with Kṛṣṇa which works like liquor in his brain. Then come others; all are described,—some tall, some short,—some playing on the flute and others on the horn, till at last we meet the stately figure of Valarāma—the elder brother of Kṛṣṇa. Though a well-known mythological personage his character has been recast in the Vaiṣṇava songs; he appears here as a living historical figure. For, as described in the songs, he is unmistakably Nityānanda himself. Chaitanya in his trances saw Kṛṣṇa, but Nityānanda in his trances saw

Çṛdāma and Valarāma.

Chaitanya. Nityānanda's whole life was a living worship to Chaitanya. He was intoxicated with the joy of Chaitanya's love so that while walking in the street he was often heard to utter the latter's name with tears in his eyes. Here in the song Valarāma is shown as stammering a little as Nityānanda actually stammered. The *pada* beginning with "কা-কা-কানাইয়া" is sung to the *Monaharsayi* tune which brings out the stuttering eagerness of the three initial *ka* syllables. Valarāma stands at the landing Ghāt and beholds his own figure mirrored in the tank. He is described as intoxicated. The Mahābhārata mentions the original Valarāma's love of wine; but the Vaiṣṇava poets really mean his ecstatic adoration of his divine companion. He looks at his own shadow in the water and exclaims: "Who art thou, proud fellow, that cometh to mimic me here; knowest not, thou mean fellow, that I am the brother of Kṛṣṇa?" Then he tramples on the earth in rage, for the shadow mimics him the more that he taunts it. His head reels and he thinks that the earth trembles under his feet. Then he grows merciful and says: "Stop, do not tremble, mother earth, I will trample no more." So saying he walks on till he reaches the courtyard of Jasodā and sounds his big horn, calling "Kṛṣṇa, my love, my adored, wilt not thou awake from sleep?" The intoxication—the fond and foolish speeches and actions—the humerous side of all human love turns suddenly to deep gravity, and the hymn ends on a solemn and elevated note.

Next we come to the Rādhā-Kṛṣṇa songs which treat of the region of the highest form of love. They tread the ways of a subtler world—the true home of divine poetry.

Rādhā-Kṛṣṇa songs.

Sometimes Kṛṣṇa appears to Rādhā as a vision—the most glorious of all.

The poets detail his beauty in the minutest detail, drawing similes freely from the flower, from music, from the blue tint of the clouds and thus display him as our highest poetic dream—a light beyond "the frontier of our consciousness"—with the flute in hand which entices our soul by ravishing notes of divine love. Sometimes they describe the pang of Rādhā—the type of the human soul of man in love with the Divine Being—in her pursuit after the glorious vision. The Māthura relates the story of the grief of parting and separation. It is the dark night of the soul,' as some of the European mystics have called it. It shows the sorrows and sacrifices of the soul, on the cross of love. For every man or woman who has loved and sacrificed himself or herself for its holy cause, is a Christ on a tiny scale, and the reward of all sacrifice is to die on a cross. Love is a gift—the giving away of all that the soul possesses. It is not a claim for a return in kind, rather is it a promise to suffer all that the soul is capable of suffering. Unrecompensed it will go. Evil will it endure in return for the good it gladly gives.—Its symbol and history is the mother's heart which takes the vow of suffering—of ever-lasting sorrows. The Māthura is the history of unreturned and unrewarded love, which triumphs after death, and whose holy flame, fed by its own inward joy, no suffering can quench.

The Māthura.

As I have stated in my previous lectures and in my History of Bengali Language and Literature, the *Kirtana* songs begin with a Gaurachandrikā or a song describing the incidents of Chaitanya's life. This is the key-note to the right interpretation of the Rādhā-Kṛṣṇa songs. It explains to

The Gaurachandrikā.

the audience what sort of things they are likely to expect. It indicates that the Rādhā-Kṛṣṇa songs tell of joys and sorrows which the human soul experiences while striving for the right comprehension of the great problem of life. It represents the soul struggling for a true fountain of joy in the place of barren pleasures which lead us ultimately to eternal conflicts and to eternal disappointments. Far higher than the creed of "duty" as the highest aim of life, but which reduces a human being to a mere machinary—is the doctrine of loving, which gives grace to action and breathes inspiration into soul. Various forces are at work in the universe, but love alone is its sustaining power and life. The Gaurachandrikā is the key-note and message of this Gospel truth of Love.

The Kirtaniyā, often of a very humble birth and invariably without any western culture, grapples religous problems with a mastery of technical learning which is astonishing. He begins by praising Nadiā—the town where Chaitanya was born. He says that the religious ideas of this place are strange. For they are not borrowed from the Vedās. He emphasises again and again that the laws of Nadiā rise far higher than those to be found in the ancient scriptures. Devotion defeats and destroys mere dogma and doctrine, routine and rule. For the Vaiṣṇavas refuse to believe in the Brahmin and even the Veda. Every variety of Rādhā-Kṛṣṇa songs has a number of Gaurachandrikās prefixed to them as a prelude, though the events in the life of Kṛṣṇa and Chaitanya are so widely dissimilar. For instance when the Goṣṭha or the pastoral plays of Kṛṣṇa with the cow-herds are to be sung, Chaitanya's life history provides no means of likening his career to that of the divine cow-herd and his sportive existence at Vṛndāvana. For Chaitānya was a Brahmin scholar, ignorant of pastoral life and unskilled in pastoral revels, but the Kīrtaniyā sings: "Chaitanya remembers the Goṣṭha play of Kṛṣṇa and calls the cows—Çyāmalī, Dhavalī and others by their names." The singer, who is also the interpreter of his songs, improvises poetical commentaries for his audience. He says "Where are the animals that Chaitanya calls so sweetly? Is it a mad utterance? No. The beasts whom Chaitanya calls are really those who have forgot Him, and devoted themselves to ministering to their passions. It is those beasts that Chaitanya calls, as Kṛṣṇa called Çyāmalī and Dhavalī by his flute. The cows could not resist the call of Kṛṣṇa's flute and behold here how the sinner responds to the sweet call of Chaitanya." The Vaiṣṇava songs reach their climactic point of pathos in "the Māthura." A word may be needed to explain what it is. When the human baby first open its eyes, it meets the Lord of Love face to face in its mother watching it with infinite kindness. The arms of the mother are its pillars of strength. She keeps up the whole night watching the sweet smile on its lips and is not weary of beholding its beauty day and night. The mother's heart bleeds to see the child ailing and fain would sacrifice her all to remove the ailment; the mother is the Protecting God, feeling infinite compassion and love for the child. The baby, however, grows to manhood. Mother's care is withdrawn. The eyes that pursued him with breathless anxiety seeking his welfare are no longer there to watch him. Engaged in the bitter struggle of life, he remembers the great mercy and love of God that had taken shape in the mother to protect him, and feels the pang of what Browning calls in

The Māthura.

her Arura Leigh "the mother-want." This feeling of forlornness forms the ground of the Māthura songs. The Lord was so merciful and loving, that if a small thorn would pierce the baby's feet, there were those appointed to protect it, to whom it would be like a dagger to the soul. But now, alas, when a dagger actually pierces the breast, there is none to speak a word of sympathy. God has removed his hand to protect and even to bless. The Māthura songs dwell upon the great love of God and his great indifference. Infinite love and infinite cruelty are shewn by contrast, and the pathos are so great that the very strings of the poets' lyres seem to break at the high-pitched music of these songs. Māthura literally means Kṛṣṇa's desertion of Vṛndāvana and going to Mathura. To the mystic, it has a deeper meaning. The poet Kṛṣṇa Kamala and many others have wholly idealised the Māthura. Kṛṣṇa Kamala says "when the vision of God is clear, the mystic thinks that Kṛṣṇa is at Vṛndāvana, when the vision fades, he thinks Kṛṣṇa to have gone to Mathura" I have seen Kīrāniyās creating a wild scene of emotions among the audiences by the irresistable appeals of these songs; not an eye that did not shed tears, not a heart that did not feel throbs of pain and joy alternately at the references to divine cruelty and to divine love.

The orthodox Vaiṣṇavas have clothed Chaitanya's advent into the world with fascinating legends. One of these says: that once upon a time Kṛṣṇa wished to feel himself what Rādhā herself felt for his love. He said to her "Your tears, your emotions and trances have a charm, my love, that makes me yearn for tasting them myself. Here do I take my vow, I shall be born on the earth, and mad after your love shall I wander from place to place, and throw myself on the dusty ground weeping for you, and yield to trances even as you do." "No, my love," she replied "I cannot endure the sight of your dear body falling on the dusty ground to its hurt; I will cover you with my body so that when in your trances you fall, the hurt may be mine and not yours." Chaitanya, they say, is Kṛṣṇa born again. But Kṛṣṇa's colour was dark-blue, whereas Chaitanya had a bright fair colour. The legend reconciles the anomaly by saying that it is fair Rādhā's body that covered him in his new incarnation bound by the vow to suffer and take upon itself the hurts of her divine lover.[1]

(b) *The Pada-Kartās.*

Govinda Dās.

Among the Pada-Kartās of this period Govinda Dās holds undisputedly the most conspicuous position. Some of the Vaisṇava historians have mentioned the year 1537 as the date of his birth. Babu Kṣirodchandra Raychaudhuri of Cuttack believes the poet to have been born in 1525 A.D. But though I had accepted the former of the two dates in my previous works, I am now inclined, in view of new historical facts that have recently come to light, to reject both these dates. Govinda Dās, it now appears certain to me, was born at least a score of years after 1537. From an account in the Karṇānanda we surmise that he was quite a young man about 1600 A.D., when Çrīnivasa returned to Jajigrām after converting Raja Vīra Hamvīra at Viṣṇupur and had an interview with the poet's elder brother Rāmchandra Kavirāja. The old writers have often

[1] See Narottama Vilāsa by Narahari Chakravarty.

mentioned the month and the *tithi* of important historical events but in many such cases they have omitted to mention the year. We trust we are right in holding that Govinda Dās was born some years after 1550 at Kumārnagar. The reason which makes us reject the year of his birth as accepted by the modern Vaiṣṇava historians also stands in the way of our believing 1612 A.D. to be the year of his death, as given in those historical treatises. With greater accuracy we may say that his life which was a long one according to all records, covered the latter part of the 16th and the earlier half of the 17th century.

Govinda Dās's grandfather on the mother's side was Dāmodara, a resident of Çrīkhanda in the southern part of the district of Burdwan. Dāmodara was a Sanskrit poet of repute. His daughter Sunānda was married to Chiranjīva Sen of Kumārnagar. The latter was a companion of Chaitanya and adopted the calling of a physician—the profession of his caste.

Chiranjīva Sen's two sons, Rāmachandra Kavirāja and Govinda Kavirāja—the poet of whom we are speaking—deservedly held the front rank amongst the men of letters of an age noted for its gifted men. Rāmchandra Kavirāja's scholarship almost equalled that of Çrīnivāsa—the most illustrious of the Vaiṣṇavas of his time in point of learning. There were numerous Brahmin disciples of Rāmachandra though he was a Vaidya by caste. Govinda Dās became an equally great personality amongst his contemporaries by his superior poetical talents which have won him great fame in his own land.

His conversion.

Many writers have described the wonderful impetus which his poetical powers received from his conversion to Vaiṣṇavism at a rather advanced period of his life. Rāmchandra had for sometime lived at Jajigrām with Crinivāsa. There he received a letter from Govinda Dās saying that the latter suffered from dropsy and was on the point of death. Rāmchandra, devotedly attached to his *gura,* could not be persuaded to leave his company and heeded not this urgent call from home. A second letter came from Govinda Dās who implored his elder brother not to delay in coming home any longer. "For," he said, "my illness is serious and if you do not come quickly you may not see me alive again." He also requested Rāmachandra to bring Çrīnivasa with him if the latter would condescend to do so out of compassion for one who was declared by the physicians to be on his death bed.

Rāmachandra and Çrīnivāsa both came to Kumārnagar and the former's medical treatment and the latter's blessings brought the hopeless patient back to health. The impression created on Govinda Dās by the faith and scholarship of Çrīnivāsa was so profound that he too, like his brother, abandoned the Çākta creed and adopted Vaiṣṇavism. Çrīnivasa initiated the poet into the new faith and the latter studied the Bhaktirasāmṛta Sindhu and Ujjala Nīlamaṇi with his Guru for some time. The poet was a profound scholar in Sanskrit, so that he mastered the Vaiṣṇava scriptures quickly. The story of Chaitanya's life as related to him by Çrīnivāsa breathed a lofty inspiration into the soul of Govinda Dās as he listened to it with tears. He begged permission of his Guru to render it into vernacular songs. Çrīnivāsa, however, said "Vāsudeva Ghosh, the favourite companion of the Master has composed songs of unmatched beauty dwelling on every incident of his great career. The descriptions are vivid for he was a constant associate of the Master. Compose songs on Rādhā-Kṛṣṇa love and I offer you my blessings; I hope ere long to see you achieve remarkable success in performing this task." Govinda Dās wrote the Sanskrit work Sangīta Mādhava, but he has acquired immortal laurels by his Rādhā-Kṛṣṇa songs in the vernacular.

The appreciation of his songs.

Karṇānanda says, "The earth was flooded with his music." In the great festivities of the Vaiṣṇavas, these songs were sung by Çrī Dās and Gokul Dās, two reputed Kīrtaniyās of Kanchangoria, and Vīrachandra, the leader of the Vaiṣṇava community, often embraced the poet before large audiences in token of his high appreciation of the merits of these songs. Jīva Goswāmi, about whom I have already written fully in my previous lectures, the greatest Indian scholar of the age, wrote many letters to Govinda Dās from Vṛndāvana extolling his poems. It appears that the poet used to send his new songs to Jīva for approval. In one of his letters Jīva writes:—

"সম্প্রতি যৎ শ্রীকৃষ্ণ বর্ণনাময়স্বীয়গীতানি প্রস্থাপিতানি পূর্ব্বমপি যানি, তৈরমৃতৈরিব তৃপ্তাবর্ত্তামহে। পুনরপি নূতন তত্তদাশয়া মুহুরতৃপ্তিঞ্চ লভামহে।"

(I have received your new poems on Kṛṣṇa. It was very kind of you to send them to me now as you kindly did in the past. These poems have the power of charming the soul like divine nectar. I long to read your new poems and hope that you will fulfil my expectations in future.)

Govinda Dās used to refer his difficulties in reading the Vaiṣṇava scriptures to Jīva Goswāmi. A letter has been preserved in which the poet refers to Jīva his difficulty in regard to the meaning of the passage beginning with

সেবাসাধকরূপেণ in the Bhaktirasāmṛta Sindhu. The poet writes from Teliā Budhari and Jīva explains the text from Vṛndāvana.

Narottama and Rāmachandra had, by this time, acquired many Brahmin disciples. The former was a Kayastha and the latter a Vaidya. The orthodox community of Kumārnagar, by their persistent hostility, made it impossible for the brothers to dwell in that village any longer. The Bhaktiratnākara mentions that one day Rāmachandra Kavirāja called Govinda Dās to his chamber and said "Brother, our ancestral home of Kumārnagar is no longer a fit place of abode for us. On the banks of the Padmā there is a beautiful village called Teliā Budhari. There our grandfather Dāmodara lived for some time and the people there are friendly to us. Let us go away from here and settle there. We need not grieve at losing our small landed property at Kumāranagar. Peace of mind will more than compensate the loss of mere wealth in land."[1]

Persecution and abandonment of home.

[1] "নিজানুজ ভ্রাতা শ্রীগোবিন্দ বিদ্যাবান।
কার্য্যেতে চাতুর্য্য চারু সর্ব্বাংশে প্রধান॥
অতি স্নেহাবেশে তারে কহয়ে নিভৃতে।
যাইব শ্রীবৃন্দাবনে রজনী প্রভাতে॥
এবে হেথা বাসের সঙ্গতি ভাল নয়।
সদা মনে আশঙ্কা উপজে অতিশয়॥
আছয়ে কিঞ্চিৎ ভূমি বহুদিন হৈতে।
তাহে যে উৎপাত এবে দেখহে সাক্ষাতে॥
শীঘ্র এই বাসাদিক পরিত্যাগ করি।
নির্ব্বিঘ্নে অন্যত্র যাব হয় সর্ব্বোপরি॥
তাহে এই গঙ্গা পদ্মাবতী মধ্যস্থান।
পুণ্যক্ষেত্র তেলিয়া বুধরি নামে গ্রাম॥

Accordingly they went to Teliā Budhari and settled there. This village is only a few miles from Kheturi—the city where Narottama lived. This may have served as an inducement to the brothers in choosing their residence.

The occupation of his last years.

The Bhaktiratnākara mentions that Govinda Dās during the last years of his life busied himself in making a collection of his songs at Teliā Budhari.[1] In his youth he had paid a visit to the village Vhisfi in the Darbhanga district and had collected a large number of Vidyāpati's songs. In the colophons of some of these he cleverly put his own name side by side with that of Vidyāpati, introducing by humorous half-lines poetic suggestions of curious beauty. Radhāmohana Thākur, who edited those vernacular songs in Sanskrit in the 18th century, has thus explained the occurence of the names of both poets in the refrains.

Govinda Dās was for forty years of his life a Çākta; and then turned Vaisnava and began his poetical career. He died about the middle of the 17th century at the age of 76.

অতি গণ্ডগ্রাম শিষ্ট লোকের বসতি।
যদি মনে হয় তবে উপযুক্ত স্থিতি॥
শ্রীমাতামহের পূর্ব্বে ছিল গতায়াত।
সকলে জানেন তেঁহ সর্ব্বত্র বিখ্যাত॥
তথা বাস হৈলে অনেকের সুখ হয়।
গোবিন্দ কহেন এই কর্ত্তব্য নিশ্চয়॥"

The Bhaktiratnākara, p. 572. Berhampur edition. It is stated later on in the Bhaktiratnākara that the brothers settled at Teliā Budhari in a part of it known as the Parçhima Pārā (the western ward).

[1] "নির্জ্জনে বসিয়া নিজ পদরত্ন গনে।
করেন একত্র অতি উল্লাসিত মনে॥"

The Bhaktiratnākara, the 14th Taranga.

Govinda Dās was a great friend of Santoṣa Rāy— brother of Chānd Ray of Rajmahal. Govinda Dās was also a dear friend of Santoṣa Datta of Kheturi who inherited the Kheturi state on Narottama's taking the vow of Sannyās. Rūpnārāyaṇa, the scholar and the Court-Pundit of Nrisiṁha Rāy, the Rājā of Pakkapalli, was also on terms of great intimacy with the poet, who has referred to those three friends in the colophons of some of his songs.

Some of his songs.

I shall try to translate here some of the songs of Govinda Dās. The poetic beauty of the originals will not be found in the translation but this is inevitable, particularly so in the case of Govinda Dās's poems, as these are characterised by a sweetness of language which is matchless even in the mellifluous Bengali tongue.

Rādha speaks of Kṛṣṇa's love for her to her maids.

"He knows that at noon day when I go to bathe, the sandy pathway on the Jumna side is hot. He steals thither and waters the path for me ; and as I behold him doing this, my heart feels the silent pang of love. When alone I go to the bathing ghāt he sees my foot-prints and kisses them. My heart again feels the pang of silent love. But abashed I stand aside, thinking what will the people say ".[1]

[1] "সিনান দুপুর সময়ে জানি।
তপত পথেতে ঢালে সে পানি ॥
লাজে হাম যদি মন্দিরে যাই।
পদ চিহ্ন তলে লুটে কাহ্নাই ॥
প্রতি পদচিহ্ন চুম্বয়ে কাণ।
তা দেখি আমার আকুল পরাণ ॥
লোকে দেখিলে কি বলিবে মোরে।'

A stranger has no means of entering the inner court of the Hindu Zenena to meet his love. The woman has to go out covering herself with the darkness of the night to meet him. Her difficulties are great. She is unaccustomed to walk in public paths. But even these have to be avoided for fear of detection and she has to tread unbeaten paths, full of thorny plants, infested by snakes and dangerously slippery during the rains. Rādhā trains herself before going out in the dark to meet her Kṛṣṇa."

"She covers the path of her own courtyard with thorns and makes them slippery with water. Her anklets she ties with her cloth lest they jingle, and then with feet tender as lotus-buds, she softly treads the slippery and thorny path, she has herself made. Thus does Rādhā, sleepless all the night, practise the art of Abhisāra for thee, Oh Kṛṣṇa. She covers her eyes with her hands as she walks all alone, in order to learn to walk in darkness. Snake-charmers she rewards with presents of her jewelled bracelets of gold, and learns from them the antedote for snake bite. She heeds not the words of her elders and gives them replies that sound strange to their ears. If her friends give her any advice, she smiles like one distraught.[1]

Govinda Dās here refers to the austerities which the soul willingly endures for the love of God. The royal

[1] কণ্টক গাড়ি কমল সম পদতল মঞ্জীর চীরহি ঝাঁপি।
গাগরি বারি ঢারি করি পিছল চলতহি অঙ্গুলি চাপি॥
মাধব তুয়া অভিসারকি লাগি।
দূরতর পন্থ গমন ধনী সাধয়ে মন্দিরে যামিনী জাগি॥
করযুগে নয়ন মুদি চলু ভামিনী তিমির পয়ানক আশে।
মণিকঙ্কণ পণ ফণী মুখ বন্ধন শিখই ভুজগ গুরু পাশে॥
গুরুজন বচন বধির সম মানই আন শুনই কহ আন।
পরিজন বচনে মুগধি সম হাসই গোবিন্দ দাস পরমান।

road of the world is to be shunned ; the convenient paths do not lead to Him. The thorny and slippery path must be trod. But all toil and danger will the soul sweetly suffer for the sake of the Beloved One. The elders are not to be respected, nor even the Scriptures. The virgin soul in the dawn of love listens only to the flute of its God. Wise friends offer to teach the road of worldly success. But Govinda Dās says the pious soul will smile wildly, for the wisdom of the world is not that of the soul that has heard the call of the Divine musician's flute.

Govinda Dās writes in a poetic dialect created by a combination of Hindi and Bengali—the Braja Bhāṣā. He is a finished master in the art of giving expression to tender thought and his literary diction is delightful. He possesses in a remarkable degree the charm and appeal which characterise the poetry of Vidyāpati. The writer of these lectures recollects many evenings on which he listened to the Avisāra songs of Govinda Dās (especially those which incidentally describe the rainy season), with eyes sometimes moist with tears and at others open wide, as if to catch the sight of Rādhā stealing forth secretly in quest of her Beloved One. The rainy season, associated with the fair plumed peacock's dance and the many coloured rainbow, vividly appeared before the mind's eye. As one listened to verse and music one could see the solitary wanderer, with her whole soul turned towards Kṛṣṇa, following with listless steps, the signal of the divine music played on the flute of her lover. When Rādhā meets Kṛṣṇa at last, her lover approaches her in ecstasies of joy, and holds her to his breast. With his lotus-hands he wipes the dust from her feet and fixes on her face a thirsty gaze that knows no satiety. With a lotus-leaf he fans her and again and again enquires of the dangers of her coming. He puts betel-nut between her lips and murmers love-speeches in her pretty ears. With the border of his garment he wipes her face and cools it with *kumkum* powder. He braids her hair himself, and puts on her brow the lucky red mark that signifies love ; jewelled anklets he offers for her feet and a necklace for her bosom. The black collyrium enhances the brightness of her eyes ; to her thus bedecked he offers his body and soul. Humbly he applies to her lotus-feet the scarlet dye Altā, and Govinda Dās wonders that Kṛṣṇa, the lord of the universe, does for her all this menial duties.

And Rādhā brings scented water and washes the feet of her love, and wipes them with her own beautiful hair. She beholds his face with insatiate gaze and says in soft murmuring accents, "I was angry with you, Kṛṣṇa, what a silly girl am I ? They say that you love me, and my mind is filled with pride. It is your love that has increased my humble worth. Who is there who can diminish it while you love me ? Oh my beautiful Kṛṣṇa, forgive all my shortcomings and faults. My life I dedicate to your feet. Govinda Dās says "Kṛṣṇa listened to her words with tearful eyes."[1]

[1] সুবাসিত বারি ঝারি ভরি তৈখনে আনল রসবতী রাই ।
দুখানি চরণ, পাখালিয়া সুন্দরী, আপন কেশেতে মোছাই ॥
অঙ্গক ধূলি বসনহি ঝাড়ই, অনিমিখে হেরই বয়ান ।
তুহুঁ সনে মান করনু বরমাধব হাম অতি অলপ পরাণ ॥
রমনীক মাঝে কহই শ্যাম সোহাগিনী গরবে ভরল মঝু দে ।
হামারি গরব তুহু আগে বাঢ়ায়লি অবহু টুটায়ব কে ।
সব অপরাধ ক্ষেমহ বরমাধব তুআ পায় সোঁপিলু পরাণ ।
গোবিন্দ দাস কহ কানু ভেল গদ গদ হেরইতে রাই বয়ান ॥

The sweet words and the tender pathos they suggest, by means of associations that are familiar to a Vaiṣṇava's mind remind him of the ecstasies of joy which Chaitanya felt while in his trance he embraced a Tamala tree saying "I have got Him" and from his closed eyes tears fell showing the silent but deep feeling of inward enjoyment. In popular belief, Chaitanya was inspired with the emotions of Rādhā.

Some of the songs of Govinda Dās do not soar so high in their mystic imagery, but have a charm of their own. I quote one of them below. Rādhā was angry and did not talk with Kṛṣṇa for some time. The latter comes to her house disguised as a Yogi.

"The false anchorite sounded his horn, which, when Jatilā[1] heard, she stepped out to give him alms. The holy father all silently shook his head and Jatilā knew from this that he declined her offer. Then she asked him what was it that he wanted. And the anchorite explained himself. 'My vow is to take alms from one who is a wife, and not from a widow as you are'. Glad was she to hear this, and forthwith went to the young wife in the house and said to her, 'At the gate waits a holy father of noble presence, and wise is he beyond doubt. Go with a golden plate filled with alms and humbly offer them to him'. Rādhā, hearing this, cried out 'How foolish! How can I go to a stranger?' Jatilā said 'Not

[1] Jatilā was the mother-in-law of Rādhā and always suspicious of her secret love for Kṛṣṇa. She is deadly hostile to the latter, and the humour of the poem lies in the fact that without recognising the Yogi who is no other than Kṛṣṇa himself, Jatilā herself introduces Rādhā to him.

a bad man, I swear, for his looks are saintly. Virtue will you acquire by a sight of him.' So Rādhā filled a plate with flour, and a golden cup did she take full of clarified butter, and with joint palms did she stand before the anchorite saying in sweet accents, 'Be pleased to take these, oh Yogi.' And as she said this, she trembled in shame at having spoken to a stranger. The false anchorite shook his head and told her 'Nothing of these will I touch. Only a request have I to make. You are angry, oh princess, with Kṛṣṇa who adores you. Tell me that you pardon him and I will go away well-satisfied, at hearing this from your lips.' And Rādhā drew her veil and hid her face as she recognised his face. And Govinda Dās says Kṛṣṇa gladly returned home rejoicing in the success of his mission."[1]

[1] "গোরখ জাগাই শিঙ্গা ধ্বনি শুনইতে জটিলা ভিখ আনি দেল।
মৌনী যোগেশ্বর মাথা হিলায়ত, বুঝল ভিখ নাহি নেল॥
জটিলা কহত তব কাঁহা উঁহু মাগত, যোগী কহত বুঝাই।
তেরা বধূ-হাত ভিখ হাম লেয়ব, তুরঁ তহি দেহ পাঠাই॥
পতিবরতা ভিখ লেই ঘর, যোগীবরত না হোয় নাশ।
তা কর বচন শুনিতে তনু পুলকিত, ধাই কহে বধূ পাশ।॥
দ্বারে যোগীবর, পরম মনোহর, জ্ঞানী বুঝিনু অনুমানে।
বহুত যতন করি, রতন থারি ভরি, ভিখ দেহ তছু ঠানে॥
শুনি ধনি রাই 'আই' করি ওঠল, যোগী নিয়ড়ে নাহি যাব।
জটিলা কহত, যোগী নহে আনমত, দরশনে হোয়ব লাভ॥
গোধূম চূর্ণ পূর্ণ, থারি পর, কনক কটোরি ভরি ঘিঁউ।
করযোড়ে রাই 'লেহ' করি ফুকারই, তাহে হেরি ঘরঘরি জীউ॥
যোগী কহত, হাম ভিখ নাহি লেয়ব, তুয়া মুখ বচন এক চাই।
নন্দ-নন্দন পর যে অভিমানসি, মাপ করহ ঘরে যাই॥
শুনি ধনি রাই, চীরে মুখ ঝাপল, ভেকধারী নটরাজ।
গোবিন্দ দাস কহ, নটবর শেখর, সাধি চলত নিজ কাজ॥"

(c) *The peculiar excellence of the Vaiṣṇava songs.*

A very large number of poets composed songs on Rādhā-Kṛṣṇa love during this period. Jñānadās, Balarāma Dās, Çaçi Çekhara, Jadunātha Dās, Jadunandana Dās, Rājā Vīra Hamvīra, Rājā Nṛsiṁha Deva and many others wrote verse that may still be read with pleasure. They were contemporaries and met together on various occasions especially during the great Vaiṣṇava festivities, held at Kheturi, Çrīkhanda and Kātwā. We have long accounts in various historical works describing the function each discharged in these festivities, and from these we can glean certain facts regarding them.

The Vaiṣṇva poetry in Bengal began, as I have already stated, from Jayadeva in the 12th century, or even earlier, from Umāpati. It said its last great word of love in the Kṛṣna-Yātrās which were written in the earlier part of the 19th century. But the activity of the Vaiṣṇava poets was greatest during the period immediately following that of Chaitanya, till the composition of the anthological work Padakalpataru by Vaiṣṇava Dās. We deal in these lectures with this period of the literature of the Vaiṣṇavas.

From the time of Vālmīki who wrote the earliest and the noblest epic in India, love has formed the favourite theme of our poets. In Bhavabhuti's poems love passed into those platonic regions which the western imagination might denominate as too subtle and dreamy, but which to our poets, even of a lesser note, have not appeared "a too inaccessible height."

But the love-poetry, of which we are now speaking, entirely differs from earlier or later verse of the kind. It revels in its own mystic joys and has some distinctive marks of its own. The lover's words are borrowed from the current phraseology, but it does not speak of the love hitherto described by the poets. It comes upon the soul as a rapturous joy, a surprise and a message from some unknown world. The songs are, like Solmon's Songs of Songs. It is for this reason that these poets are called Mahājanas, lit. great men, as contrasted with poets of wordly affection.

The peculiar atmosphere of the Vaiṣṇava poets.

The old Indian sculptor gave a touch to the image of his God which made heaven akin to the earth. He displayed that supernal beauty which perhaps no where else shines with such grandeur in wrought stone. The face of the image often discloses a smile like that of a child, innocent and dreamy, and a bud-like sweetness unspotted by contact with the world and indicated by an inimitable curl of the lips on which art-critics may well ponder. 'Who taught the sculptor this exquisite perfection of the expression of the divine face ?' one might ask. The reply is that he learned it from the sight of the Indian Yogi, who seated in the pinnacle of his conquest over passions, smiles like an infant, heedless of the world, heedless of death—in tranquil communion with his God. In the early times of Indian History these Yogis were very common in this country. And the sculptor got his inspiration from men who had drawn their inspiration from God.

The world has since moved to other deals. The vision of God was no longer familiar to men, and the sculptor and the artist tried to develop their scientific knowledge and gloried in the accuracy of drawing and in making the proportions of limbs and perspectives perfect. These are of course achievements worth having. But the divine vision has vanished and instead of reproducing the highest type of humanity, modern sculptors glory in drawing the meaner type, mis-named as 'real' as though the higher joys of the soul were visionary and beyond human reach. If the word 'ideal' by which we are accustomed to name all high things, means only that which rests in the idea and cannot be realised, it is an insult to the intellectual capacity of the human race.

The Vāiṣṇava poems of love, like the works of the great Indian sculptors, belong to a special period of history. Poets admired as prodigies may still write poetry in our tongue and excel in flights of imagination and observation of life, and in the minute analysis of human feelings. But we cannot conceive that any poet of modern times, unless the conditions of the present day should be changed, will be able to write such poetry as these Vaiṣṇava poets have written. The lovers of God, the mystics and the men with trances and strange visions were in their midst. Their inspiring presence gave a tone, a charm to the poetry of this school, which we look in vain for elsewhere.

(*d*) *Jnāna Dās.*

I need not dwell upon the lives of the Vaiṣṇava poets of this period. They have been noticed in my Vanga Bhāsa O Sāhitya and in my History of Bengali Language and Literature at some length. All that I can do here is to jot down stray notes on matters omitted elsewhere. A further light may be thrown upon the lives of these poets and their writings by research in the scenes where they lived and died. The native places of the poets, it may be presumed, still retain memorials of their lives and works; much information can still, I am sure, be gathered from a visit to these places. The late Babu Jagatbandhu Bhadra and Hārādhan Bhaktinidhi did excellent work in this matter, though the dates supplied by the latter seem to us frequently to be of questionable authenticity.

The prevailing belief is that Jnānadās was born at Kandrā, a village in the Birbhum District. The village now belong to the Burdwan District, though in pre-English days it was within the geographical area of Birbhum. Babu Sivaratan Mitra has drawn attention to this erroneous belief, entertained by some of the scholars who have written about Jnānadās. The village Kandrā is in the sub-division of Kātwā and under the police station of Keti.

Jnānadās was of the family of Mongal Brahmins of the place and was a great friend of Manohara Dās, the compiler of an anthology of Vaiṣṇava songs—the Padasamudra. Though we cannot accept the dates relating to Jnānadās, usually given in modern historical treatises about Vaiṣṇava writers, there is no doubt that he was present at the great festivities of the Vaiṣṇavas held between 1610 and 1625. This is stated in all the contemporary records. In the village of Kandrā there is a *matha*—a temple founded by Jnānadās. Here the poet lived as a celibate and monk all his life. His songs bear traces of the influence of Chaṇḍidās; in fact some of them look like mere paraphrases of the earlier poet's lines, but this does not materially detract from the intrinsic value of his song, for he too was smitten with a genuine love for his subject, and conceived his poetic images on the lines of his illustrious predecesssor. There is a very large number of songs of Jnānadās with which many are familiar. Their exquisite melody and spirituality of thought can hardly be conveyed in a translation; so I refrain from giving a rendering of any of them in English. I will, however, recall to you that familiar song of his in which Rādhā wants to learn from Kṛṣṇa the art of playing on the flute. She holds the divine flute in her hand and begs Kṛṣṇa to teach her his fashion of playing so that charmed nature foregoes her own accustomed ways and is forced to surprising miracles. The jack tree under the spell of its divine music yields the heavenly Parijāta flower; the Jamunā changes her course, and the six seasons appear all together; the peacock dances to the instrument's melody, the Kadamva flowers; the cuckoo sends its gayest notes to the sky, and Nature herself feels, as it were, a thrill of joy. Rādhā wants to know the magic of all these doings. Jñānadās, the poet, smiles and says, the flute knows but one sound. It has but one song, one burden and one word which is 'Rādhā'.[1] It calls to a girl bearing that name and it is

Some of his songs.

[1] মুরলী করাও উপদেশ।
কোন্ রন্ধ্রে কোন ধ্বনি বাজে জানহ বিশেষ
কোন্ রন্ধ্রে বাজে বাঁশী অতি অনুপম।
কোন্ রন্ধ্রে রাধা বলি লয় আমার নাম॥
কোন্ রন্ধ্রে বাজে বাঁশী সুললিত ধ্বনি।
কোন্ রন্ধ্রে কেকা শব্দে নাচে ময়ূরিণী॥
কোন্ রন্ধ্রে রসালে ফুটয়ে পারিজাত।
কোন্ রন্ধ্রে কদম্ব ফুটেহে প্রাণনাথ॥
কোন্ রন্ধ্রে ষড়ঋতু হয় এক কালে।
কোন্ রন্ধ্রে নিধুবন হয় ফুলে ফলে॥
কোন্ রন্ধ্রে কোকিল পঞ্চম স্বরে গায়।
একে একে শিখাইয়া দেহ শ্যামরায়।
জ্ঞানদাস কহে হাসি হাসি।
"রাধা মোর" বলি বাজিবেক বাঁশী॥

Rādhā who is charmed. From afar the music of the call comes floating in the air and the girl Rādhā loses all control over herself, tears herself from all ties of home and society in order to dedicate her body and soul to the musician. Blow the flute, Rādhā, as you will, with the sweet breath of your mouth, but whosoever may teach you, will not be able to change the tune eternally fixed in the flute. It can only sing of Rādhā and Rādhā ever more. "Awake my beloved, arise and see me" is the call sometimes heard as a musical whisper, sometimes bursting into strange and thrilling melodies which fill the whole sky. And when the human soul—(the woman of the Vaiṣṇava song) hears the melody, it knows no rest, the sound wins it far away from home or rather to its true home. This music, says Shakespeare, a contemporary of Jñānadās,—is in our eternal soul, but for the clay vesture of decay that environs it, we cannot hear it.

The beauty of the stanzas

"রূপ লাগি আখি ঝুরে গুণে মন ভোর।
প্রতি অঙ্গ লাগি কাঁদে প্রতি অঙ্গ মোর॥
হিয়ার পরশ লাগি হিয়া মোর কাঁদে।
পরাণ পিরীতি লাগি থির নাহি বাঁধে॥"

cannot be conveyed in translation. It is an expression of the soul's rapturous joy. The soul like a holy temple welcomes the lord to the senses which are the doorways for that eternal fountain of beauty, music and fragrance to enter. The soul wants to enjoy Him in a close embrace. This mystic longing is in the stanzas, and if a parallel of it were to be sought I would quote:—

"Eye to Eye opposed, salutes each other with each other's form." (*Troilus and Cressida*, act. iii, scene iii).

(e) *Balarāma Das.*

The next poet on my list is Balarāma Dās. We find him mentioned in the Padakalpataru as belonging to the family of the Kavirājas, *viz.* of Govinda Dās and Rām Chandra. The Bhakti-ratnākara says that he was a resident of the village Budhuri on the Padmā and that his title was Kavipati or 'prince of poets.' We have proved in a previous lecture that he could not be the same man as Nityānanda Dās alias Balarāma Dās who wrote the Premavilās, though I was, I have admitted, once of a contrary opinion. We know that Balarāma Dās was a comtemporary of Jñānadās and Govinda Dās, and was present in the famous Vaiṣṇava festivities which took place at Çrikhanda, Khcturi and Kātwā during 1610 and 1625.

Here is an attempt to translate one of Bālarāma Dās's songs. I need not repeat that I always feel that translation always difficult, is trebly difficult when rendering Bengali love-poetry into western speech. However I can but do my best. "Though always near me he cannot repose a moment, fearing lest he lose sight of me. He regrets that I am not a necklace to wear on his breast, that I am not the sandal whose perfumed contact he can always feel. Like one in possession of sudden wealth after a whole life's labour, he knows not what to do with me. He decorates my hair with the wreath of Mālati flowers. With a candle in his hand he wakes the whole night and beholds my face times without number, each time weeping for joy. He softly touches my feet and adorns them with the scarlet Alṭā dye."[1]

The entire passage from which I quote this short extract is given in original in the foot note below.

The priest is the lover of Kṛṣṇa in the temple. He waves the five lights before the image; burns incense and prepares floral wreaths for it. Day and night he remains absorbed in the vision of the beauty of his God. Love is not to be measured by the quality of its object; it's action is always subjective. What a Beatrice or a Rāmi was in fact we are not concerned to know. Sufficient for us to feel that they could create a Dante or a Chaṇḍidās. The image in the temple created a Govindadās, Jñānadās and a Balarāmdās. The finite brought them before the infinite just as a rivulet will waft the pilgrim's boat to the sea. Love a little child or love a Hercules, it is the love that matters. Passionate devotion breaks the barriers between the finite and the infinite, and the soul ascends to heaven from earth.

(e) *Song by a Mahomedan poet.*

The songs of these poets of the 16th and 17th centuries are as numerous as field-flowers, and I dare not hope that in the examples cited I have been able to hit those best fitted to please the Western taste. A more competent

[1] "মোর কাছে কাছে থাকে, সদা চোখে চোখে রাখে, তবু মোরে পলকে হারায়।
ও বুক চিরিয়া, হিয়ার মাঝারে, যেন বা রাখিতে চায় ॥
হার নহে পিয়া, গলায় পরিএ, চন্দন নহে মাখে গায়।
অনেক যতনে, রতন পাইয়া, সোয়াস্তি নাহিক পায় ॥
সাজায়ে আমায়, বসন পরায়, আবেগে লইয়া কোরে।
দীপ লইয়া হাতে, মুখ নিরখিতে, তিতল নয়ন লোরে ॥
চরণে ধরিয়া, যাবক রচই, আলাঞা বান্ধয়ে কেশ।
বলরাম চিতে, ভাবিতে ভাবিতে, পাঁজর হইল শেষ ॥"

man than myself, better acquainted with European modes of thought, might find many songs more in tune with western ideas of beauty. Here is surely a paradise of flowers. The white Kunda, the cup-shaped lily, the crescent Atasi, the tiny Juin, that looks like a tear drop or pearl on the slim branches of the plant, and a hundred others are here. Can we not see that all are lovely, though each of us has his own favourite? I shall not detain you any farther by dwelling on this point. For the names of these poets and accounts of them I refer to you to pp. 545-565 of my History of the Bengali Language and Literature and to pp. 291-320 of my Vanga Bhāṣa O Sāhitya. I shall close this chapter with a Vaiṣṇava song by a Mahomedan writer. It runs thus—

"You do not choose right hours and times to play on your flute, my love. Out of season you play, and my heart goes forth to you without any control. When I sit in the company of my elders your flute calls me by my name. Can you not imagine, my love, to what shame I am put? From the other bank of the river you sound your flute and I hear its sound across the stream from this bank. Do you not know, my love, that it is my luckless fate that] I know not how to swim across the river. Says Chānḍ Kāzi I weep when I hear the flute and woe be to my life if I cannot meet Kṛṣṇa."[3]

বাঁশী বাজান জান না।
অসময়ে বাজাও বাঁশী মন ত মানে না ॥
যখন আমি বৈসা থাকি গুরুজনার মাঝে।
তুমি নাম ধইরা বাজাও বাঁশী আমি মরি লাজে ॥
ওপার হৈতে বাজাও বাঁশী এপার হৈতে শুনি।
অভাগিয়া নারী আমি সাঁতার নাহি জানি ॥
চাঁদ কাজি বলে বাঁশী শুনে ঝুরে মরি।
জীমুনা জীমু না আমি না দেখিলে হরি ॥

The lines—

"ওপার হইতে বাজাও বাঁশী, এপার হৈতে শুনি।
অভাগিয়া নারী আমি সাঁতার নাহি জানি ॥"

show that the sound of the flute comes from a higher world, and not having power to control tho flesh, we cannot meet the god who plays it.

CHAPTER IV.

Theological Literature.

(a) The Vaiṣṇava Theology.
(b) The degenerecy of the Buddhists and the recruiting of Vaiṣṇava converts from their ranks.
(c) Jnanādi Sādhanā— a curious medley of the Buddhistic and Vaiṣṇava creeds.
(d) Christianity and Vaiṣṇavism.

(a) *The Vaiṣṇava Theology.*

Nature presents a spectacle of decay and ruin in her individual cases; but she is in eternal touch with some fountain of joy and life which never dries up. The eternal tree offers eternal flowers for her temple; their fragrance never ceases, and God's light peeps into this earth night and day through the high gate of heaven. This joy is the very life of the universe and permeates it, though individual lives perish and decay.

Nature is in touch with some blessed force from which emanetes a life which is but an echo of a joyous music of hope and of love. Where is the fountain of this joy that makes the tree smile with its floral treasure though its boughs be broken? Whence breathes that joy which is ever strange and new on the lips of a child and for which this world, thousands of years old, looks like the baby of to-day so that "time writes no wrinkles on its brow?"

The spiritual problem in this country has been whether man can scale the height on which Nature stands and arrive at that blessed stage where losses and crosses weigh not upon the soul, eternally happy in spite of accident and vicissitudes. The Yogi found the secret and solved the great problem of life. His ascetic training caused him pain, but when he ultimately reaches the stage of perfection, he smiles content and imparts his tranquillity to others, living for the happiness of the world.

Various are the ways by which this object may be attained. The Vaiṣṇavas discovered the fountain of this joy in the human world around them. Their theology is a comprehensive one. They have given a place to the Yogi who retires from the world, and, in happy abstraction, lives the life of a recluse. This according to them is the Çānta or the tranquil stage; but the Vaiṣṇava says that it is an inferior stage. The higher joys are for those to whom absolute bliss is revealed in the human world. According to them the next stage is the Dāsya. In this one serves the Lord as a servant. "Thou art my master and I am obedient to thy will," is the motto in this stage.

A classification of emotions.

There is another side of this stage; the devotee may consider the Lord Himself to be the Great Servant ready to serve the world, with all that is needed for its preservation. It makes, however, no difference, for what we give Him is also His. I have detailed the ways in which He, the Beloved One, is revealed to Man in his other relations with the human world, in my previous lectures. The Çānta, Dāsya, Sakhya and Vātsalya are the various stages which have their crowning end in Mādhurya, where man is the solitary hearer of the word of the Beloved One, the appreciative reader of the Arch Poet's great poem. The word of the Lord makes him burst into tears, His image is the all-engrossing object of his senses. In the Chaitanya Charitāmṛta and other works of this class these stages have been elucidated in the minutest detail. In a work called the Sādhya Sādhana Tattwa we have a classification of these five fold phases of devotion:—

The Cānta.—"শান্তে শ্রীকৃষ্ণে নিষ্ঠুর বুদ্ধিতা।" [1]

In the Çanta or "the quiet stage" the predominent idea is that God is terrible. Man is struck by terror and accepts Him as his refuge.

শান্তে নির্ম্মমতা যোগ নির্বেদ—অশ্রুপুলক রোমাঞ্চাদিবর্জ্জিত ॥

When the Yogi attains the stage, he loses all attachment for the world, becomes indifferent to sense and acquires concentration. He does not show any of those external signs characterised by tears, trembling or expressions of emotion.

The Dāsya.—"দাস্থে সেবা"

In the Dāsya the devotee offers his service to the Lord of all.

The Sakhya.—"সখ্যে নিঃসম্ভ্রমতা।"

In Sakhya man comes nearer to his god, the distance between the master and servant is removed. One thinks of his god as companion and friend.

The Vātsalya—"বাৎসল্যে স্নেহ"

In Vātsalya a tenderness and affection grows in man's heart towards God. [2]

The Ujjvala or the Madhura. "উজ্জ্বলে স্বাঙ্গসঙ্গদানেন সুখোৎপাদনম্" In Mādhurya man aspires to please his god by offering his body to his service.

[1] In the Charitāmṛta we find the line as

"কৃষ্ণে নিষ্ঠা বুদ্ধি এই শান্তের লক্ষণ"

but here we have followed the text of the Sādhya Sādhan.

[2] The notes on শান্ত, দাস্থ, সখ্য and বাৎসল্য are given in Bengali on this page, the rest I find in Sanskrit in the text.

অথ দাস্যরসঃ—ঈশ্বরঃ প্রভুঃ, সর্ব্বজীবশরণাগতপালকঃ, ভক্তবৎসলঃ ইত্যাদি। গুণঃ কৃষ্ণবিষয়াবলম্বনঃ। আশ্রয়ালম্বনা দাসাঃ চতুর্ব্বিধাঃ। অধিকৃত ভক্তাঃ আশ্রিত ভক্তাঃ পার্ষদা অনুগা চ ইতি।

The various classes of 'Dāsya'

So we come again to Dāsya. God is master—the one refuge of all living beings. He loves those who love Him. These and other qualities of the Lord are to be the constant object of thought. There are four classes of Dāsya, Adhikrita Bhakta, Āçrita Bhakta, Pārsvada Bhakta, Anugā Bhakta. Then follow a defintion of each and illustrations. There are subdivisions of the four main divisions. The Adhikrita Bhaktas are divided into three classes.

শরণ্যাঃ, জ্ঞানিচরাঃ, সেবানিষ্ঠাশ্চ etc. etc.

The classifications grows more and more refined, but we have no space here to enter into the intricacies of these distinction. But these classifications are by no means wiredrawn or merely ingenious. They show the comprehensiveness of a subtle theology, worked out with great insight and observation.

In Chaitanya, love was the fascination that attracted all men. The Vaiṣṇavas of Bengal at a subsequent period struck a new note in their theology. This is first expounded in the works of Rūpa and Sanātana, but the standard vernacular authority for it, is the Chaitanya Charitāmṛta. The sum and substance of their theory worked out in minute detail in the theological works of the later Chaitanya School is that the Lord, who is all beauty, willed to taste his own love and incarnated Himself in Chaitanya. The Gopīs represent the reflex power of the Lord by which He can enjoy his own perfect beauty. There are as many Gopīs as there are emotions in the soul to wellcome Him—the Beloved One. But the greatest of all is Rādhā who lives not for herself but for Him alone. According to these Vaiṣṇavas Chatanya when bewailing his separation from the deity is Rādhā and when he becomes one in his soul with his beloved god in his trances, he is Kṛṣṇa's self. Rādhā and Kṛṣṇa both, are thus incarnated in the person of Chaitanya, while the other Gopīs are incarnated in his followers.

The Chaitanya-cult.

This emotional religion has been expounded, by the followers of Chaitanya in intricate detail, as I have stated. But love is the motto—the root-word of their theology. Every man must offer body and soul to Him and must disdain his personal gratification. He must be prepared to carry out his Lord's will and in doing so must not shrink from any sacrifice. He will worship his image, he must talk of him, he must wreathe flowers for him, he must burn incense and wave the Chāmara in his temple and offer his services day and night to the Lord and to the world as well. Vaiṣṇavism, it must be repeated, is not the religion of the recluse, nor is it a non-proselytising creed. The Vaiṣṇava wants to elevate himself by his communion with the Beloved One, but he does not shut himself in a cell and seek salvation merely for himself. One of the cardinal doctrines of this religion is জীবে দয়া kindness to all living beings. The poet Govinda Dās emphasises this point in the following verse.

Love—the watch-word.

"What shall it avail a man to perform the rites of worship, to kindle the sacrificial fire, to give gift and practise

"কি করিবে পূজা হোমে, দান ব্রত নৈষ্ঠিকে
যদি করুণা নাহি দীনে।"

austerities or even lead a pure life, if he has no compassion for the poor and sorrowful." When Narottama, Çrīnivāsa and Çyamānanda were ordered to travel to Bengal, they expressed their desire to stay at Vṛndāvana and wept openly before the masters at leaving the sacred shrine. But Jīva told them "One of the noblest acts of religion is to give to others all that we possess ourselves." "The works of Rūpa and Sanātana must be circulated in Bengal and interpreted rightly." All personal considerations were thus set aside, and the happiness of other people was made the sole object of the lives of the three worthies. In the interesting dialogue given in Karṇānanda (Chap. IV & V) between Rājā Vīra Hamvīra and Rāma Chandra Kavirāj., there is a minute and detailed elucidation of the principles of the Vaiṣṇava creed. Rāma Chandra describes the true Vaiṣṇava as follows : "Kind without hostile feelings towards any one ; truthful in words, of faultless morals, a master of his passions, pure in heart, humble and doing good to all, quiet and resigned to Kṛṣṇa, without any lust, innocent, sagacious, conqueror of evil passions, living on spare diet, respector of all men, without vanity and entering into the meaning of all things, sympathetic and friendly to all, of a poetical frame of mind, not given to copious speech and always wishing for the company of Vaiṣṇavas"

The moral aspects.

Chaitanya had however described a true Vaiṣṇava in one line. "Know him to be the true Vaiṣṇava at whose very sight the name of Kṛṣṇa rises to the lips."

Bhakti, said Rāmachandra to Vīra Hamvīra, is of two kinds. One is Vaidhī Bhakti or faith which originates from following scriptural rules, some of which are enumerated below :

The rules. 1. To worship Kṛṣṇa and to leave all to his will.

2. Not to make too many disciples.

3. To avoid the company of the ungodly—the Avaiṣṇavas.

4. To avoid reading too many books.

5. To take loss or gain in the same calm spirit.

6. Not to abuse other religions nor the gods worshipped by others.

7. Not to be present where Vaiṣṇavas are abused.

8. Not to listen to village-gossip[1] (This translated into modern language may mean 'not to read news-papers.')

9. To refrain in thought, speech and action from wounding the feelings of all living beings.

10. To remember God's kindness.

11. (*a*) To wordship him.

(*b*) To recite his name.

(*c*) To attempt to realise his love, through Dāsya, Sakhya and by self-dedication.

Many such rules are enjoined by the Vaidhī Bhakti. "But" says Rām Chandra to the enquiring king of Visṇupur "there is a blessed stage which transcends the sphere of all these 'virtuous acts' and is not limited by the scriptures. This is called the 'Rāganugā' or that faith which follows its own course—the stage in which the recollection of the very name of God calls forth tears, the whole body trembles like a leaf, the material loses its grossness, and the body becomes spirit. The reciting of the name creates strange

[1] The word গ্রাম্যবার্ত্তা is also explained as "a talk on sexual matters."

emotions in the soul—they know no bounds and are not limited by the *çāstras*; they even appear ব্যাভিচারি—eccentric. The mouth wants to be multiplied to speak the name, the ears to be a hundred in number to hear the name which maddens the soul. It is a state where consciousness and unconsciousness meet. The thirsty ear knows no satiety in hearing the name recited. One who is in this blessed condition gives up all religious rites prescribed by the Vedās. "How can I speak of it?" said Rāma Chandra (See Karnānanda Chap. V). "The Tilak sign on the forehead indicates the greatest of fortunes at this stage. The name of Kṛṣṇa heard becomes the ornament of the ear, and the recitation of that name gives flow to the speech."

The Japa.

The Japa or the reciting of God's name is enjoined as the first thing to be done as a step towards spiritual advancement. It is merely repeating the name—the meaningless name without associations. The Buddhist of the Mahāyāna schools thought of the void—'শূন্য'. The meaningless name and 'the void' are merely the same thing. Its effect is to purge the mind clear of vain thoughts. Our mind is so full of worldly preoccupations that it may be compared to a garden overgrown with weeds. Before sowing spiritual seeds in it, weeds of worldly thought should be first removed. The reciting of the sacered name will serve that purpose. It will moreover act as the anchor of the mind keeping it fixed on a particular point. A beginner will feel that as soon as he is "occupied with repeating the name" worldly thoughts will come pouring into the soul in abundance. This will sufficiently show in what a thicket of anxieties and vanities and passions he lives. But by striving hard for years, so that no thought may enter the soul at the time of Japa, he will be gradually freed from this obsession. A mental vacuum must be created in order to rouse the dormant spiritual forces of the soul. For in a mind filled with worldly thought, truth will not dawn. Japa is a finer or subtler form of prayer. In prayer one is liable to fall into the errors of one's own thought, whereas "thoughtless" Japa will bring the mind to a higher plane by shutting the doorways on the earth and earthly things. If the mind scales a height by practising concentration through Japa, heaven comes nearer to the view and ultimately the stage comes when the very name of god uttered brings tears to the eyes. It not only gives rise to the holiest of thoughts but creates in the soul a mighty power for working good to the world. But the Vaiṣṇavas says that this should not be spoken before a non-believer. Jadunandana Dās, the author of Karnānanda, regretfully says "The mightiest force is in the name. My wicked mind, woe be to me, had no liking for it". [1]

This difficult spiritual process is not to be adopted by those who do not really feel a longing for the higher life. When Rājā Vīra Hamvīra enacted a law enforcing his subject to repeat the name of God at least a certain number of times a day, he went too far, and so did some of the disciples of Çrīnivāsa as described in the following passage of the Karṇānanda. "In the village of Kānchangoria the disciples of Çrīnivāsa took the vow that they would

[1] "সর্ব্ব শক্তি নামে দিল করিয়া বিভাগ।
আমায় দুর্দ্দৈব নামে নহিল অনুরাগ॥"
Karnānanda by Jadunandana Dās.

repeat the name of God a lakh of times each night. In the day time they did not do so, but in the night they had their hair tied with a twine to the roof of their house and sat up whole night to repeat God's name."[1] They fastened their hair with a twine in order to prevent themselves from falling asleep. If they nodded and became sleepy, their hair would be pulled and they were thus obliged to keep awake all night repeating the name of God a lakh of times.

The attitude of the Vaiṣṇavas was hostile towards the orthodox Hindu community. The biographer of Narottama rejoices that at his birth the Brahmins and Chandāls mixed freely. This sounds the death-knell of caste-distinction so far as the Vaiṣṇava community was concerned. In the Karṇānanda we find that Jadunandana Dās, a Vaidya, cooked the meal and such a good Brahmin as Çrīnivāsa ate from tha plate offered him by the former. Rāma Chandra Kavirāj, a Vaidya, ate from the same plate as Çrīnivāsa, and Jadunandana once asked Çrīnivāsa about the propriety of such conduct. (Karnānanda, Niryās III.)

The antagonism towards the orthodox religion.

Narottama wrote many books describing the principles of the Vaiṣṇavas of his times. Harichandra Ray, the robber chief of Jalandara, converted by Narottama, sat at the feet of his Guru, and received a course of instruction in Vaiṣṇava theology which was embodied in the work known as the Premabhakti Chandrikā, the most popular book of

[1] "কাঞ্চন গড়িয়া গ্রামে প্রভুর ভক্তগণ।
একেক লক্ষ হরিনাম করেন নিয়ম॥
দিবসে না লয় নাম রাত্রি কালে বসি।
কেশে ডোর চালে বাঁধি লয় নাম বসি॥"

Karnānanda, 1st Niryās.

the kind among the lay Vaiṣṇavas. The book, which is of a handy size, was written by Narottama in a single day. It sounds the trumpet of war against orthodoxy. Hari-chandra Ray asked if the Çrāddha ceremony performed by the Hindus was necessary for the salvation of deceased parents. Narottama said, it was not. "If one has" he said, "a true faith in God, that will save his remotest ancestors from hell, but no amount of outward ceremonial will." The Çrāddha ceremony at the death of a man by his nearest surviving kinsman is an imperative duty and indispensible for every Hindu. Narottama said again in answer to another query that it was better that one should meet a snake, a leech or a tiger than keep the company of those who are worshippers of many gods.[1] I quote again from his Premabhakti Chandrikā.

"To keep the company of holy men and offer oneself to the service of Kṛṣṇa, not to worship gods and goddesses, these are the rules to be observed by the Vaiṣṇavas, No other Yoga we recognise than conversation relating to Kṛṣṇa. If there are other ways of Yoga (by physical mortification etc.) abandon them, and offer your service to Kṛṣṇa alone. Visiting shrines and sacred places is only a superstition and unnecessary toil. The highest

[1] "আলিঙ্গনং বরং মন্যে
ব্যাল-ব্যাঘ্র-জলৌকসাং।
ন সঙ্গং শৈলযুক্তানাং
নানাদেবৈকসেবিনাং ॥"

"The Premavilása, the 17th Vilāsa.

bliss we can aspire at, may be found in self-dedication to Kṛṣṇa."[1]

Narottama not only preached this doctrine but by taking Brahmin disciples, being himself a Kāyastha, led the boldest revolt and defiance against popular belief. It is no wonder therefore that he became the one centre of attack from the orthodox community. We find that the image of Chaitanya (Gaura Ray) which he placed in his temple at Kheturi was stolen away by his enemies; and when he was once seriously ill at the house of his Brahmin disciple Gangānārayaṇa Chakravarti, the orthodox community reviled him in the grossest manner. We have noticed how Narasiṁha Ray, Rājā of Pakkapalli, was instigated by the Brahmins to march on a sort of crusade against him. In a manuscript of a theological work of the Sahajiā sect I came across a passage attacking the prevailing system of accepting the family Guru as one's own. The Hindu Çāstras, on no consideration, permits a man to desert his family-Guru. The descendants of the original Guru continue to be the spiritual heads of particular families for all generations to come, irrespective of the personal qualifications that such Gurus may posses. But the passage in question boldly attacks this system and urges upon all to take new Gurus. This is evidently a call to the people of the Hindu community to revolt against their family Gurus and accept Vaiṣṇava Goswāmis

[1] "সাধু সঙ্গ কৃষ্ণ সেবা, না পূজিব দেবী দেবা
যেই ভক্তি পরম কারণ।
ধর্ম্ম কথা শ্রেয়ঃ যোগ, যেবা থাকে অন্য যোগ
ছাড় ভজ গিরিবর ধারী।
তীর্থ যাত্রা পরিশ্রম, কেবল মনের ভ্রম
সর্ব্ব সিদ্ধি গোবিন্দ চরণ॥"

The Prema Bhakti Chandrikā by Narottama Dās.

in their place. Such doctrines were undoubtedly inspired by the teaching of Narottama and other teachers of his school.

Differing from the ideal that had hitherto found favour with the Hindus, viz., that the passions should all be extinguished in order to reach the stage of spiritual bliss, the Vaiṣṇavas urged that the passions were natural forces and therefore, instead of being extinguished, they should be utilised for spiritual purposes. Says the Premabhakti Chandrikā.

The passions are of great service.

"The passions of the soul are to be employed for service to Kṛṣṇa. লোভ (greediness) which is an evil passion, is not so in itself, it becomes a holy passion if it has for its object a communion with Kṛṣṇa. মোহ or grief may thus be purified if it possesses the soul when it loses the sight of Kṛṣṇa; মদ or mad attachment of the soul (for the world) would be praiseworthy if it seeks its fulfilment in the devotion to the Lord. Flowing in material channels they bring misfortunes in their train, but in the heart of a truly spiritual man, the so called evil passions only bring ardour to the soul and heighten its real felicities. Guard yourself against all evil doing. Do not fall a prey to earthly greediness or hankering after fame or popular admiration ; but let Kṛṣṇa be all to you."[1]

[1] লোভ সাধু সঙ্গে হরি কথা।
মোহ ইষ্ট লাভ বিনে, মদ কৃষ্ণ গুণ গানে,
নিযুক্ত করিবে যথা তথা ॥
অন্যথা সতত কাম, অনর্থাদি যার নাম,
ভক্তি পথে দেই সদা ভঙ্গ।
কি বাধা করিতে পারে, কাম ক্রোধ সাধ করে,
সাধু জনার যদি হয় সঙ্গ ॥
না কর অসৎ চেষ্টা, লাভ পূজা প্রতিষ্ঠা,
সার কর গোবিন্দ চরণ ॥

A list of works.

There are innumerable works which set forth these and similar doctrines written in the middle and the latter part of the 17th century. The most important ones amongst them are mentioned in the following list.

1. Svarupa Varṇana.
2. Vrindāvana Dhyana.
3. Guru Çikṣyā Samvāda.
4. Rupa Manjarī.

} by Kṛṣṇa Dās.

5. Prārthanā.
6. Rasa Bhakti Laharī.
7. Rāga Ratnāvalī.
8. Siddhināma.
9. Ātma Sādhanā.
10. Amṛtā Rasa Chandrikā.
11. Premabhakti Chandrikā.
12. Sāratsāra Kārikā.
13. Bhakti Latikā.
14. Sādhya Prema Chandrikā.
15. Rāga Mātā.
16. Svarupa Kalya Latikā.
17. Tatva Nirupaṇa.
18. Rasa Bhakti Chandrikā.
19. Upasanā Patala.
20. Ānanda Bhairava.

} by Narottama Dās.

21. Ānanda Laharī—by Mathura Dās.
22. Dinamaṇi Chandrodaya—by Manohara Dās.
23. Sidhānta Chandradoya.
24. Amṛta Rasa Vallī.
25. Vaiṣṇavāmṛta.
26. Sāratsāra Kārikā.
27. Sādhanā Upāya.
28. Rāsa Ratnāvalī.

} by Mukunda Dās.

29. Jogāgama by Jagat Kṛṣṇa Dās.
30. Tattva Kathā—by Jadunath Dās.
31. Bhanda Tattva Sāra—by Rasamaya Dās.
32. Rati Vilāsa—by Rasik Dās.
33. Sahaja Tattva—by Radhā Ballav Dās.
34. Dīpakojjala—by Vaṁçī Dās.
35. Nikunja Rahasya—by Vaṁçī Dās.
36. Sidharta Karīkā.
37. Vivarta Vilāsa. ... ... by one who subscribes himself as a disciple of Kṛṣna Dās Kavirāj.

(b) The degeneracy of the Buddhists and the recruiting of Vaiṣṇava converts from their ranks.

The Vaiṣṇavas of Bengal are divided into many sects of which the Sahajiyās possess an extensive literature in the vernacular. This sect comprises a vast body of men chiefly recruited from the lowest castes, who in all probability once belonged to the Holy Order of the Buddhists, but became fallen in popular estimation and outcasted when Hinduism revived and drove Buddhism out of Bengal. The Buddha was not willing to admit women to His Holy Order. Twice did his favourite disciple Ānanda plead in behalf of Mahāprajāpati, the Buddha's aunt, who wanted admittance to the Buddhist Order—then known as the Satdharma. Though Mahāprajāpati was distinguished for the piety of her life and for her high character and had brought up the Buddha as a child, twice did the latter decline to open the portals of his holy Order to her as a matter of principle. And when he could not resist the strong appeal of the venerable lady as she approached a third time and Ānanda again pleaded for her, the Enlightened One yielded but with an warning and prophecy. He said "Just as the insect *çvetasthikā* destroys a harvest, so will the Satdharma, oh Ānanda, be destroyed if women are allowed to live in the monasteries."[1] Aware of the consequences that the monks and nuns living together in a monastery might ultimately produce, he enacted sound but severe laws to avoid as far as possible the evil that he apprehended. Some of these laws are quoted below:

The Buddha's reluctance to admit women into monasteries.

The strict rules.

1. If a Bhikṣu (Buddhist hermit) without the express sanction and permission of the Sangha (Buddhist church) takes upon himself the task of instructing the Bhikṣuṇīs (Buddhist nuns) he shall be held guilty and must subject himself to penance.

2. If a Bhikṣu, unless by special appointment (when the Bhiksuṇī is seriously ill and cannot attend instructions in the monastery) goes to the dwelling place of a Bhiksuṇī to give instruction, he shall be held guilty and must be subjected to penance.

3. If a Bhikṣu, even with the permission of the Sangha goes to give instructions to Bhikṣuṇīs, after sunset, he shall be held guilty and made liable to punishment.

4. If a Bhikṣu, except by special appointment (such as while travelling by a path full of danger, where it

[1] Vinaya Pitaka, Chulla Vagga. 10, 1, 1—5 and 10, 1, 6.

becomes necessary to go armed) be found to make any long journey, or even from one village to another, with a Bhikṣuṇī he shall be liable to punishment.

5. If a Bhikṣu except for the purpose of crossing a river by a ferry-boat be found in the same boat with a Bhikṣuṇī either going up or down the stream, he must be punished.

6. If a Bhikṣu is found to sit by the side of a Bhikṣuṇī in a solitary place, he shall be liable to punishment.[1]

As a result of these healthy rules and strict supervision, some of the women in Buddhist monsteries rose to distinction by the purity of their lives and by devotion to religion. But gradually relaxation came and the free mixing of men and women brought on its inevitable result, even as the great Buddha had foreseen. The Buddhist monks and nuns used to shave their heads and were called Neḍā and Neḍies—the shaven men and women. This grew to be a contemptuous epithet in course of time, as the standard of morality sank low in the monasteries. Yet the teachings of a great moral religion still sounded in the ear of these people and their fall was not like that of ordinary men and women. They strove hard to keep a high ideal in sight, when the sexual feelings were found irresistible they tried to elevate them by proclaiming that sexual love was the door-way to salvation. This was the Sahaja or the natural path. We find Chaṇḍīdās to be the greatest exponent of this creed of love in the 14th century. The romantic love between unwedded persons was extolled by the Sahajiyās and elevated into a religion. We know that love between two unwedded person was

The Sahjiyā Cult.

[1] Vinaya Pitaka, Pati Mokkha and Sutta Viranga, Pāchittiya, 21-30.

also a religious creed in Europe in the medieval ages, but we have it on the authority of Hallam that this love while professing idealistic and platonic dogmas, degenerated into the ordinary vices that human flesh is heir to. The great historian thinks it possible that these courts of love in Europe may have been directly imported from Asiatic races whose influence permeated the atmosphere of Europe in those days. [1] Olivier de Magny (d. 1560) and Louise Labe (b. 1526) were poets and lovers in France, in whose writtings the lady is given far the higher rank. [2] We find the same thing in the poems of Sahajiyās. I have dealt with this matter at some length in my History of Bengali Language and Literature and in my Introduction to my "Typical Selections."

Vaiṣṇavism opened its doors to the outcast and to the Neḍa Neḍies—the popular nickname of the Buddhist Bhikṣus and Bhikṣuṇīṣ. Vīra Chandra, son of Nityānanda, first admitted them to Vaiṣṇava society, and as a token of gratitude for this gracious act they used to hold at Khardaha an annual Melā or fair which grew to be one of historic importance. I have already stated that this famous fair ceased six years ago, owing to financial difficulties. These Bhikṣus and Bhikṣuṇīs used to live promiscuously and indulge in debauchery. The Vaiṣṇava Gurus enforced marriage amongst them. Widow-remarriage and even divorce were permitted. Vaiṣṇavism improved their morals and brought a disintegrated crew, sunk in vicious degeneracy, within the bonds of discipline and order. If their social lives are still

[1] See "the Student's Middle ages" by Hallam pp. 580—582.

[2] See "the Franch Literature" in the Encyclopædia.

spotted by immorality, this only proves that the process of reformation is still unfinished.

Parakiyā or love for a person other than husband or wife is merely a symbol for sacrifice in the cause of religion. Chaitanya emphasised this point repeatedly and his great followers all echoed his teaching. Chaitanya knew that the age was full of vices which romantic sexual love, the prevailing practice of the Sahajiyās, had brought on, and he was rightly very strict with those who showed any imprudent tenderness towards young and beautiful women. We have shown elsewhere that his attitude towards the junior Haridās was not only severe but verged on cruelty. He knew the vicious weakness of the age, and had no faith in the romance of love preached with so much eloquence, but which mostly led to gross immorality. "These people" (he said) "are mad after love, but they know not what true love is. It is only when the sexual instinct disappears and men and women lose the attraction for each other, due merely to sex, that true love will grow."[1]

Love in the ordinary sense is a narrow view of a universal truth. Chaṇḍī Dās says that spiritual love grows in one who begins by loving an individual, but Chaitanya would not admit that. Probably he apprehended that if once romance in ordinary love was given a place in religious instructions, it must produce disastrous evils in society in the long run. The Sahajiyās, however,

[1] "প্রেম প্রেম বলে লোকে প্রেম জানে কিবা।
প্রেম করা নাহি হয় রমণীর সেবা॥
অভেদ পুরুষ নারী যখন জানিবে।
তখন প্রেমের তত্ত্ব হৃদয়ে উদিবে॥

Kadcha by Govinḍa Dās.

took Chaṇḍīdās to be their great authority, and went so far as to say that love for God was impossible unless a man or a woman, as the case might be, was loved with the whole soul's ardour. They invented stories to prove that Rūpa and Sanātana and even the venerable Kṛṣnadās Kavirāj and the stern ascetic Raghunātha Dās passionately loved women *in their hearts* and thus fitted themselves for tasting God's love. [1] The literature of the Sahajiyās is almost criminal in such sweeping allegations, utterly base and false. One of them goes so far as to say that a widow should treat her Guru as her husband, nay every Brahmin, every Vaiṣṇava or Sādhu that may come to her should receive the same attention. It is only by offering her whole hearted service to them, that she may expect to find a place in Kṛṣṇa's heaven. If she does not do so she is a sinner.

(c) *Jnanādi Sādhana—A curious Medley of Buddhistic and Vaiṣṇava Creeds.*

That this Sahajiyā creed is a remnant of the Buddhist doctrines, under a thin and superficial veneer of Vaiṣṇava faith, is obvious from the following interesting passage and a dialogue between Teacher and An inquierer as introduced in a Sahajiyā work.

"The child, as soon as he is born, forgets the true nature of the soul, and is caught in the snares of illusion created by the false Brahmins of India, and becomes accustomed later on to their ways of thought, Under their

[1] See "Typical Selections from old Bengali Literature," Part II p. 1650

false advice he takes the sacred thread at the dawn of youth, and goes on performing evening and morning rites as prescribed in the Vedās. Then in the hope of obtaining four-fold blessings, viz : spiritual rewards, wealth, satisfaction of desires, and emancipation from earthly bonds, he goes on praying to God, and worshipping Him under the instructions of his religious preceptor. But he never sees the God he worships. He reads in his false and unreliable Çāstras that Kṛṣṇa dwells in the so-called heaven called the Vaikunṭha, and never having seen his Deity he makes his image in stone and clay and worships it. The false Brahmins tell him on the authority of the false Vedās, that if he can perform the Açvamedha and other sacrifices and make gifts of cows (to the Brahmins), he will have a place in heaven after death. He does as he is bidden, but not knowing the true nature of God and merely performing the acts recommended in the false Vedās he does not advance a step, but suffers the repeated agonies of births and deaths by passing through a never-ceasing cycle of births.[1]

"The Sādhu asks the Inquirer, 'How do you obtain a knowledge of the Deity?

"The Inquirer says, 'I obtain a knowledge of my god Kṛṣṇa through my mind.

"The Sādhu, 'When the mind acts in concord with the five senses, such as the ear, the eye, the tongue etc., then only can it perceive sounds, object of sight and taste etc. When the mind does not join with the senses, it cannot perceive the external objects. Tell me then how

[1] The Buddhistic theory of transmigration of soul is here emphasised

without the relative action of the five senses, can you perceive God by your mind alone ?

"The Inquirer 'I now understand that without the help of the five senses the mind alone can have no conception of the Deity. I understand it quite well now but beg to submit my reasons here. When the mind acts with the help of the ear, it becomes cognisant of the sound which is the virtue of the sky. So through the ear the mind cannot realise God. When the mind acts with the help of the skin it becomes aware of touch which is the virtue of air. But this does not give one any conception of the Deity. And so on. I now fully understand that the five senses cannot help in the realization of Divine quality. I therefore feel that I am without any knowledge of God and that to me therefore the existence of God is unreal.

"The Sādhu 'If a child after coming to this earth from his mother's womb has never heard a sound owing to his deafness, can he read the letters Ka, Kha, Ga, Gha etc., when he is in his 25th year ? Or can he call his father and mother by the usual terms 'papa' and 'mamma' ? I also want to know from you whether a man who is born blind can contemplate the dark blue colour ascribed to Kṛṣṇa, which, as they say, is like that of the newly formed cloud ?'

"The Inquirer 'The man who is born deaf and has never heard Ka, Kha, Ga Gha etc. and 'papa' and 'mamma' uttered by others can never read Ka, Kha, Ga, Gha, as we do, or call his parents 'papa' and 'mamma' like us. And one who has never seen any object of dark-bule colour like that of a newly formed cloud can never contemplate the dark blue colour attributed to Kṛṣṇa."

"The Sādhu 'How then did you say that without the help of the senses one could realize Kṛṣṇa, the god of the universe? A man born deaf cannot read the letters, nor call his parents and friends by the terms by which they are called, and a man born blind cannot contemplate the dark blue colour of Kṛṣṇa like that of a new-formed cloud. So one who has not a true knowledge of the Deity within him cannot realise God by his mind alone which is the receptacle of the impressions produced by the five senses. Now do you tell me whether you do possess a knowledge of God or not."

"The Inquirer—'I am without any knowledge of God. I never heard God speak to me, nor ever felt His touch on my person, nor did I touch the food partaken first by Him. My nose never smelt the sweet scent emanating from His person. And now I understand that the existence of Kṛṣṇa is unreal to me.'

"The Sādhu—'You had formerly heard that tha Vedās originated from the mouth of God and that in them is written what is good and what is evil. Tell me if you consider the Vedās to be true.'

"The Inquirer—'As Kṛṣṇa, the God of the Universe, is now unreal to me, the Vedās which are said to have emanated from Him are necessarily unreal. So are the definitions of vice and virtue given in them. It is written in the Çāstras of the Brahmins themselves that vice and virtue are unreal and so are father and mother, and one's own self, and all that one says and does. Now I shall be silent and speak no more. I only want to hear what your Holiness will be pleased to say."

"The Sādhu—'Tell me when does a man become silent for ever in this world."

"The Inquirer—'When a man dies he becomes silent for ever."

"The Sādhu—'As you profess yourself to be silent, tell me whether you are living or dead?'

"The Inquirer—'I have not been able to realise God by my five senses, so you may take me for dead."

"The Sādhu—'Now the life of your ignorance is dead, and now forget for ever those false doctrinces which you read in your false Çāstras. You will now be born anew with true knowledge which I am now going to give you." [1]

The attacks on Brāhmanism and even on the worship of Kṛṣṇa, are clearly put and need no comments. The wonder is that the Sahajiyā preacher calls himself a Vaiṣṇava, though he preaches the doctrines of Buddhism.

(c) *Christianity and Vaiṣṇavism.*

Various arguments have been advanced by some of the European scholars who have tried to trace the legend of Kṛṣṇa's childhood as described in the Bhāgavata to that of Christ as related at least in the earlier chapters of St. Mathew's gospel. The points of similarity may thus be summarised :—

Similarity between Vaiṣṇavism and Christianity.

1. The striking similarity of the names—Kṛṣṇa and Christ.

[1] I have inserted the elaborate discourse from which the above extract is taken with some omissions in my "Typical selections from old Bengali Literature" published by the University of Calcutta. (Part II. pp. 1630-1637). The whole of the dialogue, which will be found interesting from many points of view, is contained in a Ms. copied in the year 1750 A.D. which is now in the Library of the University. As the cataloguing of the old Bengali Mss. belonging to that Library has not been yet finished, I cannot give the number and other particulars about this Ms.

2. Herod massacres innocent children and Kaṁsa massacres children at Mathurā.

3. Kṛṣṇa as a baby is taken to Gokula and Christ carried to Egypt.

4. St. John, the Baptist, of supernatural birth, comes as fore-runner of Christ and so does Vala Rāma as the fore-runner of Kṛṣṇa.

5. Dr. Lorinser in his German version of the Bhāgavata Gitā points out many coincidences of the Vaiṣṇava tenets with those of the New Testament, and Mr. Growse says that "the Harivaṁsa which is possibly as old as any of the Vaiṣṇava Purāṇas was certainly written by a stranger to the country of Braja, and not only so, but it further shows distinct traces of a southern origin, as in its description of the exclusively Dakṣini festival, the Punjal; and it is only in the south of India that a Brahmin would be likely to meet with Christian traditions. There the church has had a continuous, though feeble and struggling existence, from the very earliest Apostolic times down to the present, and it must be admitted that there is no intrinsic improbability in supposing that the narrative of the gospel may have exercised on some Hindu sectarian a similar influence to that which the Pentateuch and the Talmud had on the founder of Islām. Nor are the differences between the authentic legends of Judaism and the perversions of them that appear in the Kuran very much greater than those which distinguish the life of Christ from the life of Kṛṣṇa." Attempts have also been made to prove that the Çvetadwipa or 'White man's island' from which Nārada, the earliest Vāiṣṇava apostle, is said to have introduced the Vāiṣṇava tenets of salvation by faith, is identical with Christian Europe. Some

scholars have held that even the Panchādhāya of the Bhāgavata which describes Kṛṣṇa's amours with the Gopīs echoes the impassionate and glowing language of 'the Song of Songs' which is Solomon's.

Mr. Growse says in reference to the first argument :— "It is absolutely certain that the name of Kṛṣṇa, however late the full development of the legendary cycle, was celebrated throughout India long bofore the Christian era. Christos (Christ) is a Greek as Kṛṣṇa a Sanskrit formation, and the roots of the words are entirely different."[1]

In regard to the history of the Harivaṁça being written by one who was a stranger to Braja, four arguments are put forward to support it, showing some topographical discrepancies in the account of Vṛndāvana given in that book. Such errors, it is urged, could not have been made by one who had visited the country himself. They shew that the earliest Vāiṣṇava authority came from Southern India where Chritian influence was already at work.

1. Kṛṣṇa and Vala Rāma, it is mentioned in the Harivaṁça, were brought up at a spot on the bank of the Jumnā near the hill Govardhana (Canto 61). Now that hill is 15 miles from the river.

2. Gokula and Vṛndāvana are several miles further distant from the ridge and on the other side of the Jumnā, though the two places according to the earlier authorities were described as on the same bank of the river.

3. Tālavana is described as lying on the north of Govardhana (Canto 79). It is south-east of that hill.

[1] Growse's Mathura (1882), pp. 68-69.

4. Bhāndirvana is represented in the Harivaṁça as being on the same side of the river as the Kāliya Damana-Ghats. but now it is nearly opposite to it.

The four arguments will, I hope, be covered by one reply.

The course of a river so often shifts in India that these discrepancies become inevitable. Nadia, the birth place of Chaitanya, and Nadia as it is now, offer far greater dissimilarities to the puzzled pilgrims who visit the place after having read the biographies of Chaitanya, and yet it is a matter of the lapse of only 400 years. Those places which are represented in well-authenticated biographies written by the children of the soil as lying on the other bank of the Ganges are now not so, but on the same bank. When a river changes its course near a holy city, many of its sacred spots are washed away and form the bed of the river, but the priestly class cannot afford to lose their income. They get hold of the images and sacred relics and select a new part of the city to lodge them in, and mark it with well defined boundaries. They preserve the sacredness of the shrine and their own sources of income by continuing to name the new place after the old name of the shrine.

In regard to some of the festivities which are now prevalent in Southern India, there is no historical proof to show that they were not once performed in Northern India.

Regarding the coincidence of events between the lives of Kṛṣṇa and Christ, much undue emphasies has been put on them. We hold with Mr. Growse who says 'But after all, all that can be urged is that there is no historial basis for the supposed connection between the two narratives, which would probably never have been suggested but for the similarity of the names (Kṛṣṇa and Christ)."

Much stress has also been laid on the ecclesiastical tradition that the gospel which St. Thomas, the apostle, brought with him in India was that of St. Mathew and that when his relics were discovered, a copy of it was found to have been buried with him. But Eusebius disputes the point and holds that the apostle who visited India was not Thomas, but Bartholmew. The Lalita Vistāra, which is anterior in date to the Christian tradition, relates the Buddha's victory over the assults of the Evil One, and this is exactly parallelled by the story of the Temptation in the 4th Chap. of St. Mathew's Gospel. Mr. Growse holds that this is merely a chance coincidence and that "all the supposed connections between Christ and Kṛṣṇa is equally imaginery."

Though we dispute any wholesale importation of a foreign legend and its incorporation with one of the great Indian religious cults, it seems probable that in the natural process of evolution of such religions, certain ideas and stories may have been adopted from foreign sources. For in the Indian atmosphere the seed of any religious thought, if it carried any worth of its own, was not allowed to be lost, but generated and developed and became a part and parcel of one or the other of the great religions which prevailed at the different epochs of Indian history. These religions have thus never been allowed to be fossilised but fresh life has been infused into them without their losing the stamp of Indian character and individuality.

Whether the Kṛṣṇa legend is indebted to the Gospel in any of its minute features cannot easily be determined now. But there is such a strange coincidence between the various stages of mysticism, both Christian and Vaiṣṇava, that we are naturally led to believe that there was an interchange of ideas between Asia and Europe in spiritual matters on this point at least. India has been the soil of mystic ideas. They are not matters of bygone interest in this land. From time immemorial visions have been beheld by the Sādhus, truths have been revealed to the soul earnestly engaged in the contemplation of the Deity, and people have never lost their faith in such revelations and mystic visions. In view of these facts we consider this country to be the original home of mysticism, though it is not improbable that some special features of it may have, been from age to age, imbibed from her contact with similarly endowed seers of other countries, as it is also probable that from India herself, such ideas may have floated afar, influencing the spiritual atmosphere of foreign lands fit to accept them.

The word Çvetadwipa has been proved to mean Christian Europe by Col. Wilfold in Asiatic Researches (vol. 9), and many other scholars have accepted this meaning of the word. Growse admits this sense of the word in his celebrated work "Mathura District Memoirs."

Now the Chaitanya Bhāgavata by Vṛndāvana Dās, written in the year 1573 A.D., mentions in more than one place[1] that among those who admired Chaitanya and joined his Kīrtana processions, there were some people who belonged to the Çvetadwīpa. The writer says that it is a marvel that such people should be attracted by the Kīrtana and join it. The anecdote refers to the time between 1508 and 1511, and there is no doubt that the

[1] The Madhya Khanda, Chap. XXIII, and the Antya Khanda Chap. IX.

European Christians had already visited India and built their church in Bengal by the time, not to speak of those erected on the Malabar coast in the early centuries of the Christian era.

The Chaitanya Bhāgavata, as I have already stated, is one of the standard biographies of Chaitanya and seldom errs in its ordinary historical accounts.

INDEX

A

		Page
Abdur Navi	...	17
Abhinava Jay Deva	...	2, 7
Abhisara	...	204, 205
Achyuta	...	162
Acvamedha	...	239
Adhikrita Bhakti	...	222
Adikecava	...	43
Adilila	...	59
Adimalla	...	108
Advaita	...	15, 21, 51, 69, 78, 79, 90
Advaitavada	...	47
Agra	...	24, 52, 107
Ajodhya	...	102
Akbar	...	26, 48
Akrura	...	162
Alamganj	...	181
Allahabad	...	91, 97, 102
Amara	...	28
Ambika	...	102
Ambika Kalna	...	161
Amritalal Sen	...	75
Amṛta Rasa Chandrika		232
Amṛta Rasa valli	...	232
Ananda	...	233, 234
Ananda Devi	...	81
Anandalatika	...	81
Anandamahodidhi	...	36
Anandananda	...	162
Ananda Vṛindavan Champu		74
Annakuta hill	...	20
Antalila	...	59
Anuragavalli	...	23, 25, 178
Arabic	...	28
Arati	...	149, 150
Arura Leigh	...	196
Atmaram Das	...	
Atmā Sādhana	...	
Aufrecht Prof.	...	2, 4
Aurangzeb	...	17

B

		Page
Backergunj	...	28
Bagbazar	...	71
Bagdi	...	108
Baikuntha Chakravarty		75
Balaram Das	...	215, 216
Balasore	...	50
Ballava Bhatta	...	61
Beluchar	...	156
Bamciciksha	...	68
Bamci Das	...	182
Bankura	...	111
Bartholmew	...	246
Beatric	...	216
Benares	...	2, 29, 42, 61, 91, 96, 178
Bengali	...	52, 58, 81, 85
Benkata	...	102
Berhampur	...	178
Berakuli	...	181
Bhagavatamṛta	...	38
Bhagavan Das	...	53
Bhavabhuti	...	209
Bhagvata	...	13, 35, 38, 47, 50, 77, 88, 89, 91, 115, 116, 117, 160, 242
Bhagvatakumar Castri		182
Bhagyavati	...	182
Bhakti	...	21, 57, 117, 148
Bhakti-castras	...	42
Bhakti-cult	...	60, 148
Bhakti Latika	...	232
Bhakta Mala	...	52, 54, 55, 56
Bhaktirasamṛta Sindhu		103, 159, 191
Bhaktisindhu	...	55
Bhaktiratnakara	...	14, 43, 68, 86, 113, 121, 122,
Bhandirvana	...	16, 245
Bharajit	...	161
Bhramara Gita	...	122
Bhugarbha	...	55, 58, 59
Birbhum	...	160, 212
Bonaparte	...	189
Brahmin	...	38, 49, 50, 117, 118, 125, 126, 137, 138, 140, 150, 151, 152, 153, 156, 164, 165, 194, 195, 198, 201, 230, 238, 239
Braja	...	244
Brajamandala	...	17
Brhmabaivarta Purana		54
Browning	...	195
Buddha	...	93, 94, 234, 235

PAGE.

Buddhism ... 164, 165
Buddhist ... 226, 233, 234, 235, 238
Buddhist Bhikhunis 164, 234, 235, 236
Buddhist Bhikhus ... 164, 234, 235, 236
Buddhistic thought ... 36
Budhuipada ... 174, 175
Burdwan ... 13, 49, 50, 62, 76, 146, 172, 212

C

Cachi ... 66, 68, 88
Cakta creed ... 199
Calcutta ... 71, 152, 164
Cankhachuda ... 31
Cankhachudavadha 31
Canta ... 220, 221
Car Festivity ... 12, 60
Castra ... 126, 230, 239
Catherine ... 184
Cheta Deviha ... 243, 247
Chaitanya Bhagvata 60, 62, 67, 74, 76, 77, 79, 247, 248
Chaitanya Cataka ... 74
Chaitanya-cult ... 163
Chaitanya Chandrodoya ... 73
Chaitanya Charit ... 70, 73
Chaitanya Charitamrta ... 30, 31, 32, 36 38, 51, 62, 63, 65, 67, 70, 74, 77, 78, 105, 111, 220, 222
Chaitannya Chattaraj 160
Chaitanya Das ... 72
Chaitanaya mangala 67, 77, 80, 81, 82
Chakandhi ... 87
Chandal ... 228
Chandi Das .. 9, 69, 129, 133, 146, 160, 187, 212, 235, 237, 238
Chandra Cekhara Acharya 99
Chandrakanta Nayapanchanana ... 152
Chand Roy ... 135, 146, 149, 184, 203.

PAGE.

Chandravali ... 31
Chandravalililabha ... 31
Charles V ... 189
Chataka hills ... 61
Chenwa ... 101
Chhakari Chatto ... 182
Chota Nagpur ... 107, 108
Chiranjiva Sen ... 198
Christ ... 184, 189, 193, 242, 245, 246
Christianity ... 242
Christian Europe ... 243
Christian Scripture 188
Christos ... 244
Civa ... 189
Civacharan Ciromoni 152
Civananda ... 65, 71
Civa Sima, ... 2, 4
Craddha ... 229
Cridama ... 189
Cridas ... 200
Cridhara ... 117
Crikhanda ... 65, 88, 90, 174, 178, 209, 215
Crinivasa ... 15, 39, 43, 44, 84, 85, 86, 87, 89, 90, 91, 92, 95, 100, 119, 105, 114, 115, 116, 117, 118, 120, 121, 122, 123, 124, 125, 128, 134, 147, 148, 150, 151, 155, 156, 157, 158, 159, 160, 170, 171, 172, 173, 175, 176, 198, 199, 227, 228
Criparvata 21
Crivasa ... 24, 65, 66, 75, 87, 184
Cromwell 189
Cudra ... 125, 152
Cupid 131
Cuttock 197
Cyama Das 62
Cyamadas Acharya ... 44
Cyamali 195
Cyamananda ... 15, 84, 101, 103, 105, 107, 124, 132, 134, 161, 162, 163, 178, 181, 224.
Cyāmsundara Ray ... 166, 167

D

PAGE.

Dadikhanda 79
Daksini 243
Damdora 71
Damodora 201
Dandakecwara 101
Darbhanga 202
Dasya ... 222, 225
Dean Inge 159
Deccan 60
Dehanirupana 81
Delhi 136
Denur 23
Devidas Kirtaniya 128
Dewali 115
Dhananjaya Vidyanivasa ... 87
Dharendra 161
Dharmamangala 116
Dikprakacika 38
Dikvijayi 46
Dinamani Chandrodaya ... 232
Dipokojjala 233
Dolonga 163
Drupadi 157
Dukhi ... 101, 104, 105
Durgama Sangamani ... 43
Durgapuja 136
Durllavasara 81
Dwaraka 102

E

Eastern Bengal 23
Eastern Bengal State Railway ... 74
East India 2
Edwin Arnold, Sir 9
Egara Sindūra 44
Europe 184

F

Fakir 166
Fateyabad 28
Faujdar 136

G

Galhad 189
Ganadvecadīpika 36
Gadadhara ... 22, 78, 80, 89

PAGE.

Gakula 244
Ganeca 189
Gamvila 127
Ganganarayan Chakravarty ... 126, 127, 154, 156
Gangadas Pandit 23
Ganges ... 68, 87, 90, 152, 182, 245
Gaudiya Vaisnava 9
Gaur ... 1, 26, 27, 28, 40, 96, 109, 184
Gaurachuḍa 99
Gauranga 97
Gourangapriya 157
George Grierson, Sir ... 2
Gaura Roy 149
Gouridas 82
Gouridas Pandit 100
Gauritirtha Vihar 31
Gaya ... 78, 88, 102
Gitagovinda 9
Gitavali 160
Gokulchandra Goswami ... 156
Gopala 19
Gopal Bhatta ... 37, 38, 44, 57, 58, 59, 85, 86, 106, 111, 158
Gopal Champu 43
Gopal Dās 157
Gopal Micra 128
Gopalpur ... 94, 110, 157
Gopal Singha, Raja... ... 52
Gopinath Pattanayaka ...
Gopiballabh Dās 181
Gorokh Dās 53
Gostha ... 188, 189, 191, 194, 195
Gouradvar ... 135, 136, 140
Gourangavallabh 129
Gour Charit Chintāmani ... 178
Govardhana 244
Govardhana hill 22
Govinda 180
Govinda Dās ... 44, 53, 197, 198, 199, 202–208, 215, 216, 223
Govindaji 128
Govindalīlamṛta 63
Grammar 115
Growse ... 18, 52, 53, 54, 100, 244, 245

H

	Page.
Hallam ...	... 236
Hamsaduta ...	35, 160
Hamvira ...	... 109
Haribhaktivilāsa ...	36, 37, 57, 111
Harichandra ...	126, 156
Haricharan Dās ...	... 120
Haridās ...	... 78
Harihara ...	... 27
Harināmāmṛta Vyākarana	... 42
Harinarayana Vicārada	... 28
Harivamsa ...	243, 244
Haṣtināpur ...	... 102
Hemlata Devi ...	64, 112, 160
Hercules ...	... 216
Hindi ...	... 205
Hindu ...	37, 38, 53, 152, 157, 228, 231
Hinduism ...	... 233
Historical and Ethnological aspect of the Burdwan district	108
History of Bengali Language and Literature ...	171, 176, 178, 182, 193, 211, 217
History of Mathurā ..	52, 100
Holy Grail ...	... 184
Hṛdaychaitanya ...	101, 161
Hugli College ...	... 182
Husen Sāhā ...	... 29

I

Içana ...	90, 135
Içan Nāgara ...	... 23
Içani ...	... 162
Içwari ...	... 157
India ...	16, 78, 93, 102 111, 122, 151, 211, 238
Indus ...	... 102
Iswara Puri ...	21, 78

J

	Page.
Jaçoda ...	113, 189, 192
Jadunandan Dās ...	63, 64, 150, 177, 209, 227, 228
Jadunāth Dās ...	... 209
Jagai ...	78, 136
Jagannāth ...	12, 28
Jagat Bandhu Bhadra	... 212
Jagat Guru ...	... 27
Jagat Kṛṣṇa Dās ...	... 233
Jahnavi ...	... 90
Jahnavi Devī ...	128, 172
Jaipur ...	... 180
Jajigrām ...	90, 147
Jalandara ...	... 228
Jamunā ...	16, 17, 18, 19, 132, 213, 215, 216
Jasodālāl Talukdār...	169, 173
Jatilā ...	... 207
Jayadeva ...	1, 2, 3, 6. 9, 160 209
Jayānanda ...	7, 12
Jaymangala ...	... 90
Jaymontapa ...	... 163
Jerusalem ...	... 18
Jessore ...	... 23
Jhamatpur ...	... 62
Jharikpanda ...	... 108
Jīva Goswami ...	10, 29, 32, 34, 38, 41—44, 46, 47, 54, 55, 58, 92, 100, 102, 103, 105—107, 113, 119, 155, 157, 176, 224
Jīvan ...	49, 50
Jñana Dās ...	15, 213
Jogāgam ...	233
John (St. the Baptist)	... 243
Jordan ...	... 18
Judaism ...	... 243
Jugala Kishore ...	... 54

K

Kaçināth Tarkabhushan	... 152
Kalamar Gāon ...	... 50
Kālī ...	11, 143, 144
Kālidaha Ghāt ...	... 52
Kalī Dās ...	... 35
Kālidās Chotto ...	.. 151
Kālī Worship ...	... 12
Kālkut ...	... 81
Kalnā ...	... 161
Kalyan Dās ...	... 53

PAGE.

Kamalā Devī 44
Kamalā Kar 81
Kāmrūpa 44
Kañchangonā 200
Kanchanlatika Devī ... 160
Kanchdāpara ... 71, 74
Kapuri ... 51, 52
Karauli 52
Karcha ... 11, 67, 71
Karnananda ... 64, 68, 112, 148, 158, 171, 174, 175, 176, 197, 200, 226, 227, 228
Katlu Khan 109
Kātwa ... 90, 209, 212
Kavīkarnapura ... 72, 74, 85
Kavīvidyapati 29
Kayastha ... 125, 127, 138, 140, 150, 156, 178, 201, 230
Keçava Devī 17
Keçava Kāçmiri ... 78, 87
Khaḍdaha ... 163, 164, 166, 167
Kharda 90
Kheturi .. 74, 94, 95, 124, 125, 127, 134, 140, 141, 145' 149, 153, 154, 155, 156, 161, 202, 203, 209, 215, 230
Kirtaniya ... 59, 191, 194, 195, 196
Kirtaniya Gokula Dās 130
Kogram ... 81, 82
Krama Sandarbha 42
Kṛṣṇa Dās ... 48, 50, 52, 55, 56, 58, 59, 62, 64, 65, 70, 74' 77, 95, 104, 105
Kṛṣṇa Karnamṛta 43
Kṛṣṇanda Datta ... 94, 96
Kṛṣṇanda Roy 141
Kṛṣṇapriya Devī 160
Kṛṣṇavallabha ... 114, 115, 116
Kṛṣṇer Janmatithi 35
Ksettrī 51
Kshīrod Chandra Rāy Chowdhiri ... 75, 197
Kulin ... 44, 173

PAGE.

Kumara Devī 28
Kumārhatta ... 78, 87
Kumār Nagar ... 146, 151, 198
Kumarpur ... 153, 154
Kumuda Chattorāj 160
Kuvja 51

L

Laghutoshini ... 38, 39, 43
Laksminarayan 44
Laksmipriyā ... 87, 90
Laksmi Tīrtha 19
Laksman Sen 1, 3
Lalitā 31
Lalit Ghosāl 151
Lalita Mādhava ... 31, 111, 159
Lasang 6
Lavanga Latikā 99
Lagrām 108
Lochana Dās ... 12, 67, 81
Lokanāth Goswami ... 13, 19, 23, 24, 25, 58, 59, 68, 97, 98, 106
Lucknow 124

M

Maddhi Sect 19
Madhāi ... 78, 136
Mādhāipur 28
Mādhava ... 20, 21
Mādhava Miçra 22
Mādhavendrapuri ... 19, 21, 22, 60, 84
Madhurya ... 30, 220, 221
Madhyalila 59
Magha 107
Mahādeva 49
Mahānanda 28
Mahānirbāna Tantra ... 190
Mahāprajapati 233
Mahāvana 17
Mahāvārata 75
Mahayana School 226
Mahecvara Sinha, Raja .. 7
Mahomedan ... 51, 151, 161, 164, 166, 167, 217

PAGE.

Mahomedan Invasion ... 16
Maithil Court 1, 2
Maithili 3
Mala Bhum 161
Malati 162
Maldaha... 28
Malihati.. 175
Mamgachi 76
Manikchandra Chohar ... 53
Manimanjari 159
Mankar 49
Manohar Das 212
Mansingh ... 27, 39, 86
Mantrecvara 76
Maratha Brahmin ... 45, 57
Margaon 50
Matha 212
Matthew (St.) 242
Mathura ... 16, 17, 18, 29, 30, 56, 51, 100, 102, 178, 193, 195, 196, 243
Mathura Mahataya 54
Mayurbhanj 162
Meghaduta 35
Memoir of Chaitanya ... 26
Metaphysics 45
Midnapur ... 108, 181
Mir Habul 40
Mithil 2
Modan Mohana ... 51, 52, 91
Modarayana 7
Moghul 109
Mongol Brahmins 212
Moslem Army 1
Moslem Court 29
Mridanga 129
Mukunda 28
Mullhara 43
Multan 51
Murari Gupta ... 13, 28, 67, 70, 71, 79, 81
Mursed Ali 17
Muttra 97

N

Nadia 66, 70, 75, 76, 87, 244
Nagpur 74
Naihati 28
Nalin Acharyya 74

PAGE.

Nandihati 7
Narada 243
Narahari ... 65, 66, 81, 88, 91, 129, 177, 178, 179, 180, 181,
Narahari Chakravarty 14, 23, 85
Narahatta 71
Nara Singha, Raja... 172, 174
Nara Sinha, Ray 152
Narayani ... 74, 76, 96
Narottama ... 85, 94, 95, 97, 98, 99, 106, 107, 112, 113, 125, 126, 128, 130, 133, 137 —141, 144—146, 148, 152, 153, 154—156, 184, 187, 201, 224, 229, 230
Narottama Charit 68
Narottamavilasa ... 23, 100, 178, 179
Nityananda ... 21, 60, 75, 76, 78, 79, 90. 128, 172, 183, 191, 192
Nityananda Das ... 64, 85, 176, 215
Nityananda Vamcavistara ... 79
Nasipur 179
Navadvip ... 23, 179
Navaji 48, 52, 54
Nonkaran 54
Northern India 46
Nrisinha Chakravarty, Maharaja ... 179, 203
Nayapanchanana 152

O

Oldham 108
Orissa 68, 43, 101, 161, 162, 163

P

Pada 129, 183, 185, 187, 189, 191, 192
Pada Kalpataru ... 81, 123, 182, 209, 215

PAGE.

Pada Samudra 212
Padma 95, 97, 146, 201, 215
Padmanath Chakravarty ... 23
Padmapur 109
Padmavali 34
Padmavati 157
Paikpara 152
Pakkapalli ... 152, 153, 163, 174—176, 230
Panchadhyaya 244
Panchakota 109
Panchvati 110
Panda 12
Paracara 75
Parakiya ... 103, 176
Paramananda 72
Paramananda Gupta ... 82
Parsvada Bhakta 222
Pathan 109
Pathan King ... 135, 138, 140
Pantha Das 172
Pentaterich 243
Perg 94
Pergariath Ahedi 145
Persian 29
Poet Laureate 2, 47
Poona 45, 175
Prajuktasa Chakravarty ... 35
Prankrishna Chakravarty ... 82
Pratappur 68
Pratap Rudra Roy 30, 68
Pratap Sinha Roy ... 7
Prembhaktichandrika ... 156
Premratnavati 63
Pratatali 94
Premvilasa ... 13, 23, 25, 40, 44, 51, 63, 68, 77, 85, 86, 100, 102, 103, 107, 111, 112, 120, 122, 136, 138, 140, 149, 152, 156, 166—172, 14775
Probodhananda ... ...
Pundarika Vidyanidhi 21, 79
Punjab 243
Purana 75
Puri 12, 21, 30, 45, 56, 61, 68, 69, 72, 86, 89, 90

PAGE.

Purnea 24
Purusottoma Gupta... ... 81
Purusottoma Siddyantavagica ... 182
Purvaraga 186

R

Radha Abhisara 31
Radha Krishna Acharyya 160
Radhamohana 162
Radhamohan Thakur ... 202
Radhaprasadhana 31
Radha Ramana 57
Radha Sangama 31
Raganugalahari 81
Raghabendra Roy ... 135, 137, 139, 142, 145
Raghunandana 69
Raghunath 59
Raghunath Bhatta ... 10, 58
Raghunath Siromoni ... 7
Raghunath Das ... 9, 57, 61, 72, 94, 107, 130, 187
Raghunathpur 110
Raghunath Sinha 108
Raja 154
Rajamuhal ... 24, 135, 136, 203
Rajasthan 17
Rajghat... 96
Rajput 100
Rajshahi District 163
Ramachandra Kaviraj 146, 189, 149, 151, 199, 224, 225, 226
Rama Das ... 51, 72
Ramajaya Chakravarty 151
Ramakeli 37
Ramakrishna 126
Ramakrishna Chattoraj 160
Ramananda Roy ... 60, 81
Rama Roy ... 30, 112
Ramchandra ... 138, 148, 149, 151, 199, 224 226
Ram Chandra Das ... 15, 172
Ramchandrapur 61
Ramnarayana 63

	Page.
Ramnarayana Pandit ...	35
Ramnarayana Vidyaratna ...	170
Rani ...	212
Ranigunj ...	6
Rasapanchaddhyaya	116, 122
Rasikamangala ...	102, 181
Rasika Murari ...	162
Rasikananda ...	44
Rasikarangada ...	34, 63
Rayani ...	161
Reapur ...	179
Revati ...	28
Rhetoric ...	114, 126
Rupa ...	9, 27, 28, 31, 32, 36, 39, 40, 44, 47, 53—58, 61 68, 70, 89—92, 94, 103, 104, 111—113, 164, 171, 177, 222, 224
Rupamala ...	155
Rupanarayan ...	44, 45, 47, 153, 156, 163, 172—174
Rupanarayan Saraswati	46
Rūpāstāka ...	56

S.

	Page.
Sadanandi Devi ...	81
Sadgopa ...	161, 162
Sadhyu Sadhana Tattva ...	221
Sahajiya ...	63, 230
Sākār Mullick ...	28
Sakhya ...	220, 221
Saksī Gopal ...	60
Sanatana ...	9, 27, 28, 29, 32, 37, 39, 40, 44, 46—59, 61, 68, 70, 86, 89—92, 94, 104, 131, 148, 176, 224
Sandamuni ...	172
Sangito Madhava ...	200
Sankhepa Bhagabatamṛta ...	35
Sanskrit ...	10, 29, 30, 42, 57,71, 81, 147, 158, 176, 177, 198—200.
Santala ...	162
Santasa Datta ...	203
Santhal Parganati ...	108
Santipur ...	90
Santosh Ray ...	124, 125, 127, 141, 145, 203.
Saptagram ...	72
Sarasarama ...	8
Saraswati ...	45
Sarvananda Bachaspati ...	28
Sarva Samvadini ...	43
Satgaon ...	29
Satgopa ...	101
Satsandarva ...	42, 43
Satyavāmā ...	30
Satyavāmāpura ...	30
Sayamutsava ...	31
Sekandar Lodi ...	17
Sen Dynasty ...	1
Sen Kings ...	8
Shapur ...	23
Shajahan ...	17
Shakespeare ...	214
Sherkhan ...	161
Sisirkumar Ghosh ...	23
Sita ...	38
Sivaratan Mitra ...	212
Skanda ...	160
Solomon ...	210, 244
Song of Songs ...	244
Southern India ...	25, 27 46
Stavamala ...	35
Sultan Mahmud ...	16, 17
Sananda ...	146
Surya Ghat ...	47
Sutramāhlika ...	43
Suvalachandra Thakura ...	175
Suvarnarekha ...	161
Svakiya ...	103
Swarupa Damodara...	71

T

	Page.
Tajpur ...	24
Taigoria ...	23
Talmud ...	243
Talsana ...	244
Tamar ...	110
Tamluk ...	153

PAGE.

Tantra ... 153
Tarikhi Jamina ... 16
Tattvavilāsa ... 79
Telia Budhari ... 201, 202
Thames ... 246
Tipperah ... 109
Tirodhana ... 66, 84
Tod ... 17
Tol ... 23, 126
Trailakyanath Bhattacharyya 29
'Tritkuptpayana ... 102
Troilus ... 215
Tulusi ... 16
Typical Selections ... 176

U

Uddhavasandeca ... 35
Ujjalnicomani ... 103, 111
Umapati ... 2, 4, 5, 6, 209
Under Hill, Miss ... 159
University ... 109
Upanishad ... 42, 57, 154
Upper India ... 92
Urcha ... 17
Uttara-Champu ... 43

V

Vaidhi Bhakti ... 73, 103, 225
Vaidya ... 62, 76, 198, 228
Vaidyanath Bhanja ... 181
Vaisnava Das ... 209
Vaisnavastaka ... 63
Vaisnava Toshini ... 38
Vaisnava Vandana ... 79
Vakrecwara ... 102
Valarama 191, 192, 243, 244
Valarama Das ... 15, 174
Valaram Micra ... 125
Vallala Sen ... 172
Valmiki ... 209
Vamcavistara ... 166
Vana Malla ... 109
Vanavisnupur ... 107
Vanecwara ... 162
Vangabhasa-o-Sahitya 178, 182, 211
Vastutattvasara ... 81
Vasudeva Datta ... 76
Vasudeva Ghosh ... 199
Vasudeva Sārvabhauma 7, 60

PAGE.

Veda ... 45, 153, 189, 194, 226, 241
Venkata Bhatta ... 57
Venuharana ... 31
Vhisti ... 202
Vicvakosha ... 170
Vicvanath Chakravarty ... 179
Vicvarupa ... 78
Vidagdha Madhava... 31, 159, 177
Villamangala ... 63, 177
Vira Bhadra ... 173
Vira Hamvira ... 110, 113, 121 — 123, 125, 128, 147, 148, 157, 158, 170, 171, 209, 227.
Virchandra ... 34, 128, 155, 156, 163 — 168, 170, 179.
Vira Sinha ... 17
Visnukanchi ... 102
Visnupriya Devi ... 134
Visnupur ... 107, 113 — 115, 119, 134, 147, 157, 158, 163, 171, 197, 225.
Visnupur Rajas ... 170
Vraja Parikrama ... 10
Vrndā ... 16, 18, 188
Vṛndavana ... 10, 15, 17, — 21, 23 — 26, 29, 39, 39, 44, 46, 47, 49, 51, 55—58, 61 — 65, 67, 68, 70, 75, 77, 79, 85, 86, 89 — 92, 97, 98, 100, 105, 108, 111, 112, 119, 135, 147, 157, 170, 172, 178, 179, 195, 196, 200, 244.
Vṛdavanacharyya ... 160
Vrndavaṇa Das ... 13, 63, 74, 76, 77, 79, 80, 247.
Vyasa ... 75, 78
Vyāsachārya ... 44, 115

W

Wiefold ... 247

Y

Yogo ... 172